May 1993

Thanks for your support

signature

THE RESILIENT SELF

THE RESILIENT SELF

HOW SURVIVORS OF TROUBLED FAMILIES RISE ABOVE ADVERSITY

Steven J. Wolin, M.D.
and Sybil Wolin, Ph.D.

VILLARD BOOKS
New York . 1993

Owing to limitations of space, all acknowledgments of permission to reprint material are on page 237.

Library of Congress Cataloging-in-Publication Data

Wolin, Steven J.
    The resilient self : how survivors of troubled families rise above
adversity/by Steven J. Wolin and Sybil Wolin.—1st ed.
        p.   cm.
    ISBN 0-394-58357-4 (acid-free paper)
    1. Adult children of dysfunctional families.   I. Title.
    RC455.4.F3W62 1992   92-50493
    158—dc20

Manufactured in the United States of America on acid-free paper
9 8 7 6 5 4 3 2
First edition
This book was set in 11/14 Berkeley Old Style Book
Book design by Charlotte Staub

To our children,
Jessica and Benjamin,
who stayed true from
journey's start to
journey's end

PREFACE

We wrote this book for everyone who grew up in a troubled family, an unknown number of people we call survivors. Our subject is resilience, the capacity to rebound from hardship inflicted early in life. Until now, most information about this topic has been limited to academic books and professional journals. Our purpose is to put what has been learned about resilience into the hands of those who can most benefit from the knowledge—survivors themselves. The news is good. While early hardship can cause enduring pain, often it is also a breeding ground for uncommon strength and courage. If you are a survivor, you probably already know a great deal about the pain. This book is about the strength and the courage.

While writing, we also had in mind therapists, educators, and policymakers who have been exposed to a widespread image in our society of survivors as damaged goods. Here you will read about survivor's aspirations and accomplishments, which are often remarkable and just as often overlooked. We hope that the research and insights we have assembled will become the basis for new and better instruction, treatment, and programs for the survivors in your care.

When we first decided to write a book together, we struggled with the question of whose voice to use. Though we were relating both of our thoughts and experiences, we did not want to confuse our readers by switching back and forth between Steven and Sybil, he and she. Nor did "we" make sense, since most of the events we tell about happened to one or the other of us. As you will see, we settled on the singular "I." It is a device that mingles both of our voices, what each of us thinks, and the places each of us has been.

Steven J. Wolin, M.D.
Sybil Wolin, Ph.D.
Washington, D.C.

ACKNOWLEDGMENTS

We thank Paul Mahon for his wise counsel, sense of humor, and wholehearted care and attention to this project; Elizabeth and John Zinner for finding a title on the beach at Ocracoke; Nan Brooks for conceiving the Resiliency Mandala; Sheila Harty for refining the Mandala and for advising us during a determining draft; Susie Crowley, Jonathan Agronsky, and Linda and Rich Kenney for reading and commenting on the manuscript in its various stages and for easing us through rough times; the Center for Family Research at George Washington University for stimulating and supporting the alcoholism research that seeded our interest in resilience; Diane Sollee for providing the first public forum for presenting these ideas; Virginia Rutter for fostering continued interest in our work; Judy Piemme for attending to myriad details and keeping our wastelands in order; our team at Villard for transforming a waterlogged manuscript into a finished book; Diane Reverand for urging us to be a "bit more prescriptive"; Emily Bestler, our editor; Amelia Sheldon, our intermediary; and Jonathan Dolger, our agent. We have deep regard for the survivors who told us how they rose above adversity. Their stories are the heart of this book. We will always be grateful to them for sharing themselves with us.

The Resilient Self is based on clinical interviews with twenty-five resilient survivors conducted by both authors and on case material from Dr. Steven Wolin's private practice and previous research. Though the stories presented here are composites, they are psychologically accurate. All names, identifying characteristics, and other details have been changed in order to preserve privacy.

CONTENTS

Contents

Part One

PAIN AND OPPORTUNITY

A king once owned a large, beautiful, pure diamond of which he was justly proud, for it had no equal anywhere. One day, this diamond accidentally sustained a deep scratch. The king called in the most expert diamond cutters and offered them a great reward if they could remove the imperfection from his jewel. But none could remove the blemish. The king was sorely distressed. After some time, a gifted craftsman came to the king and promised to make the rare diamond even more beautiful than it had been before the mishap. The king was impressed by his confidence and entrusted the precious stone to his care. And the man kept his word. With superb artistry he engraved a lovely rosebud around the imperfection, using the scratch to make the stem.

We can emulate the craftsman. When life bruises us and wounds us, we can use even the scratches to etch a portrait of beauty and charm.

> —Jacob Kranz,
> "The Dubner Storyteller"

Chapter One

THE CHALLENGE OF THE TROUBLED FAMILY

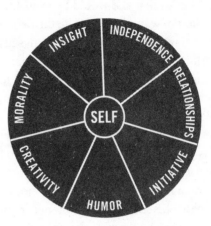

"**H**ave you ever noticed the differences in mirrors?" a good friend once asked. "The mirror in my office bathroom is lit by a fluorescent bulb that accentuates my worst features and my olive complexion. I avoid it. I might even go to the expense of replacing it. But the bathroom mirror at home I like. The lighting softens the angles of my face and tones down my sallow skin color. More and more, I find myself lingering at that mirror when I comb my hair in the morning to take comfort from an image that seems to be saying, 'You look pretty good.'"

I know my friend's motive well. The same irrepressible urge to look good moves me to tear up snapshots of myself that I don't like and to throw away the negatives. The identical need lends special significance to a photograph of Barbara standing in front of a columned university hall, wearing a cap and gown and thrusting her arms out in joy.

A survivor of a troubled family, Barbara was neglected by her parents and harangued by them into thinking that she didn't have the brains to get through college. You have probably lived some variation of her childhood. With three young children at home, Barbara mustered the courage and strength to meet the challenge of her troubled family. She silenced the hurtful words that were still ringing in her ears long after she had left her parents' home and become a mother herself. She made a schedule, bought a desk and enrolled in a local university to earn a bachelor's degree. For six years, on more nights than she cared to remember, Barbara studied and wrote papers until two and three in the morning so that she would be available to her children during the day. She did not want them to taste the deprivation she had known as a child.

"This is my favorite picture of myself because it captures my moment of triumph over my parents," Barbara explained. "It shows just how wrong they were about me. But I had to doctor it a little before I could frame it and hang it in the house. I cropped off my hands.

"You see," she said, pointing first to her wrists at the edges of the photo and then to the missing hands beyond the frame, "with each one, I was giving my family 'the finger'—two fingers—one for my mother and one for my father."

Barbara's accomplishment did not completely obliterate the pain of her past. She confided that whenever she looks at her graduation photo, she fills in the fingers she is giving to her parents and hears their repetitious cruel remarks. But she also has the satisfaction of knowing that by trimming the picture, she put the emphasis of her story in the right place. She could have permitted the hands to show and, with them, the anger she felt toward her parents for preventing her from going to college earlier. But she didn't. She exercised another choice. She centered the frame on her beaming smile and her arms outstretched in joy, and she pushed the fingers of revenge outside the border where they didn't detract from her triumph.

RESILIENCE

Deep inside all of us is the need to look good. As a survivor, you have probably shared Barbara's struggle against an unacceptable image of yourself pieced together from hurtful and belittling experiences with your troubled family. And, like her, you probably also have achievements to your credit that have proved your parents wrong. This book is an invitation to consider your victories over despair, to savor your accomplishments, and to frame a picture of yourself with your successes in the middle and your pain, disappointments, and anger at the invisible edge.

I am writing to give a full and fair account of surviving, one that includes both sympathy for your hurt as well as recognition and praise for your ability to rebound. On the one hand, I cover the isolation, degradation, fear, and anguish that survivors can often feel. Though these themes are, by now, very familiar to us, no book about survivors would be complete without them. But my real interest is in resilience, your capacity to bounce back: to withstand hardship and repair yourself. I believe that by learning about resilience, you can become resilient. You can:

- master your painful memories rather than tripping the Victim's Trap by compulsively rehashing the damage you have suffered
- accept that your troubled family has left its mark and give up the futile wish that your scars can ever disappear completely
- get revenge by living well instead of squandering your energy by blaming and fault-finding
- break the cycle of your family's troubles and put the past in its place

Research shows that children of disturbed or incompetent parents learn to watch out for themselves and grow strong in the process.[1] Young survivors figure out how to locate allies outside the family, find pleasure in fantasy games, or build self-esteem by winning recognition in school. Over time, the capacity to rise above adversity by developing skills such as these expands and ripens into lasting strengths or aspects of the survivor's self that I call *resiliencies*. There are seven.[2]

INSIGHT: The habit of asking tough questions and giving honest answers.

INDEPENDENCE: drawing boundaries between yourself and troubled parents; keeping emotional and physical distance while satisfying the demands of your conscience.

RELATIONSHIPS: intimate and fulfilling ties to other people that balance a mature regard for your own needs with empathy and the capacity to give to someone else.

INITIATIVE: taking charge of problems; exerting control; a taste for stretching and testing yourself in demanding tasks.

CREATIVITY: imposing order, beauty, and purpose on the chaos of your troubling experiences and painful feelings.

HUMOR: finding the comic in the tragic.

MORALITY: an informed conscience that extends your wish for a good personal life to all of humankind.

Resiliencies tend to cluster by personality type. A survivor who is outgoing and gregarious, for example, will have a different array of resiliencies from one who is serious and introspective. Few survivors can claim all seven, completely closing off the past. For the majority—most likely, in you—resilience and vulnerability are in steady opposition, one holding you up and the other threatening to pull you down. The inner life of the typical survivor is a battleground where the forces of discouragement and the forces of determination constantly clash. For many, determination wins out.

Unfortunately, the professions of psychiatry and psychology, as well as a growing self-help movement in this country, have done a lot to alarm you about your vulnerability but not nearly enough to inform you about your resilience. Everywhere you can hear news of your damage, but reports of your competence are sparse. You are being bombarded by frightening predictions that neglected and harmed children—like you and Barbara—are destined to repeat the past by becoming abusive and neglectful adults.

Regrettably, the assumption that mental illness travels across generations is sometimes the case. But fortunately, the transmission of family troubles from parent to child is by no means the rule. In more than two decades as a therapist and family researcher, I have seen that many survivors are like desert flowers that grow healthy and strong in an emotional wasteland. In barren and angry terrain they find nourishment, and frequently their will to prevail becomes the foundation for a decent, caring, and productive adult life.

I believe the damage alert is an overstatement and a disservice to you. Convinced, you will be caught in the Victim's Trap, bound tightly to the very past you want to escape from. You will be preoccupied with your faults and weaknesses, blinded to the variations in your life, and robbed of satisfaction with your achievements. Your energy will be depleted by fault-finding and blaming your parents for events that can never be changed.

My message to you is to avoid labeling yourself as "damaged." The promise of sympathy that comes with victim's status is enticing bait. But if you take it, you will be helplessly hooked to your pain.

Although resilience may be hard for you to contemplate at first, the idea can liberate you. As a survivor, you are probably much more conscious of your anguish than of your morality, insight, or initiative. You may disregard the distance you have already traveled from your troubled family. Despite your accomplishments, you may yearn to return to childhood and do your past over the "right" way. You may feel cheated, or you may fear that you will not be able to give a spouse or a child the love and attention you never had. You may believe that you are living a lie and that sooner or later someone will discover that you are very much like your parents. Like almost every survivor I have known, you may be envious of the happiness that you imagine children in other families enjoyed.

The pain associated with these feelings is sharp and deep and can spread its influence across your life. But you can also put limits around your pain and release yourself from the Victim's Trap.

Go out in search of your resilience. Look for the times you outmaneuvered, outlasted, outwitted, or outreached your troubled parent. Find the dignity you have mined from a degrading past. In the process of discovery, I have seen many survivors replace pain and doubt with self-respect, pride, and a new awareness of their own accomplishments. You can do the same.

UNCOVERING YOUR RESILIENT SELF

Begin the search for your resilience by reading how successful survivors regard themselves. In a poem he calls "Taste the Fire," Dwight Wolter, an adult child of an alcoholic, describes his courage, growth, and power to forge creativity from a legacy of agony and insanity.

> I was crippled for five years as a child.
> Result: I became a poet. And I have a new joy

> in the discovery, at the age of thirty-six,
> of my body and all its wondrous abilities. . . .
> I was raised by two sick people who taught
> me insanity and fear and hatred. I was
> raised in hell. Chaos felt like home.
> Result: I learned to land on my feet in
> any situation. I can stand face to face with
> the cruelest of ogres.[3]

I believe that the assurance, grief, conviction, anger, and immodesty expressed here result from the resilient survivor's experience of being tested to the limit and prevailing. In the self-image of survivors, opposites unite. Injury and repair, defeat and triumph, fear and courage, go hand in hand. I call the unlikely mix of feelings Survivor's Pride. It floats as a faint strain through the narrations of agony that many survivors tell.

Listen to the Survivor's Pride in the stories of Janet and Faye. As children, both survivors cultivated strengths that have endured, acting like walls against their pain.

JANET

I met Janet at a workshop I gave for teachers on the topic of supporting students from troubled homes. Sitting in the audience, Janet found that the subject stirred up feelings about her own past. A week later, she wrote me a letter describing her pain and her resiliencies—creativity, relationships, and insight into her own clashing feelings.

When I was little, I was very close to my mother, a frail but playful woman, in many ways a child herself. We were best friends. When I was nearly six, she succumbed to a serious, progressive mental illness.

The event changed my life. I lost my best friend. My father, who never really loved my mother, absented himself. I spent my childhood isolated on a large estate in Atlanta. As my mother's condition deteriorated, she became more and more withdrawn and angry. I was the main target of her fierce criticism. When I was fifteen, she died. My memories of her have been filled with guilt and sadness. But I also had other feelings that I couldn't put my finger on before. Perhaps I was ashamed of them.

Even in the darkest days of my mother's illness, I took pleasure in being alive. I was lucky to have talents and I cultivated them in order to save myself. I spent my time with games and books, and when I entered high school I turned to serious sports and music. Today my cello is a steady source of joy and of comfort in times of trouble. I wonder if I would have played without my mother's tragedy.

Janet's question has no answer; nor is one important. What matters is that Janet's creativity helped her through a longstanding childhood crisis and remains a source of pleasure and strength in her life to this day. For Faye, the same protective function is served by the combination of humor and insight.

FAYE

Faye's mother had a wounding temper, especially in public. She often humiliated Faye in front of her school friends, calling her names and making fun of her "scrawny" body.

As a teenager, Faye's insight helped her to spot someone who knew how to curb her mother's temper—a local beautician. She went along whenever her mother had a hair cut and watched the beautician in action. Before long, Faye figured out that the beautician's technique was wit. The observation got her going. Undoubtedly drawing on a natural talent, she practiced being funny. Eventually, she worked up the courage to greet one of her mother's tirades with humor. Though the reward for Faye's ingenuity was not exactly approval, her mother's response was far less vicious than usual.

Over time, humor became a mainstay in Faye's personality. Her ability to laugh, to see the absurd in herself as well as in others, is one of her most attractive characteristics. Her humor and insight have also gotten her through many crises. She told me:

My mother substituted douching for sex. A whole closet in her bathroom plus the medicine chest were filled with different powders for lavage. She talked a lot about the differences in brands.

When I was in college, I developed a painful vaginal infection. I made the mistake of telling my mother about it. She took the opportunity to lash into me for being "filthy" and to say that I wouldn't have gotten sick if I douched regularly. She then added that she had been to the doctor recently and he told her that she had the cleanest insides he'd ever seen.

At first, I was seared, but then I felt the laughter bubbling up and washing away the rage. "Hey, Ma," I said, "what hole was the doctor looking in? Are you sure he wasn't looking up your nose?" The conversation ended pretty fast after that, but I swear when I got off the phone I was still chuckling, and I was as pleased with my comeback as I was hurt by her comment.

By relating how Janet and Faye survived their troubled childhood, I do not mean to minimize the ordeal that you, as a survivor, lived through in your family. Nor am I advocating that children must suffer in order to grow strong. On the contrary, I do not accept that hardship is a prerequisite for developing character. But I do propose that you were not necessarily undone by the obstacles your family put in your path. As one resilient survivor wisely told me, "You could regard my home life as a prisoner-of-war camp or as basic training. I prefer the latter."

I have observed that while survivors certainly suffered as children, they also can overcome hardships and build self-esteem. Many times you may have been challenged to develop methods for warding off harm and for finding substitutes for what your parents could not and would not give. In some ways, you may be stronger for your past. Buried somewhere deep inside you, there may be a streak of Survivor's Pride. Claim the self-respect you have earned. Do not deny your pain, but, for your own sake, also take the credit that you deserve.

FROM DAMAGE TO CHALLENGE

When it comes to understanding human nature, science has always lagged far behind literature and art. Behavioral scientists, with tests that too often miss the subtleties of our innermost thoughts and feelings, have tended to limit their inquiries to our surface behavior and our biology. Until recently, the pen and the brush have been unrivaled tools for plumbing and portraying our deeper stirrings.

Three centuries ago, William Shakespeare, one of history's most astute students of the human soul, boldly described the unlikely bittersweet twistings of adversity:

> Sweet are the uses of adversity,
> Which like the toad, ugly and venomous,
> Wears yet a precious jewel in his head . . .[4]

In the last century, the Victorian novelist George Eliot echoed a similar thought in her book *Adam Bede:*

> Deep, unspeakable suffering may well be called a baptism, a regeneration, the initiation into a new state.[5]

And early in this century, long before any scientific recognition of resiliency was made, the novelist Christina Stead anatomized the internal image of a survivor. In *The Man Who Loved Children,* she draws a portrait of Louie, the eldest resilient child of the crazed Pollit family. On almost every page, Louie suffers horribly, but she also grows, strengthens, and protects herself by transforming the family view of her as an ugly duckling into a more pleasing image of herself as the beautiful, misplaced swan.

> Louie knew she was an ugly duckling. But when a swan, she would never come sailing back into their [her family's] village pond; she would be somewhere away, unheard of, on the lily rimmed oceans of the world. This was her secret. . . . With her secrets, she was able to go out from nearly every one of the thousand domestic clashes of the year, and as if going through a door into another world, forget about them entirely. They were the doings of a weaker sort.[6]

At the end of the book, Louie, now a young woman, makes a dramatic break with her family. Leaving their grimy, dismal existence and bitter feuds behind, she heads off in search of a better life. Stead leaves us believing that Louie will succeed. As Louie turns her back on Spa House, the family home, she sees the world as she never did before, in a clear, dazzling light.

> "Good-by!" She walked away without looking back, feeling cheated and dull. . . . She walked across the market place and into Main Street, looking into a little coffee shop and wondering if she would have a cup of coffee. She had never been in there before, because it was like a fisherman's

hangout, dingy and dubious. But no, she walked on. Everyone looked strange. Everyone had an outline and brilliant, solid colors. Louie was surprised and realized that when you run away, everything is at once different. Perhaps she would get on well enough. She imagined the hubbub now at Spa House, as they discovered she was not bursting up the stairs with their morning tea. They would look everywhere and conclude that she had gone for a walk. "So I have," she thought, smiling secretly, "I have gone for a walk around the world."[7]

Only in the past thirty years have the fields of psychiatry and psychology approached the arts in understanding the Louies of the world and in unraveling the improbable, if unrequested, "uses of adversity." In 1962, the noted child psychologist Lois Murphy identified the preoccupation with pathology and problems that was then dominating the mental-health professions. In *The Widening World of Childhood,* she states:

> It is something of a paradox that a nation which has exulted in its rapid expansion and its scientific-technological achievements, should have developed in its studies of childhood so vast a "problem" literature: a literature often expressing adjustment difficulties, social failures, blocked potentialities, and defeat. . . . [T]here are thousands of studies of maladjustment for each one that deals directly with ways of managing life's problems with personal strength and adequacy. The language of problems, difficulties, inadequacies, or antisocial or delinquent conduct or . . . anxiety is familiar. We know that there are devices for correcting, bypassing, or overcoming threats, but for the most part these have not been directly studied.[8]

THE DAMAGE MODEL

I was studying to be a psychiatrist at the time Murphy published *The Widening World of Childhood.* My education was shaped by the pervasive bias toward problems and maladjustment that she described. In medical school, where my training began, I spent four years steeped in the language of disease. By graduation, I had mastered an alphabet soup of symptoms and syndromes, and I was on my way to finding illness and maladjustment wherever I went.

In my psychiatric residency that followed medical school, I glibly applied the terminology of physical disease to the "disorders" of behavior and the mind. Eventually, I became so immersed in pathology that I no longer even used the word *healthy*. Instead, I conceived of health as the absence of illness and referred to people who were well as "asymptomatic," "nonclinical," "unhospitalized," or "having no severe disturbance." In retrospect, the worst offender was the term "unidentified," as if the only way I could know a person was by his or her sickness.

The peculiar vocabulary that my colleagues and I used to describe our patients reflected our meager regard for the forces that keep people healthy and our comfort with identifying, categorizing, and labeling diseases. Although we paid lip service to "normal" psychological processes, our real concern was with the lasting damage that results from exposure to harmful influences early in life. Our orientation, which I call the Damage Model of human psychology, roughly resembles the germ theory of disease. While the model has its merits, I have found that it can also be less than useful to survivors.

In the Damage Model, shown in the diagram below, troubled families are seen as toxic agents, like bacteria or viruses, and survivors are regarded as victims of their parents' poisonous secretions.

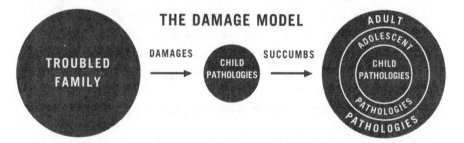

Children, according to the Damage Model, are vulnerable, helpless, and locked into the family. The best survivors can do is to cope or contain the family's harmful influence at considerable cost to themselves. Inevitably, the damage theorists say, the accumulating price of coping takes its toll and results in symptoms and behavior problems that make up the general category of pathologies. In adolescence and adulthood, pathologies are layered on pathologies, and eventually the survivor is no better off than his or her troubled parents. The role of the therapist in this scenario is to help repair the harm by understanding it.

When I first began practicing therapy in the Damage Model, I had little idea of how one-sided my approach was. I had not been exposed to an alternative view, and, despite its limits, the Damage Model had healing power that prevented me from seeing its shortcomings. I knew then, and still know now, that by listening empathically and by tracing people's woes to the troubles in their families, I could relieve some of their suffering. Therefore, as a young psychiatrist, I did not hesitate to take the Damage Model from the hospital setting, where I had been trained, into my private office, where I continued to think about my patients primarily in terms of their injuries.

Only gradually did my accumulating share of what we in the profession politely call "clinical failures" begin to dawn on me. In trying to understand why I hadn't helped certain patients, I began to see the drawbacks of the Damage Model clearly. Just as the model provided only half of a picture of human psychology, the therapy based on it was only half of a treatment.

Survivors who were my patients, and I with them, got bogged down in the Damage Model in three ways:

1. The Damage Model was leaving survivors in the lurch. With its focus on injuries inflicted in the past rather than on living well in the present, the Model offered few cues about how survivors could build and maintain loving relationships with other adults, function as effective members of their community, raise children, or treat troubled parents. For patients who had to unlearn what their parents taught them and fill in a lot of gaps, the model lacked a vital educational component.

2. The model often backfired. Instead of energizing survivors, it lured them into the Victim's Trap. By overlooking strengths and ignoring resilience, Damage Model therapy encouraged survivors to describe, dissect, and document repeatedly how they had been hurt. In the process, they solidified an image of themselves as helpless in the past, which then became the basis for fault-finding and continued helplessness in the present. Ultimately, the child-as-victim image diverted survivors away from the hard work of changing.

3. The model left many survivors who had traveled a considerable distance from the past feeling like walking time bombs. The prem-

ise that family troubles inevitably repeat themselves from one generation to the next, coupled with the model's omission of resilience, did as much to frighten survivors as it did to help them.[9]

THE CHALLENGE MODEL

No doubt, I was stuck in the Damage Model, and there was little in my education to help me out. Eventually, my research pointed me in a new direction. Investigating the long-term consequences of having alcoholic parents, I found that the transmission of addictive drinking from parent to child was not as predictable as the Damage Model and conventional wisdom imply. Numbers of adult children I interviewed had not repeated their parents' drinking patterns, nor had they fallen prey to serious psychological problems.[10] Some did surprisingly well, leaving their troubled parental homes to lead satisfying adult lives.

How had they helped themselves?

- not by dwelling on the past and the damage they had suffered
- not by blaming their parents for what was less than desirable in themselves
- not by taking the bait in the Victim's Trap

The adult children of alcoholics who were free of drinking problems and leading satisfying lives had:

- found and built on their own strengths
- improved deliberately and methodically on their parents' life-styles
- married consciously into strong, healthy families
- fought off memories of horrible family get-togethers in order to establish regular mealtime routines, vacations, and family celebrations and rituals in their own generation

The capacity for self-repair in these adult children of alcoholics taught me that strength can emerge from adversity. The lesson added a new technique to my Damage Model therapy repertoire. Now, in addition to listening empathically and looking at the damage that survivors had suffered in their troubled families, we also searched for their resiliencies and their Survivor's Pride. Together we then built on what we found. Thus, the Challenge Model of human psychology was born.[11]

The Challenge Model is represented in the diagram below.

In the Challenge Model, two forces are at work as the child and the family interact. The interplay is represented by the interlocking arrows on the diagram. The troubled family is seen as a danger to the child, as it is in the Damage Model, and also as an opportunity. Survivors are vulnerable to their parents' toxic influence, and they are also challenged to rebound from harm by experimenting, branching out, and acting on their own behalf. As a result of the interplay between damage and challenge, the survivor is left with pathologies that do not disappear completely and with resiliencies that limit their damage and promote their growth and well-being.

The contrasting elements of vulnerability and resilience in the survivor's inner self are shown by the shaded and unshaded areas on the Challenge Model diagram. The dark-light, chiaroscuro pattern is the product of an identity-forming process called *mirroring,* which I will now describe.

Distorting Mirrors and Alternate Mirrors

According to child-development experts, we all are born without any idea of who we are.[12] We piece together a picture of ourselves—first of our bodies, then of our essential nature—by seeing our reflection in the faces of the people who take care of us. Children who generally see love, approval, pleasure, and admiration in the mirror of their parents' faces construct a corresponding inner representation of themselves that says, "I am lovable. I am good."

In troubled families, the mirroring process goes awry, and children are at risk of forming an inner representation of themselves that says, "I am ugly. I am unacceptable." Twisted and bent out of shape themselves, troubled parents are like distorting mirrors that reflect grotesque images.

Distorting mirrors can delight if you know for sure that the flattened head and hideously lengthened arms you are seeing in the funhouse hall of mirrors are not features of the "real" you. But you don't have to be a psychiatrist to know that the picture you will associate with the word *I* can be shattering if distorting mirrors are your only means of viewing yourself. When parents reflect images that say, "You are bad. You are ugly. You are not lovable," then children's inner representations of themselves can be less than pleasing.

At times, you may have submitted to the spell of the monstrous images you saw of yourself in your parents' eyes. In the vain hope that the freak staring back at you would eventually reshape itself and become beautiful, you kept looking. Those times were damaging and account for your pathologies.

At other times, you may have heard your parents' message as a challenge—a call to action. You may have rallied your courage, broken free of their spell, and gone in search of alternate mirrors in which you could see a more pleasing image of yourself.[13]

For example, a teacher who watched you solve a tricky math problem and said, "You're clever," may have served as one alternate mirror. Another may have been a neighbor who said, "You're a good kid," when you helped him unload packages from his car. At times, you may even have been your own alternate mirror: walking out on a family fracas, going to the garage, fixing your bicycle, and reflecting on your achievement with the remark, "I am competent." The pleasing self-images you collected by rebounding from pain and pulling into constructive activity accumulated over time and account for your resiliencies.

On the Challenge Model diagram, your pathologies—the damage that you suffered in your troubled family—are represented in the child and adult circles by the same shading that fills the family circle. The resiliencies, or the elements of yourself that distinguish you from your troubled family, are represented by the unshaded areas. Chiaroscuros, shaded and unshaded side by side, are meant to capture the interplay of forces—

damage and challenge, vulnerability and resilience—that typify the survivor's experience and inner life.

Right now you may be thinking that there were few or no instances when you met the challenge of your family as a child. You may primarily remember your defeats. By reading this book, you can broaden your awareness of your strengths and retrieve lost memories of the times that you successfully rebounded from pain. Even if the pleasing images you found in alternate mirrors were fleeting and infrequent, they have value that you may not be considering. You can use these images to frame your life story, as Barbara did, with your triumphs in the center and the fingers of revenge at the invisible edge, where they lose their power to hook you to the past.

RESEARCH ON THE CHALLENGE MODEL

The observation of resilience in survivors is not the fabrication of novelists and playwrights or of a solitary psychiatrist.[14] Case reports of resilience are trickling into professional journals. And in the past few years, a growing number of experiments on resilience have added to our understanding of how survivors overcome formidable stumbling blocks. This research puts a serious dent in the Damage Model assumption that misfortune in childhood necessarily leads to *decreased* psychological functioning in adults. On the contrary, we are seeing that children can cope with adversity and that, ironically, an *increased* sense of personal competence can result from successfully meeting the challenges of a troubled family.

As a survivor, you deserve to know what researchers have found out about you. Their work may inspire you and give you hope. In the upcoming chapters of this book, I will describe some of this research in greater detail. Here I will mention only one particularly vivid example, a long-term study conducted by child psychologist Dr. Emmy Werner and her colleague Ruth Smith.

Since 1955, Werner and Smith have followed the lives of 698 children born on the island of Kauai in Hawaii.[15] Each one knew hardship. All were reared in poverty; almost one-third also had experienced stress either before or at birth, were raised by parents with little education, or lived in families torn apart by fighting, divorce, alcoholism, or mental illness.

Nevertheless, many of these children developed into fine human beings as measured by the familiar triple standard of mental health: working well, playing well, and loving well. Werner and Smith explain their success as a result of personal traits and "protective factors" in the environment—for example, a tie to one caring parent or to a larger cultural heritage.

Here are Werner and Smith's conclusions after watching the resilient children of Kauai grow up:

> Our findings appear to provide a more hopeful perspective than can be had from reading the extensive literature on "problem" children that come to the attention of therapists, special educators, and social-service agencies. Risk factors and stressful environments do not inevitably lead to poor adaptation. It seems clear that, at each stage in an individual's development from birth to maturity, there is a shifting balance between stressful events that heighten vulnerability and protective factors that enhance resilience.[16]

Though Werner and Smith do not employ the framework of the Challenge Model, their concept of a "shifting balance" between stress and protection, vulnerability and resilience, is closely related. I cite this passage from their work now because it drives home the optimism of the Challenge Model despite minor differences in terminology. As you begin to look at the "shifting balance" of vulnerability and resilience in your own life, that optimism may take root in you.

WHAT CAN THIS BOOK OFFER?

a new way to look at your past

a vocabulary of strengths

a method for forming a pleasing image of yourself

the right to feel Survivor's Pride

a knowledge of the latest research about you

In the 1980s in this country, the Damage Model seeped down from the professional to our popular culture in a big way. The survivor-as-victim image became the rallying point for a recovery movement that is still growing today.[17] As the movement has spread its influence, diseases, addictions, and human frailties have occupied the limelight of our awareness, and resilience has fallen into the shadows. We are fast becoming a nation of emotional cripples, incapable of managing the expectable problems that life doles out each day.

How can we restore ourselves to health? How can we escape the pessimism of the Damage Model prediction? What shall we say to our modern-day doomsayers who have reworked the ancient prophecy—"The sins of the father shall be visited upon the sons"—for popular consumption?

I think we need to hear less about our susceptibility to harm and more about our ability to rebound from adversity when it comes our way. This book is my attempt to make a start. Its heart is a mandala, a symbolic circle that stands for peace and order in the self. Called an archetype or universal form by Carl Jung, mandala symbolism can be found in cultures all over the world.[18] In Eastern civilizations, the mandala is a focal point for inducing a deep state of meditation. For the Navajo, the mandala can cure illness by bringing a sick person into inner harmony.

I have chosen the mandala to represent the resiliencies because of its mythological associations with peace, harmony, and health. In the Challenge Model, the ideal Resiliency Mandala shows all seven resiliencies forming a protective ring around the self; it is pictured on the next page

In a series of exercises throughout this book, I will help you construct your own Resiliency Mandala. Within its circumference, the dark and light themes of the survivor's self can come into balance.

In Chapter Two, we will begin where all survivors are naturally drawn, in the space around the mandala that represents your family's troubles and the damage you suffered in childhood at your parents' hands. We will assess your family's functioning and how you were hurt by their inability to provide a decent setting where you could grow. My goal in Chapter Two is to give you enough distance from your pain so that you can begin looking at your resiliencies—the skills you've used to rise above adversity.

In Chapter Three, we will turn to the Challenge Model and see the

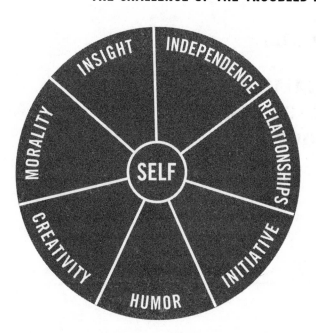

therapy technique of *reframing*[19]—uncovering new, hidden themes in old stories. Using reframing, you can revise an image of yourself as a passive victim to one of an active resistor, looking for ways to protect yourself from harm. By acknowledging the steps you took, however small and timid, to transcend your troubled family, you can offset your pain with pride.

In Chapters Four through Nine, Part II of this book, we will walk through the development of each resiliency from childhood to adulthood. These chapters are an opportunity for you to construct the individual wedges of your Resiliency Mandala by noting the times you:

- struck out on your own
- turned away from your troubled parent and sought out alternate mirrors
- rejected the distorted self-image you saw in your parents' eyes
- tipped the balance between vulnerability and resilience inside you and bounced back

I hope that by reading these pages, you will find a source of pride and confidence where you may have least expected it—in the challenges you met as a child in your troubled family.

Chapter Two

TO NAME THE
DAMAGE IS TO
CONQUER IT

Power in families rests in the hands of the parents. As a child, you came into the world small, naked, and ignorant. You were dependent on your parents to create an environment that would promote your physical and emotional well-being. In troubled families, the basic inequality between parent and child can cause great pain. Though the theme of my book is resilience, your pain is the subject of this chapter. My experience has taught me to begin here, at the beginning of your life and at the center of your Resiliency Mandala. Acknowledging your suffering, turning your anguish over and looking at it, first from one angle and then from another, will open your mind to the possibility of your strength.

In healthy families, power is shared. Parents' responses *match* the needs of their children, who are, in turn, shielded from a full awareness of their inherent weaknesses.[1] Troubled parents *mismatch,* leaving children with few doubts about their lowly position in a world dominated by often hurtful and unpredictable adults.

MATCH: I'm scared of the dark.

I'm calm and confident, and I'll show you that there's nothing to fear.

MISMATCH: I'm sad. My best friend moved away.

You're always crying. You're too demanding. You drain me. You want something to cry about? Well, here it is. *Slap!*

MATCH: I failed a math test.

Let's talk about it. Did you study? Was the test fair? What can I do to help?

MISMATCH: I got a D on my report card.

You're giving me a heart attack. What will my friends think? I'm ashamed. How can you be so stupid? You certainly didn't get your brains from me.

Matching is another way of understanding the mirroring process I described in Chapter One. The right reflection on a parent's face—a match—seeps inside a child and takes root in a deep feeling of I-can-get-exactly-what-I-need. That feeling is the nucleus of a healthy self-esteem, a pleasing internal image of oneself.

A mismatch, or distorted reflection, wounds and can leave scars. This is not to say that competent parents need to have a godlike capacity for giving or that childhood should be like an extended stay in Eden. It is to say that families should have enough goodness to go around. Parents' inner resources should be sufficient to sustain themselves and to provide an essentially loving environment for their children.

In troubled families, parents neither sustain themselves nor provide a loving environment for their children. For some survivors, the resulting sense of helplessness is held in the "memory" of lying alone in a crib, in a dirty diaper, crying and unheard. Of course, the literal accuracy of this "memory" is doubtful, for no one is likely to remember back so far; but its emotional content is authentic. Directly opposite to the I-can-get-exactly-what-I-need feeling, the image of a deserted infant symbolizes the survivor's sense of impotence and damaged self-esteem.

On the Resiliency Mandala, the self of the unheard, crying infant is represented this way:

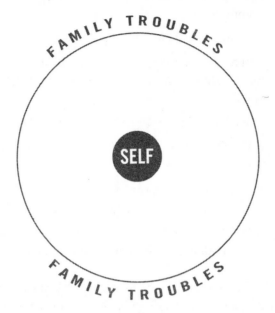

Before the resiliencies begin to develop, the space between the circumference of the Mandala and the center is empty, leaving an unprotected self encircled by the family's troubles. To the extent that this space in your mandala remained empty, and nothing stood between you and your family's troubles while you were growing up, you were damaged. You were like the emotionally needy queen in the tale of *Snow White* who turns to a magic mirror and asks a question we all pose to our parents in one form or another:

> Mirror, mirror on the wall
> Who's the fairest of them all?[2]

The mirror, like a troubled parent, frustrates the queen by refusing to give the answer she wants to hear, the answer that instills the I-have-exactly-what-I-need feeling. Rather than replying, "You are the most beautiful," it names Snow White.

Caught in her frustration, the queen returns to the mirror again and again, seeking the reply she wants. When the mirror does not change its answer, she becomes obsessed and cannot break away from its spell. In her rage, she hatches a plan, irrational and, in the truest sense of the word, self-destructive. She orders a hunter to track down and kill Snow White. The plan turns against the queen, who eventually dies, shattered by her obsession with a mirror that refused to say what she wanted to hear.

As a young child, deprived of what you wanted and needed, you may have been pulled toward your parents by your frustration, just as the queen was riveted to the magic mirror. Your futile attempts to find satisfaction added hurt upon hurt and layered pathology upon pathology. You can measure your damage by counting the times you were caught in your troubled parents' compelling spell, repeated the same question, and incorporated their mismatched answer into your inner self. You can measure your resilience by the number of times you broke free and searched for alternate reflections.

At the end of each chapter in Part II of this book, you will find specific questions to help you identify your resilience. But first we will yield to the pull of your pain, the necessary first step before you can contemplate reframing the past from the perspective of your strengths. We will face how you were injured and allow you to air your anger, frustration, disappointment, and sadness by using the Damage Inventory in the Appendix at the back of this book.[3] Please turn to it now.

The Inventory is designed to assess specific signs of psychological injury—not for the purpose of assigning blame or sending your parents a list of grievances but to begin a therapeutic process. Identifying your areas of difficulty will convert formless anxiety and a fear of the unknown into something you can understand and control. To name the damage is to conquer it.

After you have taken the Inventory and interpreted the score according to the directions in the Appendix, return here. We will proceed to look systematically at the family environment in which your difficulties were bred.

THE TROUBLED FAMILY

Writings in family therapy often cite the well-known opening line in Leo Tolstoy's novel *Anna Karenina:* "Happy families are all alike; every unhappy family is unhappy in its own way."[4]

My training, conducted in the spirit of Tolstoy's words, prepared me to make fine distinctions between the causes of people's misery—serious mental illness, substance abuse, physical violence, bitter fighting, and acrimonious divorce, to name a few. In treating survivors of troubled families, however, I have come to see that the fine distinctions we professionals make are lost in a child's immature mind.

Growing up in a troubled family, you probably recognized your unfulfilled need for a loving parent. The reasons why you were unfulfilled most likely didn't matter much. I've seen that regardless of the specific nature of the problem, the families of survivors sound the same from the child's point of view.

At a group session devoted to milestones and holidays in troubled homes, one survivor, whose mother was chronically depressed and embittered by divorce, related that his family didn't celebrate Christmas. His mother was either too tired, too upset, or too sad. Usually around the beginning of December, she retreated to the bedroom, making herself scarce until New Year's had passed. One year he appealed to his father, who became enraged. "How can you be so goddamn selfish? I'm doing all that I can. Get off my back!" he shouted.

This survivor never tried that again. Instead, each December, he borrowed Christmas books from the library to read to his younger brothers and sisters, and he saved what money he could earn during the year to buy them inexpensive gifts.

Another survivor remembered that her family didn't celebrate July Fourth because her mother saw any get-together as an opportunity for her alcoholic husband to make a scene.

> The son of a bitch would only get drunk and break up the picnic. And no one would come anyway because he's made an enemy of each and every relative.

A third survivor, the son of a workaholic business executive, remembered spending his birthday with his stepbrother and their nanny. His parents were out of town on a business trip. They didn't call or send a present. When they got home, they gave him cash.

From different social classes, family structures, religious backgrounds, and diagnoses, survivors find, when they compare notes, that they all attended the same "school":

- We rarely celebrated holidays.
- They hardly ever came to a soccer game, a school play, or a community picnic.
- There were no regular mealtimes.
- They forgot my birthday.
- The house was a pigsty.
- No one had a good word for me; nothing I ever did was right.
- They were always fighting with each other, tearing each other apart—in front of us, as if we didn't exist.

The curriculum at "survivor's school" is abuse and neglect, and the necessity of taking care of oneself.

Damaged and suffering themselves, troubled parents are consumed by the task of getting from one day to the next. They have little energy left for anyone or anything else, not even their children—often, especially their children. Rather than matching their children's needs, they act like children themselves, turning family life upside down.

On the following pages, I present a framework for you to evaluate the troubles in your family. Questions directed at you are not taken from a diagnostic manual that defines the differences in family types. My framework, instead, assumes the child's point of view, looking at the way your family functioned in five areas:[5]

- ensuring a safe environment
- providing affection, support, and affirmation
- communicating
- maintaining a positive family identity
- solving problems

Based on the insider's perspective, the five-area framework examines what you saw as a child, not necessarily what the diagnostician can observe from outside the family.

Steel yourself! Working through this evaluation will undoubtedly

27

bring back some awful memories. At the same time, completing it will give you a greater understanding of how your family functioned and why you may often see yourself as powerless and hurt.

ENSURING A SAFE ENVIRONMENT

Providing physical safety and nourishment is the family's primary obligation to its young. In healthy families, children do not question these fundamentals. They assume that tomorrow will be like today, that they will have a home on secure ground with food, clothing, and a reliable parent who cares. Survivors make no such assumptions. All too often, they are physically unsafe and see themselves as weak and besieged in a dangerous world.

Were You Physically Abused?

If you were physically abused, your parents took advantage of your size to overpower you and hurt your body.

In some trouble families, physical abuse can masquerade as discipline. One survivor told me that his mother locked him out of the house whenever he said something that was foul by her "dignified" standards. He would stand for hours on the front porch begging to be let back in, each time believing that he was being abandoned forever. He went through childhood with the fear that his right to live at home could be revoked at any moment.

Other survivors remember being "taught a lesson" with a paddle, strap, or terrifying confinement in a locked closet. Physical attacks on a child's body can also made behind a banner of religion, propriety, or safety. One survivor recalled:

> My mother was a cleanliness freak. She consumed gallons of mouthwash to freshen her breath. She swabbed her ears several times daily. I swear, the local drugstore couldn't keep up with her demand for Q-Tips. She even used two or three deodorants at once. No nook or cranny where dirt could lodge escaped her attention—even on my body. She probed my ears, my nose, my teeth, and my fingernails. She bathed me in detergent, and she monitored my bowel movements daily. When I didn't produce, she

flushed out my insides with an enema. There was no way I could protect myself against her invasions.

Other troubled parents don't bother to raise a banner of self-justification. Lacking impulse control, they openly direct rage that is meant for someone else at their children. When angry at the boss, disappointed in a spouse, or snubbed by a neighbor, these parents take their feelings out on the smallest or weakest member of the family. Listen to this example:

> Friday nights were the worst because all the frustrations of the week came out. My father went to the local bar before he came home. Around the dinner table he'd lose his temper over the smallest mistake. Fists could fly if you didn't watch your step.

Troubled parents cannot match their actions to their children's needs. They blindly strike out when children make normal demands or when they cry, nag, or defy. If your parents regularly struck out at you, no matter what reason they gave, you were physically abused.

Were You Sexually Abused?

Feeling grossly inadequate or lacking all traces of judgment, some troubled parents turn to their children for gratification they cannot get elsewhere. These parents are the sexual abusers who stalk at night and coerce their victims into secrecy during the day. One female survivor told me:

> Whenever my father was feeling sorry for himself, he slobbered all over me. He'd come into my bedroom crying. Then he would get into my bed and put his big fingers on my little genitals. He said that if I told anyone, he would never talk to me again.

The term "sexual abuse" includes the kind of explicit fondling described by this survivor as well as intercourse, exhibitionism, or posing a child for pornographic pictures.[6] It also encompasses more subtle sexual assaults that can pass for affection.

My father was still hugging, kissing, and holding me close to him long after I had developed breasts and gotten my period.

If you were sexually abused, you were treated as an object, either explicitly or subtly. You were robbed of your innocence, and you were cheated of the right to discover your sexuality with an appropriate partner at the right time for you.

Many survivors who were abused are not able to remember what happened to them. You may be one. The reasons and consequences of burying such memories deep in your unconscious are too complex to take up here, but if you want to pursue this topic further, I have listed several readings and resources in the notes at the end of this book.[7]

Were You Physically Neglected?

Often the problem is not what troubled parents do; it's what they don't do. They don't keep medicines and harmful cleaning solutions out of reach or put away broken liquor bottles. They don't take their children to the dentist or the doctor. They are absent at mealtimes, leaving their children to make dinner for themselves from old Halloween candy, moldy cold cuts, or bread and sugar. Or they don't speak up when their other children, spouse, or lover steps out of bounds. One survivor told me, "My father disappeared when my mother was on the rampage. He thought taking care of the kids was a woman's business." Another said, "My mother didn't protect me from my father because she was afraid of going to the poorhouse without his money."

You were physically neglected if your parents did not keep you out of harm's way.

PROVIDING AFFECTION, SUPPORT, AND AFFIRMATION

After physical security, a child's most basic needs are emotional. All children require love and support. A parent's pleasure imbues a child with a sense of worth and a zest for living.

In *The Art of Loving,* psychologist Erich Fromm cites a Biblical account of the childhood of humanity to illustrate our basic physical and emotional needs.[8] He notes that in Genesis, God promises His people primary security, a land of milk and honey. Milk, Fromm suggests, is our physical sustenance; honey is the love and affirmation that give sweetness to life and instill happiness in being alive.

Taking Fromm's analysis a step further, I compare healthy parents to a satisfied God who looks at His creation and says, "It is good." Troubled parents, on the other hand, have the face of an angry God who looks down on His children and bellows, "You have not pleased me. I will deliver you to your enemies."

Even if you did nothing wrong, hearing this message can lead you to accept the judgment that you are bad.

Were You Emotionally Abused?

You were emotionally abused if your parents wore the face of an angry God. Many adult survivors are still bewildered by how parents who are "supposed to love you" can be so hurtful. "Why did my mother treat me so badly? Aren't mothers supposed to love their children?" many ask.

Psychoanalyst Alice Miller offers an explanation.[9] She has suggested that the capacity to give love and support is found in people who are able to see their separateness from others. Understanding deeply that "you" have a larger purpose in life than to satisfy "me," they can tolerate differences between themselves and others.

Troubled parents balk at differences. Walls of misery obstruct their vision, and they are unable to see their children as separate individuals with needs, wants, and views of their own. Oblivious to the boundaries between self and other, these parents regard children as agents of their own desires. Their unjustified expectations are expressed in a range of emotionally abusive behaviors including the verbal assault, invasion of privacy, and inconsistent, capricious demands.

Were You Verbally Assaulted?

The most obvious form of emotional abuse in troubled families is the open verbal assault that parents too often direct at their children. They tease about chests that are too flat, hips that are too fat, ears that are too big, skin that is pimpled, and hair that is too straight or too curly. Or they lash out at their children for being bookworms, for getting low grades, for being jocks, unathletic, overly social, unpopular, not serious enough, or too serious. Children in troubled families never seem to get it quite right. No matter what they do, their parents are dissatisfied.

One survivor reported this bitter memory of his father's disappointment:

> I was shy and thin and small. My father wanted me to be a leader in the Boy Scouts. He was the master of the troop and said I was shaming him. He would call on me at meetings, and when I didn't answer he would make fun of me. At home, he would tear into me for not participating and being afraid.

In a healthier family, the contrast between father and son might have been respected as a source of family strength. In this troubled family, the father was wounded by the difference, and the son bore the brunt of the man's unfulfilled wishes.

You were verbally assaulted if your parents made unfeeling, hurtful remarks to you and did not respect you as a person separate from themselves.

Did Your Parents Affirm You?

Some troubled parents are less assaultive, but ignore their children's accomplishments and need for recognition. You were unaffirmed if your parents never sang your praises.

Many survivors recall coming home with a test paper, a project, a trophy, or a social triumph and being greeted by an angry, depressed, or distracted parent who had no interest. Often, the interaction turned to the parent's problem, and the child was expected to act as confidante or comforter. Listen to this survivor:

> I tried to show my mother a poem I had written. She took one look at the paper and started crying. She told me that she was leaving my father, that he had beaten her again. She showed me the bruises on her arms and on her legs. Then she broke down completely and said she didn't know what to do. When she put her head down on the table, I tiptoed away.

Frequently, when children press their demands—when they do not tiptoe away—a parent's self-pity may turn into an accusation or an expression of resentment. "If you weren't out so much, I wouldn't be so depressed." Or, "If you were more considerate, your father wouldn't have left me." Statements like these cut to the core and leave children feeling worthless and guilty long after the words are uttered.

Was Your Privacy Invaded?

Disrespect for the child's inner self, illustrated by the comments above, is paralleled by a disregard for privacy that is frequently found in troubled homes. Your parents did not respect your privacy if they betrayed your secrets. One survivor recalled:

> I swore my mother to secrecy the day I first got my period. When I came to the dinner table that night, my older brothers and father were laughing and asked if I was bleeding because "someone had cut my cock off." My mother joined in.

Other troubled parents invade their children's physical space. In a group session, a survivor talked about her impotent rage when her father repeatedly barged into her room without knocking and rifled through her underwear drawer while snarling, "Where are my goddamn socks? Why in hell can't your mother put my stuff away in the right drawer?"

As an adolescent, this survivor hung a DO NOT DISTURB sign on her door, but judging from his subsequent behavior, her father probably never read it. What he did read was her diary and her mail. And because he was big and powerful, he didn't ask permission before helping himself to her belongings, even those she had bought herself. Nor did he refrain from using the toilet when she was taking a bath.

This father's abuse of privacy also extended to the common spaces in the house where he would lounge around undressed. His unfeeling and arrogant response when confronted was, "I'm a free spirit. What's the matter with you?"

Your privacy was invaded if you had no place or belongings that were off limits to the rest of the family. Your privacy was invaded if your right to be alone—in the bathroom, for instance—was not honored.

Were You Besieged by Inconsistencies?

Sometimes troubled parents recognize what children need and even attempt to provide. But riding an emotional roller coaster themselves, they cannot set clear, consistent expectations. One night they require their children to be home by midnight, and the next, they barely notice when a teenager doesn't come home at all.

Other troubled parents cannot sustain an ability to give. Sometimes they are withholding and critical, and other times they are wildly indulgent or sickeningly contrite. Your parents were inconsistent if you didn't know what to expect next.

Listen to these two survivors describe the uncertainty of their homes and how they learned to mistrust.

> I would come home from school on a day that my mother had received an alimony check from my father, and she'd be in a great mood. She'd offer to take me shopping to buy something special. Then, after she spent the money, she'd panic and turn on me. She'd tell me that I was inconsiderate and selfish, that I was demanding, that I didn't care that she had to beg my father for a buck. I learned never to accept an offer.

> My father stood me up on visitation day. I'd be dressed and waiting for him, and he wouldn't show up—didn't call either. He would forget Christmas for two years straight. Then the third year, he'd call me up and cry, telling me how much he missed having the family all together. I eventually wrote him off.

Ensnared by their own troubles, parents like this mother and father cannot attend to the emotional needs of their children. If your parents were chameleons, if their shifting moods rather than logical rules were the unspoken guidelines for your behavior, if you were chronically confused, your parents did not provide a consistent, stable environment.

COMMUNICATING

Communication is the process by which people engage one another. Parents communicate with their children to teach, guide, control, help, console, achieve closeness, entertain, plan, and accomplish the practical necessities of life.

Competent parents regulate what they say and how they speak to meet their children's needs. Their conversations are clear, flexible, open, and responsive. They say what they mean, and they encourage their children to speak up and use the phrase "I don't understand." Healthy parents also permit children to disagree with them and not feel like traitors. When parents are skilled communicators, children volunteer and say, "I think," "I feel," "Why?" "I'm confused," and "I want." Family business is accomplished, and children see themselves as having a meaningful role.

Could Your Parents Communicate with You?

In troubled families, children are either silenced or driven to noisy rebellion. Parents are curt and withholding, or they sound off with no regard for being understood or for understanding anyone else. Family business is jumbled, and a child can be left standing on a street corner while a parent is waiting to pick him or her up in some other place. Communication in your family failed if conversations were confused, one-sided, or rigid. Your parents were ineffective communicators if what they said and how they said it drove the family apart and you away.

Was Communication in Your Family Confused?

Communication in your family was confused if your parent was like this father and talked with no clear purpose, just to fill a void.

> My father was a rambler. He'd start out on one subject—like how the car had to be fixed—and then he would move on to some minute details of a business deal he was working on, and he'd end up talking about life in Baltimore when he was a teenager. I knew I was supposed to respond but I was never sure how. Should I offer to take the car to the gas station? Should I admire his ingenuity as a youth? Should I apologize for my own slovenly teenage habits? Or should I wish him good luck on his business deal? I usually got it wrong.

Communication in your family was also confused if your parents, boggled by their own emotional chaos, couldn't complete their sentences or put two thoughts together in a logical sequence, or if they said one thing and meant another.

Some troubled parents hide behind a thin, brittle veneer of civility. They initiate conversations with an apparently benign comment or a question that puts their children off guard. Then the veneer shatters, and the violence beneath crashes through. Only a few repetitions of the sequence are necessary for survivors to establish a permanent state of mistrust.

> My father would come home from work and ask a seemingly harmless question like, "Do you have time to help me clean up the basement tonight?" I was taken in. I thought he meant, "Do you have time?" So I'd say, "Not tonight. I have a test tomorrow." Then all hell would break loose. "Why the hell not? I'm sick and tired of this crap." It would go on all night. No one else said a word.

Another form of saying one thing and meaning another is the family cover-up. Without the courage to face reality or the skills to tell their children the truth, many troubled parents mount disinformation campaigns. Central to the psychology of many troubled families, disinformation leaves children feeling cut off from help, frightened, and deeply uncertain of what is real and what is not.

Here is a sample of cover-up stories I have heard from survivors. The lyrics are different, but the tune is the same. Perhaps you are familiar with the song.

> When my father was out with his mistress, my mother would draw us into a lament about how hard he was working.

> My mother would be up in her room boozing, and we'd be downstairs talking about her migraine headaches.

> When my father was hospitalized for depression, my mother told me he was on vacation.

If your parents had a cover-up story and didn't speak the truth, then communication in your family was confused.

Was Communication in Your Family One-sided?

Many troubled parents have little appreciation of how their comments or diatribes fall on their children's ears. They talk for their own purposes, not for their children's. For them, communication is not a mutual interchange; it is totally one-sided.

Communication in your family was one-sided if your parents talked to display their power; if they issued dictatorial commands rather than making requests; if they interrupted, didn't listen, ridiculed, or made disrespectful comments. Here are a few examples:

> My mother took the opportunity of every conversation to be angry. She never hesitated to tell me how disappointing I was as a student or to tear into me for something I had done wrong, like picking the wrong Mother's Day gift.

> My father used the dinner table as a podium for reciting his virtues. He was a great provider, a handsome guy, a terrific father. We were supposed to chime in with examples. When we didn't he'd start cursing at us.

> My parents never *asked* us to do things. Everything came down as orders from on high that we dared not challenge. It wouldn't have been so bad if we had other kinds of conversations. But the military command was the only language that my parents knew how to speak.

> My father's standard response to anything I had to say was, "How did you ever get to be so stupid?"

A variation on one-sided communication occurs in families in which troubled parents, in conflict with each other, are blind to the fear they inspire. Rather than shielding their children or offering assurance, these parents use their children as a messenger service and force them to travel back and forth directly through the line of fire. Often, children are pressured to betray one parent by professing loyalty to the other. One survivor described her agony when her mother instructed her to "tell the bastard [her father] to sleep in the living room tonight." Another had precisely the same feeling when she was instructed to ask her father, who was on the outs with her mother, whether he intended to pay the rent or let the family be evicted.

When children are used as messengers between feuding parents, they are often left feeling "No-matter-which-way-I-turn-I'm-in-for-it." The same feeling is generated when parents barrage children with conflicting demands. As one survivor described:

> My father would tell me to go to sleep, and my mother would tell me to clean up the kitchen. They'd both be screaming, and there was nothing I could say that would keep me out of their trap. I wanted to run away from home.

Communication in your family was one-sided if your parents used you as a messenger service or tore you apart with contradictory demands.

And perhaps worst of all, communication in your family was one-sided if your parents were silent, rarely volunteering information or asking questions. Silent parents remain strangers to their children, offering little information about themselves. They fail miserably in the role of teachers, helpers, and companions. Their silence tells children that they are neither worth talking to nor valued.

Sometimes troubled parents use silence as a weapon. When angry, they punish their children by withholding words. With the silent treatment, these parents state, "My displeasure is nonnegotiable." In some troubled homes, the silent treatment can go on for weeks on end. Survivors describe the experience of a silent parent by saying they felt "reduced," "devastated," or "annihilated."

"It was as if I didn't exist," one survivor told me.

"Like looking in a mirror and seeing a blank," I responded.

Was Communication in Your Family Rigid?

Troubled families with rigid communication styles have strict rules about unmentionable subjects. Sometimes these rules are openly articulated; sometimes they are unspoken.

In some troubled families, expressing emotions is forbidden. They regard affection, hurt feelings, illness, or physical pain as signs of weakness. Other families can permit tenderness but have a taboo against anger. And still others enforce rules of propriety that exclude the "vulgar" topics of death, illness, and sex, as well as differences of opinion. If your parents restricted the content of conversations, communication in your family was rigid.

Rigid communication also determines the style of family talk. Some families go in for the indirect statement. One survivor shrewdly observed:

> My mother grew up not saying what she wanted. Around our dinner table it was always the same. She would use phrases in the third person, like, "It would be better if someone . . ." or "Your mother would like it if your father . . ." My father was intimidated, and for years they never said anything real or important to one another. They just danced around each other right into the office of the divorce lawyer.

By direct contrast, other families yell and curse. And somewhere in the middle is what I call the switchboard syndrome, which goes like this. Troubled parents who are afraid that the family might unite against them exercise tight control—like a switchboard operator—over who talks to whom. Such parents prevent family members from talking to one another, disconnect conversations once they get started, or connect people when convenient for themselves. Listen to a survivor describe the switchboard syndrome.

> In my house it was a matter of allegiance. If my brother and I talked to each other, we were traitors in my mother's eyes. If I tried to talk to my father, she would think I was taking his side in their latest battle. No conversation could be conducted, no information could be passed, without her scrutiny. In looking back on it, the amazing part is that we complied.

Communication in your family was rigid if topics of conversation were restricted or if one style of talking, such as yelling, indirect statements, or working through a switchboard, prevailed. Very different on the surface, each of these misdirected or aborted communication techniques gives children one unmistakable message: You don't count. That message can get worked into the self-image that children in troubled families carry through life.

MAINTAINING A POSITIVE IDENTITY

Historically, education of the young was a family function. From an early age, children worked beside their parents to master the basic skills necessary for their survival. Simultaneously, they learned their family history, customs, religion, values, ethics, and place in the community. This body of knowledge is what I call the family identity—the answer to the question "Who are we?"[10]

The foundation of a healthy family identity is a shared feeling of pride and kinship. Parents and children believe:

We are a good family.

Home is a safe, welcoming place.

We have a past that is a source of strength, and we have good, sound values to guide us in the future.

We are known and respected in our community.

We like each other.

We enrich each other's joys, and we support one another in times of sorrow.

Our blood runs thick; we will always be there for one another.

Troubled families are not knit together. When members gather, they intensify each other's misery in cold, hollow interchanges or fights. Family feuds, with relatives refusing to talk to each other, are common and can last long after the original cause of friction has been forgotten. Sometimes the resentments are not even buried at the grave. In some troubled families, not going to a cousin's, an aunt's, or even a parent's funeral becomes a point of honor or a matter of saving face.

A colleague summed up the problem brilliantly in a therapy session with a family torn apart by hostility. Week after week, he encouraged each member to hear the others' feelings and thoughts. No one did, and the bitterness and backbiting continued relentlessly. One day, as the family got ready to leave his office, the youngest child hung back and asked, "Whose side are you on anyway?"

He replied, "I'm against all of you. I'm the only one here who is for the family."

A family that is "for" itself takes deliberate steps to cultivate and pass along a positive identity to its children. The family keeps traditions, saves mementos, and tells stories about its heroes. These activities congeal in a proud heritage that ties the family to the past but also grows and changes to fit the present. Children in such families see themselves as part of a unit larger than themselves and take pleasure in belonging. Children in troubled families see themselves as alone.

Was Heritage a Source of Conflict in Your Family?

Some troubled families are inflexible and can't adapt the past to the present. Heritage, in this case, does not bond people together or make them proud; it strangles them on separate ropes. One troubled parent sends his son to the boarding school that he, his father, and his father's father attended even if the boy doesn't want to go. He sticks stubbornly to the plan even if it means putting the house in hock. Another refuses permission to send his brilliant daughter to college "because women in this family get married after high school." And a third drags everyone out in a blinding snowstorm "because we always go to a restaurant on Sundays."

If your parents created animosity toward the past by rigidly enforcing traditions, heritage was not a positive force in your family.

The opposite problem, disregard for the past, is also found in troubled families and can be equally destructive. Your family disregarded the past if your parents were ashamed of their origins and isolated themselves from their history.

In some troubled families, parents don't talk about the past at all, or they shower contempt on their relatives. Telling stories about misfits, losers, and rogues, they use heritage as ammunition, not as a source of pride. The point is made vividly in this memory told to me by a survivor.

> In the fifth grade, we did a project on family history. I interviewed my parents, and they didn't have one good word to say about anyone. According-ing to them my relatives were low-class boors who acted like they "just got off the boat." I didn't do the project, and I got a 0, which led to D on my report card in social studies.

Did Your Family Ruin Holidays, Milestones, and Vacations?

At no time is the problem of a negative family identity more dramatic than at holidays, milestones, and on vacations.[11] Many survivors regard these times as the worst events of their life. Surrounded by cultural expectations of togetherness and family joy, children in troubled families feel isolated and crushed when their parents mishandle celebrations. Because there is always a holiday coming up, the subject is never far from survivors' minds. Many cannot stop talking about it. Listen to a sample of survivors' accounts, and decide how badly your family ruined celebrations.

The celebration stories I've heard from survivors fall into three rough categories:

- cold, meaningless, and hollow
- angry and chaotic
- overlooked and ignored

Your family's celebrations were cold, meaningless, and hollow if, on these occasions:

- bonds were not reinforced
- the feeling that "We really know how to do this holiday right and we're looking forward to doing it again next year" did not prevail
- rituals were not revitalized with personal contributions from participants, such as a new recipe, a new Hanukkah story, or a new Christmas carol

Here are two examples of a vacation and a celebration that were cold and meaningless.

We all dreaded the obligatory family vacation, but no one had the guts to say so. We lived in Philly and the tradition was to drive west to one of the national parks. In the car we would sit for days in silence, or talk about the weather or how many more miles we had to go. When we finally got to wherever it was we were going, we'd get into a cabin. My mother would go hiking. My father would go horseback riding or fishing, and my brother and I would be given some money and told to do whatever we liked. I can't remember any attempt on my parents' part to compromise what they wanted to do or to keep us together as a family. Our vacations were hollow.

For Easter, the extended family got together at my grandmother's. It was the only time we saw one another. The conversation at the table was stilted—"Oh, this is such wonderful ham"—or competitive—whose business was doing best, whose kids were doing best, who had moved into the nicest neighborhood. As soon as dessert was over, everyone made a beeline to the door.

Your family's holidays, milestones, and vacations were angry and chaotic if:

- they became occasions for people to air old grievances and fight
- your parents were too incapacitated to celebrate—for instance, by buying a Christmas tree, making a Seder, or putting together a picnic
- there was no shared idea of how to celebrate and differences of opinion generated conflict

To hear survivors tell it:

Every vacation turned into a horror show. We would be all together in a cabin, or we'd go camping. They'd be fighting the whole time. It was worse than being at home, because there were no friends' houses to escape to.

My mother was always drunk on the holidays. One Christmas my sister and I worked for the whole day on decorating a tree. She came in and snarled, "What's so special about Christmas?" and tried to push the tree over. I grabbed her and pulled her away. Holidays were always a mess like that. Mostly she would be crying at the table, saying how unhappy she was. There was no thought for any of us, and my father was helpless.

My father refused to go to any family event on my mother's side of the family. He had a grudge against my mother's brother, and he had the idea that he was protecting our family's honor by keeping us away from "that slimy bastard." My mother would go alone, and he would pace around the house shouting that she had betrayed him. When she came back, the fight would go on and on. Only as an adult did I get to know my aunts, uncles, and cousins.

Ignoring or overlooking celebrations is, for some troubled parents, a way of expressing anger. Others are too incompetent to remember or too depleted to care. Here are some examples:

> I rarely had a birthday party. My mother was always too upset or too frazzled or too angry at me.

> My father had a dread of public places and crowds. He wouldn't come to my graduation.

> My parents were divorced. For holidays, I was supposed to be with my father, but he wouldn't send for me. My mother resented him. She'd sulk. I remember Thanksgiving. She would give me five dollars and tell me to get myself dinner. She would go up to her room and play solitaire.

Regardless of the family's style, survivors rarely forget the misery of holidays and celebrations in their parents' homes. Their recollections can be the nucleus of a lasting negative family identity.

SOLVING PROBLEMS

Life deals out its fair share of blows to both healthy and troubled families. The important distinction is *how* each handles its problems. Healthy families use constructive strategies for solving problems. Troubled families, thrown back on limited resources, are knocked out by their problems and give children the idea that life will easily defeat them.

Researchers at the McMaster University in Hamilton, Ontario, have developed a three-part scheme for categorizing the problems that occur naturally in all families.[12] At the most fundamental level, families face basic tasks, solving problems associated with providing food, money, transportation, and shelter. At the next level are developmental tasks, which include problems that arise from the family's normal development over time, such as pregnancy, the marriage of a child, aging, and death. Finally, hazardous tasks involve managing crises stemming from serious illness, job changes, moving, and sudden or unexpected loss.

On all three levels, competent families:

- define the difficulty
- accept that problems are a normal part of life and not a stigma, punishment, or sign of weakness
- come together to find a solution
- assign a leadership role to parents while allowing other members to express their views

Many troubled families cannot successfully complete these steps. They have no methods for solving problems and are unprepared for stress.

Can Your Family Acknowledge Problems?

Your family cut off problem solving at the pass if your parents couldn't admit that difficulties existed. For instance, many troubled families believe that talking about a problem makes matters worse, or that open discussion threatens the family's pride or its reputation in the community. These ideas lead to a rule of secrecy and silence that stops family members from getting help from each other or from outsiders. Listen to survivors talk about the rule of secrecy and decide if your family had one too:

> My grandfather died of cirrhosis. We were told that he had a heart condition. When my father was drinking himself to death, no one said a word. My mother made excuses instead. Now my brother is drinking too.

> My sister had a kidney problem. My parents felt that talking about it would shame her. No one explained her illness to me or told me what I could do to help her. I don't think anyone talked to her about it very much either. She became a psychological wreck.

> My father broke with his family. He didn't go to either of his parents' funerals. When I tried to bring up the topic of our own strained relationship, he stopped talking to me for days.

In some troubled families, the rule of secrecy is carried to the extreme and takes the form of total denial. If your parents were deniers, they flew in the face of reality, creating a myth that the family was happy or that the family problem was somewhere outside—for instance, with the neighborhood, with relatives, or with the school system.

The lies fostered by denial are designed to bolster a troubled parent's own damaged ego and are maintained without regard for a child's need to hear and speak the truth. The confusion parents create for their children by denying family problems can be lethal. Not only are children forced to endure the family without any hope of change, but they are also pressured to bottle up their distress, disown their feelings, and buy into their parents' myths. One survivor told me:

> My parents looked good on the outside. My mother was in the PTA, and my father had a good job. At home, they were brutal to the kids, but we were supposed to believe in their public image. They told us that they were wonderful people, caring parents. They wanted us to be grateful to them and sing their praises to our friends, teachers, and neighbors. I doubted my own senses, and I didn't know what to believe.

Could Your Family Find Solutions to Problems?

If your parents were ineffective leaders, the family probably could not solve its problems. Rather than bringing the family together around a common purpose, some troubled parents try to impose their will arbitrarily. Solutions in the arbitrary style do not enlist cooperation. Instead, one-sided decisions leave children and spouses feeling unheard, squashed, or rebellious.

> My father dictated the family budget; my mother ran us into debt by spending behind his back. There was no money left for college. I often felt that she wouldn't have done it if he had taken her into consideration.

In other troubled families, parents abdicate responsibility for leadership. Cut off and isolated from relatives and the community, they cannot guide the family to needed resources. A survivor described the isolation and its effects with this metaphor:

> I felt like I grew up in a house with no windows. I didn't know that any help was possible outside the family.

Problem solving in your family was also inadequate if your parents lacked the skills to analyze situations, listen, negotiate, or ask and answer questions. When families without these skills gather, disrespect for one another's feelings is rampant. The attempt to solve a problem can quickly deteriorate into an icy silence or a noisy free-for-all, complete with yelling, breaking dishes, slamming doors, and stomping out as people blame and criticize one another.

In other cases, the family's attention becomes so diffused by conflict that people cannot keep track of the issue that needs to be resolved. One survivor recalled:

> We'd start out discussing whether we should get a new car. Soon everyone would be shouting at each other. I didn't even know what it was about. I just knew that I wanted to put a pillow over my head and drown out their voices.

Sometimes a family's attention is all too focused, but in the wrong place. In these families, problem solving inevitably becomes an opportunity to rehash the same old grievances. Another survivor remembered:

> Every time a problem came up in my family, we reviewed ancient history. My mother reminded my father that the only reason she married him was that she was pregnant.

If your parents did not keep their attention appropriately focused, your family was probably unable to solve problems.

For whatever the reason, the end result of failed problem solving in families is the same. Resentments fester, tensions grow, and, all the while, problems that go unresolved get bigger and bigger.

THE NET RESULT OF YOUR FAMILY'S TROUBLES

When parents behave as if they, themselves, are their one and only child; when parents do not provide a stable, safe, and supportive environment; when parents abuse, neglect, coerce, and criticize; when parents do not serve as role models or offer guidance; when parents and children mismatch; then children can't be children. Instead, they become ugly, bad, and unacceptable in their own eyes.

Consider the mismatch between your parents and yourself by looking at the outer rim of the Resiliency Mandala and the space beyond that represents your family's troubles.

From the preceding discussion and your own lexicon, select the words that best describe your troubled parents. Either in your mind's eye or with a pencil, insert them along the circumference of the mandala. Use as many as you need to complete a picture of the painful environment in which you grew up. Words have therapeutic value; they change the formless chaos of your family's troubles to something you can understand and work to overcome.

Chapter Three

REFRAMING: HOW TO RESIST THE VICTIM'S TRAP

In the previous chapter, you had the chance to construct a systematic picture of your family's troubles and the damage you suffered as a child. In workshops for survivors of troubled families, I have found that this exercise causes a mix of powerful emotions. On the one hand, most participants feel heard—some for the first time—and have a predictable "wash of relief." You may share some of their feelings:

COMFORT because the secret of your family is out in the open and you are no longer alone with it

PRIDE because completing this exercise honestly is something your parents could not have done

COURAGE because identifying the extent of your family's troubles has allowed you to see that in some ways your life has already improved upon the past

VALIDATION because someone has acknowledged that there really was something wrong with your family and you were not imagining or exaggerating what happened to you

CLARITY because you know the elements of your past that need to be changed in order to build a healthy, well-functioning life of your own in the present

But these positive feelings do not predominate when most survivors review their family history. Rather, many have a heightened sense of pain from recalling incidents they had pushed to the back of their minds and would rather keep there. You may also have some of these feelings:

GRIEF because of your lost childhood

ANGER because of the indignities you suffered

LOSS because of the love and acceptance that you didn't have

FEAR because no matter how far you have traveled, sooner or later you will fall into your parents' patterns

SHAME because of your origins

I cannot promise that these feelings will ever go away completely. The wounds that troubled parents inflict leave scars on their children's spirit, and most survivors are never completely free from unfulfilled wishes and doubts and fears about themselves. As the Challenge Model suggests, the Resiliency Mandala of every survivor will have shaded and unshaded areas.

In some survivors, the past generates a steady undercurrent of uneasiness. For others, pain wells up with sudden sharpness at pressure points: in new relationships, at holidays, and when survivors have children and find themselves without a model for parenting or the energy to give what they never received. Whatever the form, survivor's anxiety tends to stick and can sometimes reach panic proportions.

Though I do not have a method for redoing your past or shedding your pain completely, I can show you a way to limit its power over you.

- Do not be frightened by the unsubstantiated myth that family problems will inevitably be perpetuated from one generation to the next. This is not true.
- Do not be lured into the Victim's Trap or believe that you will feel better by examining the damage you have suffered over and over. This will only keep the past alive and intensify the pain.
- Do not deplete yourself by continuously blaming your parents for hurting you. This will only fuel your anger and tighten your ties to your troubled family.

The alternative to nursing your pain endlessly is to demote its importance by uncovering the same interplay between your vulnerability and resilience that Werner and Smith found in the children of hardship they studied on Kauai.[1] Step back from yourself far enough so that your injuries diminish within a bigger picture that also includes your strengths. You saw this approach in action in Chapter One when Barbara framed her favorite photograph, with her triumph in the middle and the fingers of revenge on the invisible edge, when Faye took solace and even laughed at her humorous response to her mother's verbal assault, and when Janet wrote to me, taking credit for her creative solutions to a stultifying life with her mentally ill mother.

You too can make a mental shift from dwelling on your damage to recognizing the challenges you met and the times you bounced back from your family's troubles. The mandala on the next page, picturing each of the resiliencies, will be a guide throughout this book, telling you how to look for strengths in yourself that you may not have acknowledged before.

From my experience with survivors, I know that the transition I am recommending—from thinking of yourself as a damaged victim to considering yourself a resilient survivor—is far from simple. Sharp, deep, and longstanding, your pain will not easily release its hold on you. Right now, you may be both more familiar and more comfortable with a Damage Model angle on your resiliencies, seeing

- Insight as self-absorption and intellectualization
- Independence as a fear of being close or an intimacy impairment

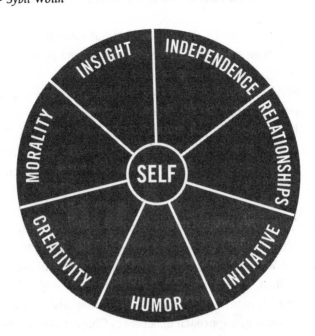

- Relationships as excessive dependency or preoccupation with the needs of others
- Initiative as overachievement
- Creativity as useless fantasy
- Humor as compulsive clowning
- Morality as guilt and overresponsibility

Used to being beaten down by your family, you may be twisting your accomplishments around and viewing them as faults. The horrors of the past and your memories of suffering might hold a far greater attraction for you, at the moment, than thinking about your strengths.

Take note. The Victim's Trap has tight springs. I believe an example might help you loosen the coils. Below, I tell the story of Noreen, a resilient survivor who stumbled into the Victim's Trap but climbed back out. The details of Noreen's story—the precise events in her life, the kind of mother and father she had, and the particulars of her response to them—may be very different from your own, but the benefits of transforming her self-image from damaged victim to resilient survivor can also be yours. I hope that you will see beyond the details of Noreen's story to the underlying progression and that her example will encourage you to make the same journey.

NOREEN

When I first met Noreen, she was twenty-four years old and in her second year of medical school. She came to see me because of a crisis in her love life. Her relationship with her boyfriend, Stewart, had fallen apart.

Noreen and Stewart had gone out for more than a year, lived together for a few months, and had begun talking about marriage. From the outset, they quarreled. Stewart complained that Noreen was tough and on a short fuse. Noreen felt that Stewart was trying to tell her what to think, to control her life, and sometimes to possess her. Nevertheless, they found ways around their disagreements, and Noreen felt that they loved each other.

After Noreen and Stewart moved in together, the little disagreements began to escalate into big fights. Noreen found herself feeling angrier and angrier about small inconsiderate acts on Stewart's part. She had a sense that she was overreacting, but she couldn't control herself.

A week prior to the breakup, Stewart had borrowed Noreen's car and returned it without refilling the gas tank. He apologized, but she couldn't back off. She was enraged and refused to talk to him for two days. By the time she came around, it was too late. Stewart, who described himself as "battle-weary," had decided to move out. Noreen couldn't dissuade him. After he left, she panicked. Flooded by guilt and self-loathing, she became convinced that no man would ever love her.

Noreen's narration suggested that disappointment and rejection had opened many sore spots. She was actually a strong person, but, swamped as she was by anxiety, she could not see herself clearly. To drive home her poor self-image, she described a series of love affairs in which she had been rejected. Her descriptions were punctuated with demeaning remarks about her worth. Her resiliencies, pushed to the back of her awareness, came out only indirectly.

From a dismal past, Noreen emerged as a well-functioning young woman. Although she had trouble when "relationships got too hot," she was able to make and keep several meaningful friendships. By dint of her initiative, she had put herself through college and was doing the same in medical school. Amid all of her hard work, she took time to enjoy life. She backpacked, played tennis, and, as much as her finances allowed, took advantage of the cultural life in the cities in which she had lived.

In the past, in her parents' home, Noreen had shown similar grit. From a young age, she saw that getting love or even the daily necessities of life from her mother and father was like "hitting my head against the wall." So she got tough. She gave up on her parents and took matters into her own hands. She did the chores left unattended by her mother, learned to cook the meals, cleaned the house, and supervised her younger brothers and sisters. By mid-childhood, she had disengaged from her parents emotionally and was well on her way to solidifying the resiliency of INDEPENDENCE.

Noreen also did well in school and won the admiration and attention of her teachers. She took after-school and weekend jobs that got her out of the house, gave her money of her own, and built her confidence that she could make it in the world. As her family moved from city to city, she was able to create a stable sense of community for herself by joining the Brownies and, later, the Girl Scouts. In her troops, she elaborated her domestic skills—cooking, home repair, and child care—and added new ones—first aid, camping, and exploration.

Noreen described all of this, emphasizing the damage to her emotions and her capacity for intimacy. She dwelled on the escape value of the Scouts and the burdens she felt as a child—the violence and abuse in her household. She belittled herself for being "Little Miss Perfect" and took none of the credit she deserved for her competence, courage, and the challenges she faced and met. The picture she painted was distorted and unfair to herself.

THERAPY

The idea of Noreen's therapy was to help her see herself as she really was. The task was not easy. She clung tenaciously to her pain and her view of herself as a victim of her past. Blind to her resilience, she could not hear the Survivor's Pride that unconsciously slipped out now and then as she told me that she was the only one in the family the babies loved and that she ran a better house than her mother ever could.

Noreen's treatment turned on reframing, a therapeutic technique for uncovering valuable, submerged themes in a patient's story. Reframing is the method Barbara intuitively used when she cropped the fingers of revenge off her graduation photo and put her big grin of success in the middle. Reframing is a method you can use to shift your view of yourself as a defeated victim of your past to a stalwart survivor with some special strengths to show for your experience.

The Damage Model Phase of Therapy

We started therapy in the Damage Model, relating Noreen's childhood to her readiness to feel rejected, to flare up, and to alienate people she cared about. Guided by her insight, she was able to ask herself the difficult question of why her relationships so often went sour.

"Fighting is more comfortable than loving," she said. Noreen could see that, for her, arguing about disappointments was safer than negotiating differences; leaving felt more secure than staying around when "things got hot." The reasons were not hard to understand as we began talking about the way Noreen had grown up.

Noreen had come from a family where alcohol was abundant and love was scarce. Her parents were incompetent to perform most of the tasks of family living I described in the previous chapter. Her paternal grandfather had died of cirrhosis; her father and mother were heavy drinkers. Family life was riddled with physical violence, verbal abuse, and neglect. Ties to a community and relatives were made impossible by frequent moves related to her father's work. One vivid description conveys the flavor of her home life:

> My father was brutal. A lot of his violence was related to his strict rules about eating. You'd be sitting around the table and you'd put your peas inside the mashed potatoes, mushing them together in some way. My father would stand up and smack you in the face, sometimes hard enough to push you off the chair, sometimes not, depending on how big you were at the time. And then he would kick you when you were down, screaming the whole time. Anybody who made a noise around the house would get

the same treatment. If you cried, you'd get another blow. You had to eat those potatoes and peas separately. If you didn't eat your spinach, he would come over and grab you by the hair and pull your head back. He'd shove the spinach in your mouth and slam your mouth shut, holding your nose closed until you swallowed it. My mother egged him on. She would point out someone who wasn't eating.

At first, opening Noreen's memories about her past did a lot to help her comprehend her damage. She could see that as a child, she had used toughness as a principal method for coping—with good reason. Her hard outer shell was an effective barrier against her parents and gave Noreen a sense of her own power to protect herself. By the same token, Noreen incurred unavoidable costs by armoring herself. She suffered both on the taking and giving sides of her intimate relationships. On Noreen's Resiliency Mandala, the relationships wedge was primarily dark, showing the extent of her damage.

On the taking side of relationships, Noreen could not tolerate the sight of herself as dependent. Nor could she stand giving up control. Seeing other people as dangerous and unpredictable, she invested herself in practical accomplishments. Unlike more socially oriented survivors, whose Resiliency Mandalas highlight relationships, Noreen did not turn to substitute parents or to peers for affirmation. Instead, the Scouts, school, and her housekeeping skills were the mirrors in which she could see an image of herself as competent.

On the giving side, Noreen did not cultivate the ways of tenderness, compromise, and forgiveness. Acts of giving, except in relationships with her younger siblings, in which she could maintain control, were a threat. Through her child's eyes, to be soft was to be vulnerable. The product of this equation was the pugnacious stance that led to Noreen's trouble with Stewart.

Understanding that her problem with Stewart was an unfortunate but expectable consequence of her upbringing diminished some of the guilt and self-loathing Noreen felt when she first came for therapy. She was relieved to learn that she was not a "bad person" with an "innate defect," but rather someone who had suffered and who had scars to show for it.

But after her first stride forward, Noreen stumbled into a dead end. She could not shake off her painful memories. Session after session, she spun out the lurid details of her childhood, as if, in the telling, she could undo them. The endless repetition had the opposite effect. Recalling her past did not ease her pain; it intensified her distress. What she needed was a blueprint for building loving relationships in the present. But stuck in the Victim's Trap, she could only tell and retell her memories of growing up in a loveless home.

The Challenge Model Phase of Therapy

I knew that Noreen's only way out was to suspend her pain, to see her past not only as a stumbling block but also as a challenge, and to recognize her own resilience. I also knew that she would resist. I remember the first time I suggested the idea to her. She was talking about her mother:

> My mother had a label for all of the kids. My sister had big breasts, so she was the "tramp." The babies—the twins—were "ugly"; my mother said she wanted to hang veils on their faces. I had something wrong with my eyes, and I had to wear a patch, so I was "defective." A lot of times I would fall or bump into things because I had an eye problem, and she would berate me for being clumsy and out of control. I wouldn't let myself cry. I would stare at her and think of something else . . . like, "I'll know how to be a good mother. I'll do the opposite of everything she does, and my children will love me, and maybe then, I'll finally have a family."

Noreen related the incident for the same reason she had told other similar stories in the past: to let me know about her mother's verbal abuse, the total absence of support and love in her family, and her own suffering. Certainly all of this was present in her story. I knew the pain she was feeling, and I would never want to dismiss or minimize any of it. But from my outside perspective, I also recognized the affirmation that could be salvaged from her story, and I knew that she would benefit from seeing that side of her story too. I forged ahead and reframed the story to reveal its submerged themes.

"I find it remarkable," I ventured, "that under unbearable stress you could exercise terrific self-control, see your siblings' plight, and keep your hopes for yourself alive."

Noreen balked. She needed more time to unhook from her pain and see herself from a new and different point of view. A contemptuous smile crossed her lips. "That's nice for you to say," she came back at me. "You probably had a mother who loved you."

Several more attempts at reframing Noreen's experiences fell on deaf ears, but eventually my prodding made an inroad. Noreen was talking about her father.

> He could go into a rage over anything. When you played a game with him you had to let him win. You had to look like a weakling and let him feel like he was boss.

Again we went through the pain: her father's brutality, how she always had to be on guard, how she had to be the parent and could never be the child. Then I reframed the story to emphasize Noreen's knack for figuring out her father, controlling herself, and outwitting and cleverly maneuvering around him.

"You were pretty shrewd about your father," I proposed casually. "How did you figure him out?"

Noreen looked at me for a long moment. I waited for her to dismiss me again, but this time she didn't.

"I watched him carefully," she answered, "and I figured out what made him tick. I could read the expression on his face. I could tell the kind of mood he was in from the way he walked. I knew the difference between the drunk and sober times. I never got taken in."

A well-developed, protective part of herself that she had never owned before was now out on the table.

"It sounds like you had some kind of tactic for managing your father and a lot of insight into him, besides," I said.

"That's right," she returned. "I knew what was going on, and I knew what I had to do to survive."

With these words, Noreen retrieved a recurrent childhood fantasy:

> Sometimes I would lie in my bed in the dark after my mother had been on the warpath against me. I would pretend I belonged to this tribe of Indians who had to live in a hostile white world. I had been in this incredible

massacre, and I was the last survivor. I was tortured and humiliated. But like all good Indians, I was a stoic. Afterward, I wandered alone through the wilderness, fending for myself, and I was at peace.

The fantasy was a perfect bridge for getting to my point because it captured both sides of Noreen's survivor story—her pain and her immense will to overcome adversity. Drawing power from its deep truth, the fantasy freed Noreen's memory and helped her to see the value of her toughness as well as its potential for causing trouble in her life. She now could recall how she armored herself as a child, broke away from her family, and won many victories: the academic accomplishments, the sense of community and achievement she had found in the Scouts, her self-reliance in the adult work world, and her competence in taking care of a household.

As Noreen's focus broadened to include the challenges she met as well as the defeats she suffered, there was also a profound shift in her identity. She went from labeling herself as a casualty to regarding herself as a strong person who had suffered but who had also successfully withstood the blows that life had dealt her. By taking the credit she deserved—by laying claim to Survivor's Pride—she gathered courage to risk trying something new and scary, just as she had been willing to stick her neck out in the past. With small, tentative steps, she tested the ways of tenderness and healthy dependency that had been closed to her in childhood. And with small steps she learned the art of loving.

REFRAMING

Our lives are a story.[2] There are as many stories as there are lives, and each of our stories is many stories. As authors; we are free to script and cast ourselves as we choose. Out of our complicated and varied experiences, we each select the events that have meaning for us and interpret them to fit our inner picture of who we are. Then we arrange the details in a plot that defines us—our problems, our strengths, and our possibilities. In turn, the story we write exercises a powerful influence on how we feel and behave. As we construct our story, it constructs us.

In the story of Noreen, you saw that when she viewed herself as a helpless victim in the past, she was powerless in the present. When she reframed her story to include her resilience as well as her "faults," she found power in herself to change.

You can find two instances of successful reframing in Noreen's story. Both times, she used incidents from childhood, with embedded evidence of her strength, to convey her suffering. In the first, Noreen talked about her mother's verbal abuse. By shifting the emphasis of the story, we could see Noreen's courage to withstand an attack and the morality and sensitivity she maintained toward her brothers and sisters through the assault. In the second instance, Noreen recalled her father's brutality. In the *reframed* version, we uncovered her insight, shrewdness, and ability to watch out for herself.

To further illustrate the technique—and power—of reframing, I offer the stories of Hal and Julie.

HAL

Hal described how he cowered in the corner each night as his mother and father went on the warpath, cursing at each other and throwing dishes. Most evenings, Hal said he was driven out of the house by his fear.

Reframing started with a question. "Where did you go?" I asked.

"I went to my friend's house," he recalled.

"The same friend every time?"

"Yes."

"Wasn't it late at night? How come they took you in?"

"My friend's father really liked me."

And now Hal's social agility—his way with people—which he had ignored when he first told his story, emerged. Knowing his own need to escape from home, Hal ensured that he would have a place to go. He cultivated a relationship with his friend's father, who was a member of the school board. Hal combed the newspaper every morning, looking for school news, so that he would always be ready to strike up an interesting conversation. His strategy won him a staunch ally, sympathy for his plight, and an open invitation to stay whenever he had to.

Hal's Resiliency Mandala is dominated by the relationship wedge.

JULIE

Julie's parents also were fighters, but her strategy for protecting herself was different from Hal's. On her Resiliency Mandala, morality is one of several dominant wedges.

When I first asked Julie what she did when her parents fought, she gave a standard victim's response. "Their behavior disgusted me. I was miserable. I did anything I could to get away, anything at all."

"What exactly did you do?" I asked.

"Nothing important. Typical teenage stuff. It doesn't matter. I couldn't face the reality of my parents' lives and what they were doing to me, so I blotted them out by denying and running away."

"Teenage stuff? Running away?" I asked, imagining her staying out all night. "Did you get into trouble? Sex? Drugs?"

She was jolted and covered her mouth, trying to stifle her laughter. "Me? Never!"

The shift in her mood, which now bordered on giddiness, was an opening. I pursued the fine points in Julie's definition of "typical teenage stuff." "Don't make any judgments," I said. "Just reconstruct the scene. Tell me exactly what you mean by running away."

My questions led to reframing Julie's portrayal of herself as an air-headed teenager, running around aimlessly. Now her story revealed her conscience—a morality that gave direction to her life—and self-approval, which filled in for the guidance and affirmation that her parents withheld.

"I worked one night a week at the blood bank," she said. "I read to a blind woman in the afternoon. I volunteered to work with a crew, cleaning up the creek in a local park."

No sooner did she get started than she tried to undercut herself again. "I was attracted to places where people didn't ask any questions. Keep moving and keep up the denial: That was me."

"Moving and denying is one way to frame your activities," I agreed, "but there's another way to look at this. I prefer to say that you were on a rescue mission for other people and for the world. Your choices seemed to be based on a strong sense of morality, generosity, and decency."

Honing in on Julie's response to her parents' fights revealed her fine values. Her unselfish devotion to good causes hauled her out of her parents' degeneracy. In the projects she picked, in the places she "ran" to, she became, in her own eyes, someone who could change things for the better. By rescuing others, she was also rescuing herself.

In the previous chapter, we used the outer rim of the Resiliency Mandala to represent your family's troubles. The point of this chapter has been to begin focusing on the center of the Mandala, the part that represents you. It is here that the work of reframing begins. Based upon the examples of Noreen, Hal, and Julie, you may want to try the technique yourself.

Begin by recalling an incident from your family life when you felt injured. Think of what you did—the actions you took—not how badly you felt. Focus on specifics, not on generalities. What exactly did you say? Whom did you talk to? Where did you go? Where did you get the idea of doing what you did?

Recalling these details, you may look at an old scene from a new angle and see a meaning that eluded you before. Use what you observe to make an interpretation of the incident that emphasizes how you successfully helped yourself, not how badly you were hurt.

YOUR RESILIENCY MANDALA

Look at the Resiliency Mandala pictured on the next page. The dark rings represent the times you succumbed to adversity; the light rings, the times you rebounded from pain. The contrast is meant to remind you that nobody is strong all the time. Resilience ebbs and flows. All survivors have vulnerable times, and none escapes the past totally unharmed.

Expect to enter both your damage and your resilience on the Mandala and to see a similar pattern of dark and light emerge. Do not focus on the dark or feel discouraged by it. Instead, regard the contrasting rings as a symbolic picture of your inner life—one that is balanced and realistic, and includes your distress as well as your determination to prevail.

In Part II of this book, we will work to fill in the light sections of your Mandala, your resiliencies. By describing research and offering examples of successful survivors, I will illustrate how the seven resiliencies— insight, independence, relationships, initiative, creativity, humor, and

morality—evolve over time, from childhood to adolescence to adulthood. Using this information and the technique of reframing, you may start to see the development of your own resilience and build a fence around your pain.

Remember that resiliencies tend to group and that some of your wedges will be primarily light while others may be darker. For instance, a survivor with initiative, like Noreen, will have a different light/dark pattern on her mandala than someone like Hal, who has a talent for making relationships. The purpose of this book is to help you discover your own mandala, a symbol that may diminish the burden of being a survivor and lead you to greater peace and harmony in yourself.

Part Two

SEVEN RESILIENCIES

One discovers that destiny can be directed, that one does not have to remain in bondage to the first wax imprint made on childhood sensibilities. Once the deforming mirror has been smashed, there is a possibility of wholeness. There is a possibility of joy.

—Anaïs Nin

Chapter Four

INSIGHT: FOREWARNED
IS FOREARMED

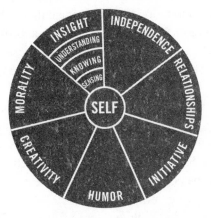

DEFINITION: INSIGHT is the mental habit of asking searching questions and giving honest answers. The development of insight begins with *sensing* or an intuition that family life is strange and untrustworthy. Alert to danger, resilient children soon see the meaning of telltale changes in a parent's walk, dress, breath, or tone of voice. With the intellectual growth of adolescence, sensing deepens into *knowing* the full extent of the family's troubles, including its personal implications. In adulthood, the psychological awareness of resilient survivors ripens into a penetrating *understanding* of themselves and other people.

A family of three children was interviewed as part of a research project conducted by psychoanalyst Dr. E. J. Anthony on the consequences of growing up with severely emotionally disturbed parents.[1] Their mother suffered from paranoid schizophrenia. Convinced that someone was poisoning the food at home, she ate all her meals at a restaurant. A twelve-year-old daughter accepted her mother's delusion and always went out to eat. Another daughter, who was ten, ate at home when her father was there, but otherwise, she too would go along with her mother to a restaurant. The youngest child, a seven-year-old boy, was undaunted by his mother's strange fear. He made a habit of always eating at home. When asked to explain his confidence that he would be all right, he shrugged and replied, "Well, I'm not dead yet."

Anthony's case illustrates how troubled families both threaten *and* challenge their children. The example shows also that insight is a lifeline that can pull a survivor out of the family maelstrom. By refusing to submit, by meeting the challenge of a parent's bizarre ideas with skepticism, survivors can differentiate themselves from a troubled family and ensure their own healthy growth and development.

The mother in Anthony's case, whose thinking was twisted and pulled out of shape by her schizophrenia, was not able to teach her children how to live effectively. Instead, she provided "training in irrationality."[2] She altered facts to suit her own emotional needs, and, like a distorting mirror, reflected disturbing illusions. The world she pictured was dangerously out of joint and required her to take extraordinary safety precautions. She saw her children, like herself, as the targets of a nefarious plot, and she portrayed her pressure to eat in restaurants, rather than at home, as a loving and protective act.

The eldest child was not resilient at all. Having no insight, she asked no questions, accepted her mother's delusions, and refused to eat at home. Research has shown that she is, by far, the exception; most children of schizophrenic parents do not develop disordered thinking and become schizophrenic themselves. In fact, only about 10 percent succumb.

The second daughter, far more typical than the first, lived in a shifting balance of resilience and vulnerability. Gathering strength from her father, she was able to withstand her mother's pressure most of the time. When her father was present, she ate at home, secure in the belief that she would be safe. When her father was absent, however, she was drawn in by the magnetism of her mother's paranoia, and she succumbed to fear. As a young adult, this daughter did not become schizophrenic, *and* she developed some clear strengths. In her Resiliency Mandala, damage and self-repair—shaded and unshaded areas—existed side by side. She separated from the family, went to college, and did well. By the same token, she tended to take a dependent role in her interpersonal relationships. Like many survivors, she had essentially bounced back from the effects of her mother's illness, but she had some scars to show for her experience.

The youngest child, the boy who always ate at home, was the most resilient. He did not require the outside support of his father to bolster his confidence. Relying on his own insight, he saw through his mother's irrationality and dismissed her bizarre ideas. His accurate and sophisticated judgment surrounded him like a protective shield. As he matured, competency was layered upon competency in his Resiliency Mandala. According to Anthony, the child developed into a talented thinker who clearly mastered the corrosive presence of his mother's illness. Though awe-inspiring, his resilience is not rare.

Indeed, after studying 208 schizophrenics and their families for thirty years, noted Swiss psychologist Manfred Bleuler found that only a minority of the children were "abnormal" or "socially incompetent." The majority were healthy despite miserable childhoods. He stated:

> It is surprising to note that their spirit is not broken, even of children who have suffered severe adversity for many years. In studying a number of the family histories, one is even left with the impression that pain and suffering has a steeling—a hardening—effect on the personalities of some children, making them capable of mastering their lives with all its obstacles, in defiance of all their disadvantages.[3]

How did the children Dr. Bleuler studied rise above their daily hardships? How did insight inoculate the boy in Dr. Anthony's example against harm and the Damage Model prediction that his mother's illness would be repeated across generations? How did the Challenge Model drama play itself out in the boy's head? Let's attempt to reconstruct his mind-set.

Start with Anthony's observation that the boy, like all children, wants deeply to feel and behave like his peers. He is also curious. So he looks around and observes that other families in his building are fearless. They eat at home and seem to be just fine. In a TV advertisement, he sees kids like himself chowing down Ho Hos right out of the kitchen cupboard without falling dead to the floor. Perhaps he also visits friends' houses, where everyone eats together showing no apparent signs of terror.

Everywhere the boy turns, his mother's warped, paranoid vision of life is assaulted. His observations set off an alarm in his head. Her strangeness starts to close around him like prison walls. While he wants to fit in and be a regular kid, she is trying to make him stand out and be different. The challenge for him is to recognize what she is doing and to resist her pull. Urged on by pain, he breaks away from the spell of her distorting mirror and turns inward. There, he finds the perfect device for solving his dilemma: a self.

The unique and valuable feature of the self for this boy is its capacity to be observer and observed at the same time.[4] In Challenge Model terms, you can think of the self as a mirror in which the boy can vary his reflections as freely as he can try on different hats. An alternative to his mother's distorting mirror, the boy's metaphoric inner mirror offers unlimited, pleasing possibilities for contemplating himself. He leaps to the opportunity, experimenting with his appearance and evaluating how he feels with each change he makes.

First, he calls up a scene of a restaurant where he is seated across a table from his mother. Aware that his friends are eating at home, he flashes back and watches himself being dragged out of his house in protest. His heart sinks. Next he sees a friend pass by the restaurant, look in the window, and spot him sitting with his screwy mother. The boy cringes, slumps down in his chair, covers his face with a napkin, and mutters under his breath, "That kid thinks I'm just like her. It's curtains for me."

The series of clips makes the boy feel awful. His discomfort challenges him to experiment with a more acceptable sequence of scenes. His resilience is the will to meet his mother's challenge instead of giving in to embarrassment and despair.

Timidly at first, he projects a picture of himself taking over his mother's role. He asks his father for money, goes shopping, returns home, puts together a simple meal, and sits down at the kitchen table to eat. All goes well until he hears his mother's frantic command on the soundtrack. "Stop," she screams. The boy freezes, his arm suspended in midair, bent at the elbow, lifting a forkful of SpaghettiOs to his expectant, open mouth.

The boy can't accept what he sees. The image is too demeaning and too irrational for his taste. To fight back his mounting hesitation, he switches scenes to the advertisements for food he has seen on TV, his friends and their families eating at home, and his intrepid neighbors who hardly ever go to restaurants. The support he gets from these clips emboldens him to act.

The boy actually begins to prepare his own meals and finds, as he suspected, that he dies neither of loneliness nor of poisoning. His estimate of himself soars. Next time he looks in the mirror of his self, he is proud and courageous. The image he sees is full of Survivor's Pride, and he shouts with relief, "I am competent. I can take care of myself. I am not susceptible to the poisons in my mother's delusional world. I can reject what she tells me." Finally, after repeated experiences of success, the boy incorporates these conclusions into his self, where they take form in a lasting resiliency.

Insight—confronting the self with difficult questions—can protect survivors of troubled families and all children from harm. This observation, says psychologist Jerome Kagan, fills a void in our understanding of children that was long left empty by science and Damage Model thinking.

In his book, *The Nature of the Child,* Dr. Kagan points out that for years scientists, overlooking the power of subjective thinking, have tried and failed to uncover a set of principles that relates children's characteristics to their parents' objective actions.[5] This is not to say that parents have little or no effect on their children. It is to say that the precise nature of a parent's effect on a child has eluded us. We have little cause to think we can tell how children, coming from different environments, will fare. Though we have a moral obligation to say how we think children should be treated, we have little scientific evidence to back up our contentions.

Kagan proposes that some of the mystery might be resolved if scientists stopped viewing children as passive objects, Damage Model–style, and started crediting them with an active part in their own lives, Challenge Model–style. For a fruitful line of inquiry, he offers the question: What role do children's perceptions of the events in their life play in their subsequent development?

From Kagan's perspective, it's not primarily what parents do to children that matters; it's also how children understand what happens to them. Thus, Kagan says:

The effect of an emotionally significant experience—like a father's pro-longed absence or a bitter divorce—will depend on how the child inter-prets these events. . . . Rarely will there be a fixed consequence of any single event—no matter how traumatic—or special set of family condi-tions.[6]

In other words, three children of the same paranoid mother can be given an objectively identical message, but they can interpret that mes-sage in widely different ways. The variations have important implications for their individual behavior and self-images and may be more important than the message itself. The variations also show the protective power of insight.

To measure your resilience, look at the way you interpret yourself and your family. Do you accept their distorted views or have you developed your own explanations of events? Do you walk into the Victim's Trap by considering yourself a lifelong casualty of your parents' troubles? Or do you see yourself as a person with difficult but solvable problems? Do you submit and "go to the restaurant"? Or do you cook for yourself and eat at home alone, secure in the belief that your insight can keep you safe?

SENSING

Imagine yourself in the following scene. The central character is Alan, who today is a husband, a father with children of his own, and the senior partner in a commercial real estate brokerage firm. At the time of this incident, he was seven years old. If Alan's story is not directly familiar, you have probably lived some variation on its basic themes: confusion, fear, thinking a mile a minute, and reaching a correct conclusion about your troubled family. You are not happy because the pieces of the puzzle you put together do not make a pretty picture. But you do get the satisfaction of being right, seeing yourself as clever, and finding a way to protect yourself. This scene could be an early source of Survivor's Pride.

You are about seven years old. It's a summer evening, and you hear the bells of the ice cream truck coming up the street. Your mother is in the kitchen, doing nothing in particular. Off guard, you run up to her and ask for some change to buy ice cream. No response. So you ask again, this time tugging on her arm.

Now she turns on you, shouting that she has no money and that you should get away and leave her alone. You slink off to your room, climb into bed, and stick your head under the pillow, trying to stifle your sobs.

At your young age, you surely feel damaged by your mother's rejection. Wanting and needing to believe that your parents are good and fair and wise, you might concoct an explanation that you are bad. You might think, "Mommy is angry at me. I must have done something wrong. I don't deserve an ice cream pop. Good Humor is for good kids, not for me."

Or you could follow a different line of reasoning. Like Alan, you could entertain the idea that your mother's outburst has little to do with you and a lot to do with something going on inside her. Then you could refuse to write yourself off as bad.

When resilient children are hurt unfairly, the wheels of their minds start turning, thinking, and interpreting. They speculate, "Maybe the problem isn't in me. Maybe the trouble is inside my mother or my father." Spurred on by the natural curiosity that all children have about their parents, resilient children begin to observe closely and to test their hypotheses. Their parents become suspects rather than sages, guardians, agents of mercy and compassion, protectors, and idols to be admired and loved. Sensing, the earliest sign of insight in resilient survivors, is the intuition that your family is not what it's supposed to be. Sensing is a "nose for trouble."

For instance, in the ice cream episode, you may have recalled uneasily that the night before, your father didn't come home to eat. You asked where he was, and your mother snapped at you. When your father finally arrived, long after the dinner hour, his lip curled in a certain menacing way that you recognized. Soon there was a lot of yelling. You couldn't understand most of it, but the words *paycheck* and *whore* and *crazy bitch* stood out in your mind because you had heard them flying around in screaming bouts between your parents before. You put these words together with your mother's changing moods and her frequent requests to borrow money from your aunt.

You sense a pattern, and a crucial piece is that you get hurt. You're too limited to grasp, at age seven, that your mother is manic-depressive. And you're too innocent to see that your father, a cad at heart, is escaping into an affair and draining the family funds to buy his lover expensive gifts.

73

But you're intuitive, and you spot the individual details that signal an explosion between your mother, who is in a low phase, and your father, who is depleted at the end of a spending spree. Weaving a safety net of impressions, you find protection from fear and confusion and convert a barrage of senseless, unconnected incidents into something you can master. You learn to be vigilant, to anticipate trouble, to steel yourself, and to make yourself scarce.

A sizable body of child-development theory[7] with a damage bias portrays young children as patsies, insightless[8] fall guys for their parents' faults. Wanting protection in a world that is big and scary, children will not question a parent's actions no matter how unjustified. Instead, they reason, "If I'm being punished, I must have done something to deserve it." In order for their parents to be "good," the developmental experts say, children are willing to be "bad."

I accept that young children sometimes purchase pseudo-safety at the cost of truth, but they also can be psychologically sophisticated—even at very young ages—and sense their parents' flaws.

"What do you think of that idea?" I asked Dr. Ruth Davis, co-director with Dr. David Berlin of an educational program geared to teaching children not to blame themselves for their parents' drinking.[9]

"That's a hard one," she said. "We discourage blaming."

"I don't mean blaming," I replied. "I discourage that as well. I mean *sensing*. A lot of theory says that kids in the age range of your programs can't accept the idea that a parent might have a problem. Both of us have heard, often enough, how the 'immature mind' will buy protection at the cost of illusion—seeing even a rotten parent as perfect."

"That's the company line," she said. "But maybe people working from a resiliency framework are opening their eyes to something else."

"Exactly how have your kids responded to a curriculum that goes around more traditional theory by saying, 'Mommy and Daddy drink too much, and that's because they have a problem'?"

"They lap it up," she said. "They keep coming back and asking for the same stories over and over."

"How come?" I asked. "Shouldn't this stuff be too threatening for them to handle at their age?"

"Not at all," Davis replied without a hint of uncertainty. "The kids trust us, and they trust what we tell them. I think they can accept our message because it's not news; it honors what they know in their bones."

On the research front, psychologist Dr. Robert L. Selman has confirmed Davis's impressions.[10] In a study looking at social, or interpersonal, development, he showed that young children can acknowledge that parents are fallible. Asked hypothetical questions, seven-year-olds differentiated between the justifiable actions and the mistakes of their parents. In their opinion, punishment is not necessarily deserved just because a parent metes it out; rather, it can be warranted or unwarranted. The seven-year-olds who spoke to Selman were capable of skepticism toward parents, saying it's wrong to punish children without considering the reasons for their behavior, thoughts, and feelings.

Alan, like the children in Selman's study, identified his parents' fallibility early in life. He saw an objective pattern of trouble *outside* himself, and he did not fall into the error of locating the reason for his parents' misery *inside* himself. Alan did not try to buy comfort by deceiving himself with the judgment "I am bad." By the time he was eight, Alan could read the signs and predict his mother's cycle although he lacked the vocabulary to name what he was seeing.

"What were the cues?" I asked.

"I could always tell when she was going to be low. The night before, she would pace the floor. I would be woken up several times by the sound of the toilet flushing. The bathroom backed on the same wall as my bed. In the morning, she'd have a distracted look in her eyes, and her voice was heavy and low. The first sign that she was cycling into her high phase was also her voice. She would say my name in this high-pitched tone, with a singsong quality that would go up at the end. And she would call me Aleeeeee," he imitated.

"How did sensing the cycles help?"

"Help? You've got to be kidding. I was miserable when she was low and acting like I was not there, and I was miserable when she was high, running around the house in her nightgown. I never knew what she would do next—what mortification she would bring to the family."

"I know you were miserable. How could you be otherwise? But you've spent a lot of time telling me what an astute observer you were. You're describing a skill, and there's a lot of pride hidden in your words."

75

"It's embarrassing to admit," he replied after a long, awkward silence. "But I knew I was the smartest one in the family, because I was the one to tip everyone else off about what was coming up with my mother. Somehow or other, they seemed to be missing the point about her."

"Is that all?"

"Maybe not. I started to discount what my mother said early on. When she was high and loved me more than anything in the whole wiiiiiiide world, I knew her words were as meaningless as the times she ignored me or struck out . . . like the ice cream episode."

The experience of sensing that Alan related to me also reverberates in Noreen's story of growing up in a brutal, alcoholic family. Noreen pegged her parents by the time she was seven too. Listen to Noreen describe her astute ability to pick out the signs of trouble in her father:

> I could tell before I even laid eyes on him. I could hear that he was having trouble turning the key in the front door. Once he got inside, I could see him stagger and smell his breath. Anything could roll out of his mouth. Some of the time, he succeeded in making me miserable. But most of the time, I kept him from getting to me. I sensed that his vile words were part of a pattern made by his smell, stagger, skin color, and words. I later learned that the pattern was alcohol and the bile that flowed out of his mouth had more to do with his drinking than with anything in me.

Sensing that trouble is at hand does not give children the power to change their circumstances. But picking up a pattern of trouble in your family you probably:

- counteracted your family's distorted reflections of you
- located the problem where it rightfully belonged
- reduced your anxiety by making the unexpected predictable
- removed yourself from the line of fire

For resilient children, forewarned is forearmed.

KNOWING

A fourth-grade boy attending a school-based alcohol-education program run by Davis and Berlin was fascinated by the story of a dog named Pepper.[11] In the story, Pepper is sad because his master regularly forgets to feed him and take him out for walks. Eventually, Pepper sees that his master is alcoholic and sick. In an unexpected turn of events, the dog begins to feel better. When the children in the alcohol-education group were asked what improved Pepper's feelings, the fourth-grade boy responded, "Knowing what the matter was."

Knowing, the second stage in the development of insight, is seeing beneath the signs of trouble in your family to an underlying explanation. Knowing is giving a name to what you see. Your progress from sensing to knowing was made possible by emotional and intellectual changes that come with normal development in all children.

First, the emotional need for your parents naturally diminishes over time. As children grow and mature, their bonds to the family weaken. Teenagers typically invest themselves in separating and differentiating themselves from their parents. Looking for justification, they can expend considerable energy piling up evidence of their parents' faults.

Second, thinking powers expand dramatically in adolescence. The capacity to move out and observe the world beyond the family; to collect, categorize, and classify information; and to make judgments all grow. The result for you was an increased ability to organize, confirm, and label your earlier impressions of your troubled parents.

To the extent that you capitalized on your diminishing dependence and your growing intellect to pose the painful question—What's going on here?—and to answer that question intelligently and honestly, you were resilient.

From the E. J. Anthony research project I mentioned earlier[12] comes the example of George, the only son of a schizophrenic father.

George sensed his father's illness and strove to know more about it. By reading, George learned about schizophrenia and contrived a theory that his father's mind restricted incoming information. George pictured the situation as a "crowding at the gates" and postulated that items entered and exited his father's brain randomly, without any order or logical connection.

George's theory led to a plan. He thought that, in order for his father to function, the daily demands of his life had to be limited and simplified. Consequently, George colored and numbered a series of cardboard boxes. Each one contained a task for his father to complete before going on to the next. The system worked for a while and supported George's theory of schizophrenia. After three months, however, George's father lost interest and reverted to chaos.

Nevertheless, George continued his rational existence. His analytical, intellectual approach distanced him from his father and insulated him from harm.

Alan, the survivor I mentioned earlier with a manic-depressive mother, also found protection as a child by resorting to his intellect. He said:

> In the late fifties, I saw a television program on the lithium breakthrough for manic-depression. Everything that was described fit my mother to a tee. Going two miles an hour at certain times and a hundred miles an hour at other times. Crying for weeks on end, hardly saying a word; and then suddenly going out and spending wildly, wearing flashy clothes, and talking, talking, talking out of control without making any sense. "That's it," I said to myself. "My mother is manic-depressive." I went to a medical library, read about the illness and talked to the psychologist in my school. Then I knew for sure. The bitter disappointment came when I tried to tell my father and he wouldn't listen.

Noreen, the medical student who, as a child, filled in for her alcoholic parents, didn't need a medical library or the extensive research that Alan did to name her family's trouble. She just needed to find a few other teenagers like herself. When Noreen was in high school, her parents' problem—alcoholism—was not nearly as esoteric as manic-depression had been in the late fifties when Alan was growing up. Noreen told me:

> I'm not sure how we recognized each other. We must have sniffed each other out and compared notes. One guy had been to Alateen. He told us about the meeting and that opened the floodgates. We all sat there and unburdened ourselves of a terrible secret. Our parents were alcoholics. The word formed a bond between us, and we drew strength from one another.

Sick . . . troubled . . . crowding at the gates . . . schizophrenia . . . manic-depressive . . . alcoholic . . .

Knowing and using these labels can cause problems for survivors. Some children feel ashamed, and putting a name to what they know adds to the hurt. They feel as if they're watching something they're not supposed to see, like an X-rated movie, or as if they're being forced to face the reality of not having what they desperately want—a "regular" parent. But labels also protect, and the willingness to assign one to troubled parents is a resilience verified by research.

The protective value of knowing was identified by Dr. William R. Beardslee and Donna Poderefsky in a study of fifteen- to eighteen-year-old resilient survivors of parents with severe emotional disturbances.[13] Observant and reflective, the successful young men and women in this research were all deeply aware of their parents' illnesses. Yet they remained safely outside its orbit. All distinguished themselves clearly from their sick parents. In interviews, they were open and eager to talk, freely discussing their dawning awareness of family problems and noting changes in both themselves and their sick parents over time. None felt guilty, blamed himself for his parents' difficulties, or lived in fear of repeating history. On the contrary, these survivors had come to terms with their home life, achieved peace, and enjoyed a healthy self-image. Thus protected from within, many could afford the luxury of viewing their parents' plight with compassion and empathy.

As Beardslee and Poderefsky's research suggests, and as Alan, Noreen, George, and other resilient survivors demonstrate, knowing and accepting that a family is troubled can help a survivor break the compelling spell exercised by a sick parent. Instead of hanging on, waiting—Snow White–style—for a magic mirror to say, "You are beautiful," resilient survivors use the "troubled" label to free themselves in various ways. They:

- see themselves as different from their parents
- remain relatively free of guilt because a parent's illness cannot be a child's fault
- filter and evaluate the information disturbed parents pass along
- hold images of themselves and of the world they inhabit that are more pleasing than the ones their parents project

UNDERSTANDING

"How has living with your knowledge about your parents—seeing the truth about them all along—affected you?" I've posed this question many times to resilient survivors who traced their growing awareness, from childhood, that something was wrong with their families.

One survivor responded:

> I had chronic envy for other children. Now I envy adults who have decent relationships with their parents. A few days ago, a friend told me that she was looking forward to a camping trip with her seventy-five-year-old mother, her twenty-three-year-old daughter, and herself. What a blessing, I thought. I could barely stand to listen and to face the comparison between her family and my own.

Predictably, survivors' answers to inquiries on the long-term effects of sensing and knowing start at the rim of their Resiliency Mandala, with the pain. "I felt robbed of my birthright and I still feel that way," Alan said. But he didn't stop with the emotion of loss. Following his own instinct for reframing, Alan probed deeper and unearthed the challenge side of his story. He added:

> But I also have something to show for my suffering. I've come away from the past with insight. I can think straighter than a lot of other people. I understand myself and other people, and I can tell the difference between what's important and what's not.

Understanding, the adult phase of insight, is a reflective frame of mind. Understanding results from spending your childhood examining evidence, sorting out the truth, and protesting illusions.

When:

- you inhabit a confusing and contradictory world
- your mother tells you that the water in your apartment house is poisoned, but everyone else is drinking it and seems fine
- your father repeatedly promises to buy you a bike but never has the money because he's spending wildly on his mistress
- your parents tell you that your uncle is a bum, but he's the only

one in the family who ever gives you a decent word or takes you to a baseball game

Then:

- you need to think a mile a minute to keep things straight inside your head
- you become skeptical and learn not to leap to conclusions
- you rely on your own thoughts and not on what other people tell you
- you separate yourself from the lies around you by becoming a truthful person

As the research of Beardslee and Poderefsky on resilient adolescents suggests, awareness of a parent's illness and self-awareness travel together. Resilient adults do not take people, themselves, or life at face value. Striving always to understand, resilient survivors process their experiences, look for meanings hidden beneath the surface of events, and confront themselves honestly.

The power of understanding was a major source of self-esteem for Alan, who learned early on to predict his mother's mood swings and to carry on without support from either her or his father.

> Can you imagine how affirmed I felt when my mother was finally diagnosed as manic-depressive and hospitalized? When I was vindicated? When I realized that I was the one who had seen the truth while my father was papering it over?

He was eyeing me to see how I would react. He seemed to be sizing up how I regarded his relief. Did I consider self-affirmation a strange or inhumane response to having his mother pronounced mentally ill and being put in the hospital?

I allayed his uneasiness. "Yes," I answered. "I've heard about that feeling from other adult children of troubled families. I call it Survivor's Pride."

"Survivor's Pride," he repeated, turning the words over in his mouth as if he were savoring every syllable. "It tastes sweet."

He continued with renewed energy:

I was living in chaos and terrible confusion. My mother's wild mood swings totally disrupted our household. I never knew what was coming next. On top of that, my father acted like everything was fine. "There's nothing wrong with her. She's on the rag," he'd say and then disappear, leaving me and my two younger brothers alone in the turmoil. When I pushed the issue, as teenagers do, he'd yell and storm out the door. I felt his actions were worse than my mother's illness. I thought he was trying to drive me crazy by denying what was plain as day.

Undermined as he felt, Alan was not dissuaded. "My devotion to the cause saved me. I went on a crusade to make my father see the truth."

Alan persisted. He waited. And he actively looked for confirmation of his perceptions. When he was a sophomore in high school, he found the endorsement he needed.

Once I saw that show on manic-depression and lithium, I knew for sure what was going on. I started to look for articles and clip them, and I left them all over the house where my father could see them. I even mailed a few to his office. I kept battering away at him, and finally, when I was eighteen, just getting ready for college, he took my mother to the psychiatrist who diagnosed her.

Alan buttressed his healthy identity with the affirmation he won by confronting his father. As a young man, he rested his self-esteem squarely on his ability to see and to speak the truth.

When Alan got out of college and became a real estate salesman, he was put to a test. Wet behind the ears and eager to make money, he experimented with the hard-sell tactics of the salesman at the desk across the aisle. When showing properties, he talked fast and glossed over potential problems. Using this method, Alan made some big commercial sales. His career looked promising, but the routine went against his grain. After a few rounds, an alarm went off in Alan's head. When he looked at himself in the mirror, he disliked what he saw. He also didn't sleep too well at night.

To keep the past in its place, Alan needed to keep up his identity as an honest person—someone different from his father. His integrity was his most valued asset. In the role of the hard-selling real estate agent,

Alan was losing his worth in his own eyes. He understood that the self-esteem he had earned as a teenager by confronting his father's denial would not be enough to sustain him as an adult.

Alan's response was quick, self-protective, and growth-producing. He asked himself some difficult questions.

Can I continue to do this? Am I willing to risk a great start by trying out a different approach? How long will it take to get booted out of here if I start losing sales? What will I do then?

In answering his own questions, Alan insisted on no less than he wanted from his father—the truth. He forced himself to admit that he was unhappy despite the money he was making. He risked trying out a new tactic: straight talk. The gamble paid off. At the time I met Alan, he was the senior partner in a highly successful commercial real estate brokerage and building company. He said:

My name is golden, and it's gotten me where I am. I don't try to give anybody the idea that I have the ear of the city or the county for getting road access or zoning exceptions and I certainly don't try to lure a guy who's trying to open a small shop in one of my malls by saying that I've booked Macy's or Bloomingdale's when all I have from those shops is a promise to consider. The banks trust me. The insurance companies trust me. The subcontractors trust me. And the customers trust me. And that's because I don't bullshit anyone. And I consider that my biggest accomplishment.

The challenge of the troubled family does not end when survivors walk out the door of their parents' house. Understanding the pull of the past, resilient survivors like Alan take deliberate measures to ensure that life for them will be different and better than it was for their parents. As children with a "nose for trouble," resilient survivors become adults with insight. Unafraid to ask hard questions and give straight answers, they keep themselves on track.

Barbara, the mother of three young children who put herself through college, understood that anger at her parents could twist her into a bitter person. She saw clearly that, in order to find peace, she needed to curb her wish for revenge. So when she framed her graduation picture, she trimmed off the "fingers" she was giving her parents and let her smile of triumph dominate the scene. Barbara tries to live by the same principle she used to frame her graduation picture. She is insightful, making every effort to face herself squarely, to identify the parts of herself that resemble the troubles of her past, and to institute the necessary trimming.

Noreen saw the breakup with her live-in boyfriend, Stewart, as part of a self-destructive pattern in her relationships. When feeling vulnerable, she attacked. Noreen could have blamed Stewart for their ruined relationship, as well as each of the other people she'd had trouble with in the past. But she didn't flinch from her suspicion that she had a hand in her own misery. Though going overboard with self-blame at first, her insight eventually led her to a reasonable question: "Why am I souring my relationships?" As Noreen began to look for honest answers, the darkness on the relationship wedge of her Resiliency Mandala began to lift.

Yet another survivor was embroiled in chronic conflict with his daughter and found himself using the silent treatment as a way of expressing his dissatisfaction. "When I caught myself in the act," he said, "my own father's face flashed in front of my eyes. I felt terrified. I knew it was time to change."

"Were you able to shift gears?" I asked.

"Yes. By sheer force of my will," he replied. "I wouldn't tolerate turning into my father."

Resilient survivors cannot afford to act blindly and stumble backward toward the past. Relying heavily on an internal mirror, they watch themselves in action.

Some of the scenes they see give incredible pleasure. Barbara told me:

My parents never went on vacation. I make a point of planning a regular vacation for my whole crew. When I watch myself relaxing in a rowboat, or going on a horseback ride with my husband and the kids, or just reading a book on the front porch of a cabin, I understand what my life could have been and just how far I've come. It's a terrific feeling.

Other scenes are harder to take, but resilient survivors don't wince. They stand firm, process what they see, and rise to the challenge at hand. Alan said:

There's been a lot of tension in my office recently as the real estate market has begun to fall apart. With the mounting pressure, I'm getting to be more and more of a bulldozer at home. I think I'm resorting to the same stubborn insistence on getting what I want with my wife and kids that I used years ago with my father. It's not working. We're fighting a lot; home life right now is not a pretty picture.

"What are you going to do about it?" I asked.

"I guess I'd better get hold of myself," he returned without breaking stride.

Whether watching yourself in action brings pleasure or pain, insight will protect you against the ravages of the past. Individual pleasing clips of yourself—like Barbara's horseback ride—can fuel your resilience. And disturbing questions with hard-to-take answers—like you're turning into your father—are easier to accept when you ask them yourself than when you hear them from someone else.

As one survivor told me:

The past is a reference point that helps me control the course of my life. In some semiconscious way, I'm always comparing what I do to my parents' life—the choices I make, the way I treat my kids, how I talk to my friends. When there's a big difference, I feel safe. But when similarities crop up, I hear a siren and get to work.

History has many uses. We can learn from the past how to be and how not to be. As a species, we have not put the past to especially good use. We are as plagued as ever by problems of war, poverty, and injustice. Perhaps resilient children are, in the words of Dr. Norman Garmezy, "the keepers of the dream,"[14] our best hope for learning how to use the lessons of the past to help ourselves in the present.

PATHS TO YOUR RESILIENCE

This is the first of a series of exercises that appear at the end of each remaining chapter. Its purpose is to help you shift your view of yourself from a damaged victim to a resilient survivor. At first, your attempts at reframing the story of your life may be frustrating. Clinging to evidence

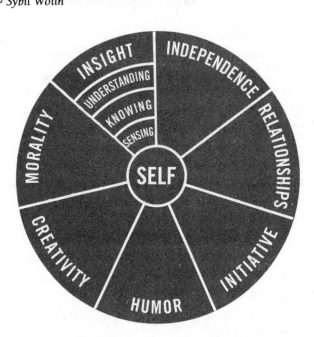

of your damage may be more natural than looking for signs of your resilience. You may be helped by looking back over the chapter, finding the examples of survivors' stories that hit close to home, and trying again. You may even want to read entirely through this book first, immerse yourself in the idea of resilience, and, only then, return to the reframing questions.

Look at the Resiliency Mandala above, focusing on the insight wedge. Rerun the stages of this resilience in your mind. Remember the times that you were painfully aware of the troubles in your home. Try to frame your memory around your insight rather than your pain. The questions below about sensing and knowing will remind you of the early signs of your insight. The questions about understanding can help you gain greater insight into yourself and others now.

Sensing

In early childhood:

1. were you a careful observer of your parents' behavior?
2. did you detect patterns in their behavior that spelled trouble on the way?
3. did that awareness help you stay out of harm's way?
4. did you sense that something was wrong with your family?

Knowing

In middle childhood through adolescence:

1. did you label your family "troubled" in one form or another?
2. did you make efforts to learn more or to gather information about their particular difficulties?
3. did you disassociate from your troubled family and see yourself as healthy?
4. did you protest if and when your family denied its problems?

Understanding

As an adult:

1. do you watch yourself in action, contrasting your successes with your parents' failures? Do you take pleasure in the difference?
2. are you on the active lookout for signs of your parents' behavior in yourself?
3. can you accept the role you play in your own difficulties rather than blaming others?
4. do you consider that your childhood was a good training ground for developing insight?

Chapter Five

INDEPENDENCE: A DELICATE NEGOTIATION

DEFINITION: INDEPENDENCE is the best possible bargain you can drive among competing needs: your right to safe boundaries between you and your troubled parents, the dictates of your conscience, and your longing for family ties. The first sign of independence in young children is *straying* away from painful family scenes. Realizing that distance feels better than closeness, older children and adolescents work at *disengaging* from their families emotionally. As adults, resilient survivors master their hurt feelings and succeed in *separating* themselves from their troubled families. With the achievement of separateness, survivors relate to their family out of freely chosen, rational beliefs rather than conforming to their parents' unreasonable demands.

As a son and a father, I know that families exert a powerful pull for togetherness—a pressure for members to endorse the family's collective identity and to gratify and affirm one another. No outsider—friend, acquaintance, or colleague—can arouse the same intense emotions as a parent, a child, a sibling, or a spouse. Family feelings are in a category of their own. My two children can drive me farther up the wall and fill me with more pride than anyone else in the world. And my aging mother can tie me up with a mixture of exasperation and sympathy like no one else.

My experience as a therapist and researcher conforms to my subjective impressions as a father and son. Patients who have satisfying relationships with their parents, volunteers in my research, and survivors all relate complicated and ambivalent feelings that bind them to their families and push them away at the same time. In resilient survivors, pain and rage mingle freely with a saddened regard for the struggles of a troubled parent. The contradictions are wrenching.

For example, Noreen said:

> My parents were almost totally incapable of love, and I wonder if the ache of abandonment that I still feel will ever go away. I can't forgive my parents the pain they've caused, but I do know they were suffering themselves. When I think about the emotionally impoverished lives each of them led, I actually feel sorry for them. Inside my head, my rage and my sympathy for them face off in an interminable debate.

For better or for worse, blood runs thicker than water. Therefore, even in the best of circumstances, achieving independence from one's parents is a demanding challenge. Troubled families add to the trial.

In healthy families, the togetherness pull makes members strong by fostering support, care, concern, intimacy, and love. Aware of the hazards and benefits of the togetherness pull, healthy parents instill their children with the confidence to stand alone and be independent. At the same time, they maintain a warm, welcoming home base where children will want to return and can leave feeling renewed.

Troubled parents, shattered inside, cling. Rather than fostering your independence, they make messes that threaten to engulf you. Troubled parents:

- squander their money and ask you to pay their debts
- demand that you don't invite a favorite aunt to your birthday party because they're not talking to her
- insist that you go into the failing family business instead of pursuing the career of your choice
- complain to you about one another
- protest that you'll kill them by leaving

Even when troubled parents reject you and refuse to see you, they exercise a psychological hold, for their criticisms are thinly disguised demands. "I can't stand the woman you're planning to marry" translates easily to "Marry someone I like." Somewhere deep inside, you may even have a passing thought to oblige.

If you could somehow "outgrow" the togetherness pull, you might easily ward off your troubled family's attempts to enmesh you. But the wish to belong does not fade with age. This is why independence is such a difficult achievement for children of troubled parents. Even as adults, survivors, feeling the family pull, cannot readily dismiss their mothers and fathers. Like everyone else, survivors remain attached to their parents, want their love, and are vulnerable to their criticisms, demands, or smothering "love."

Driven by a need to "fix" things, you may try to win over your troubled parents. Or, overcome by pain, you may try to make a clean break. Or, unsure of your own mind, you may alternate frantically between the two extremes.

My experience is that none of these approaches leads to true independence or brings survivors much peace. Rather, resilient survivors, who successfully work out their struggles for independence, master the conflicting feelings that bind them to their troubled parents and push them away at the same time.

A clinical study I conducted in the mid-1970s with my colleague anthropologist Dr. Linda Bennett,[1] showed that the achievement of independence is a key difference between adult children of alcoholics who repeat their parents' drinking patterns and those who break the cycle of addiction. Sixty-eight young married couples, all from alcoholic families, volunteered for the study. On the average, they had been married for eleven years and had one or two children. Approximately two thirds of the couples were not problem drinkers. I considered them the more resilient group. In the other third, either the husband, wife, or both were abusing alcohol. I considered them the more vulnerable group.

What made the difference? Did the parents of the resilient couples drink less or have fewer hospitalizations? Or had the resilient couples, as a unit or as individuals, developed strategies and skills for rising above the insults of the past? A preliminary run through the data showed that the amount of alcohol consumed by their parents did not explain why some couples resisted drinking and were more resilient than others. On the contrary, the alcohol-free couples had parents with drinking problems that ranged from moderate to very severe.

Next, I turned my attention to the couples themselves. My first efforts were devoted to developing two interviews. One, for use with the husbands and wives individually, included questions on growing up in an alcoholic home. The other, a joint interview, explored the paths each spouse had traveled as an adult as well as their shared decisions and life-styles together.

The interviews, administered to both the resilient and vulnerable couples, showed that maintaining close ties to alcoholic parents may perpetuate drinking problems from one generation to the next, which translates to: Keeping your distance from a troubled parent may be an effective self-protective maneuver for you to consider.

A subset of interview questions that I labeled "level of contact" asked couples how far they were living from their parents and how frequently the family got together. As a group, the resilient couples were living farther away and seeing their parents less often. The magic combination appeared to be: Locate more than two hundred miles apart and visit no more than twice a year. Reviewing my results, I thought of the survivors I had in therapy at the time and wondered what the implication of this finding was for them.

The two-hundred-mile/twice-a-year rule of thumb was tempting to pass along. But I hesitated to apply a formula—even one taken from my own research—to any one survivor's complex struggle for independence. Like all statistics, this calculation represented an average that obscured the individual differences among the couples. Besides, I suspected that another elusive element lay hidden between the deceptively neat rows and columns on the computer printouts piled on my desk. So, before advising anyone to move, get an unlisted phone number, or cancel Christmas plans with their parents, I felt obligated to learn more about the subtle shadings of the "level of contact" factor that my research had uncovered.

In therapy and in interviews with resilient survivors, I began to pay closer attention to the issue of distancing from troubled parents. Some of the survivors I spoke with were the adult children of alcoholics. The rest were from families that had other problems, but were equally as incapable as the alcoholics at performing the tasks of daily living that I described in Chapter Two.

The diagnostic distinctions among families didn't matter. Uniformly, the stories I heard confirmed that resilient survivors choose to stay away, but, as I suspected, the physical distance they had put between themselves and their troubled parents was only a small part of a much larger psychological achievement. In addition to leaving, these resilient survivors had, to a great degree, withstood the pull for togetherness exerted by their troubled families. As our talks deepened beyond airplane tickets and long-distance phone rates, so did their definitions of the word *distance* extend beyond physical space to independence in the self. The shift captured the invisible, subjective element that had eluded my computer printouts and crystallized a piece of advice I could consider worth passing along: Leave your troubled family, but attend carefully to the noisy commotion of your own feelings while making your exit.

Listen to two resilient survivors talk about mastering the inner feelings that surrounded their decisions to leave home. The first, Jeffrey, was able to leave only after extricating himself from the belief that if he tried hard enough and said the right words, his troubled father would change for the better. The second, Anna, spared herself the guilt of precipitating permanent alienation by pouring out her rage, reciting the gory details of her parents' failures to them, and storming out the door while her parents shouted, "Don't you ever show your face around here again. We're through with you."

JEFFREY

Jeffrey's mother died when he was five, leaving three children. Jeffrey was the oldest. As an adult, Jeffrey had no clear memories of her. His father, who never remarried, earned a good living. He paid the bills and employed housekeepers to take care of his children's physical needs. Lacking insight into other people, he had little awareness that his children also had emotional needs, and paid little attention to the personalities or qualifications of the people he hired and less to the conditions necessary to keep them on. Expectably, a string of people came and went. Some did an admirable job while they stayed but left in exasperation.

Others were unsavory types. One watched television all day and ignored Jeffrey and his two sisters, failing to get them to school a couple of times a month. Another molested the middle girl.

As the oldest child in his family, Jeffrey played the role of his father's confidant. He listened nightly as the man bemoaned his loneliness, his business problems, and the trials of raising three children without a wife. "I don't have one memory of my father ever expressing any interest in how I was feeling or doing," Jeffrey said. "I think he felt that his only obligation as a parent was providing the cash."

When it was time for Jeffrey to go to college, he was still convinced that his loyalty and devotion would eventually prevail and heal whatever ailed his father. Feeling duty-bound, he chose a local school so that he could continue to live at home. But during Jeffrey's sophomore year, the light dawned, and his internal psychological balance tipped toward his resilience. He began to feel an urgent need to break his tie to his father and to pursue his own independence. Realizing that his father was not changing and probably never would, Jeffrey concluded that he should leave. He transferred to a college in another state and never lived at home again.

In our interview, Jeffrey explained his decision to go:

I took an inventory of life with father from my earliest memory, and I saw that I was as stuck in a warped sense of loyalty as he was in self-pity. I was going under, closing off every opportunity for my own happiness, and he wasn't changing one iota. This was a no-win situation, and I decided to get out. But I knew I was vulnerable to guilt, and I wanted to leave in good conscience so I wouldn't be burdened to the point of feeling that I had to go back.

First, I spoke with my two younger sisters. I told them why I was going and prepared them to decline the role of parent-to-my-father that I was about to vacate. I told them that I would always be available to them and that they should call or write or visit whenever they had to.

Next, I turned to my father. I told him what I was going to do. I *didn't ask* for his permission or approval. I just told him. Since his whole justification for being was the cash he provided, I gambled that he wouldn't use money as leverage, which turned out to be correct. When I left, I did feel guilty—there was no escaping it—but the feeling was held in check by my certain knowledge that I was doing the right thing for myself, that I hadn't deserted my sisters, and that in reality, staying was doing nothing at all positive for my father and probably was making him a lot worse.

Jeffrey was a realist with profound insight. Before leaving home, he had asked and honestly answered some hard questions about his relationship with his troubled father. He knew the risks involved in staying around as well as the cost of suppressing his own need for togetherness and the strivings for decency that were solidly rooted in the morality wedge of his Resiliency Mandala. A clean escape was an idle daydream, a childish fantasy. Jeffrey's resilience was to face his situation squarely and to drive the best possible bargain between his need to go and the obligation he felt to stay.

ANNA

Facing a different set of family problems and personal issues, Anna also achieved independence by artfully balancing her conflicting needs. Unlike Jeffrey's widowed father, Anna's mother and father were meddlesome, domineering people who were never satisfied. In their eyes, nothing Anna did was good enough, and they expressed their displeasure with her lavishly, frequently, and, often, viciously. Anna's parents filled her with understandable fury. However, her revenge fantasies did not jive with her wish to be a decent, healthy person.

Listen to Anna talk about negotiating her conflicting inner feelings at the time she decided to leave home:

> I had this irresistible urge to tell them off and to cut them off forever—to never see them or talk to them again. At first, the thought made me smile smugly because I felt so justified. But then the idea started to twist around on itself. I had an awful sense of loss that seemed so ironic because my parents had given me so little. Another hooker was that I wanted—no, desperately needed—to think of myself as respectable, different from my parents.
>
> "What kind of person has no contact with their mother and father?" one part of me asked.
>
> "Mean, bitter people, like my parents," the other part of me answered.

The dialogue nagged me and nagged me. I was haunted by the picture of myself in a doctor's office, giving a medical history and being asked about my parents' health status. In the scene, I avoided the doctor's eyes and mumbled, "I don't have that information." I couldn't tolerate the shame and knew I had to find another solution.

Like Jeffrey, Anna had penetrating insight and knew there was no easy route out of her troubled family. Rather than looking for the impossible, she embraced the challenge of leaving with her head held high.

"What did you do?" I asked.

Her answer evoked the imagery of a dancer whose flowing movements conceal enormous efforts. She said:

> I stopped rattling my chains. I accepted that although I was leaving, I needed or wanted to keep up my contact with my parents. I knew that venting my rage and cutting them off could become a draining preoccupation. And I appreciated that to avoid an ugly free-for-all, I had to choose my words carefully and most of all to hold on to my anger. So I toe-danced out the door, making an especially graceful exit.
>
> Once I got out of my parents' house, I knew I was all right because I found that I had this terrific ability to compartmentalize them. I boxed off a few days a year for visits and a couple of fifteen-minute segments for phone calls. I actually entered all of this in a date book so I could see how little time they were taking up in the context of my whole year. During the time that was left over, I crowded them out with better things.

The question of the proper distance to keep from troubled parents puts survivors on their mettle. On the surface, my research statistics were suggesting that a solution could be found in flight. This turned out to be partially true. Physical distance can help to disentangle you from the family knot. But as survivors with insight and morality, like Jeffrey and Anna, demonstrate, physical distance is not enough. Like all simple solutions to complex problems, making tracks creates its own complications. The big hitch here is that you have to take yourself along. So my advice to you is this: Follow Anna's example, and go gracefully.

STRAYING

The decision to distance yourself from your troubled family can occur at any time. Some survivors, like Jeffrey, leave only after years of frustration caused by trying to change an intransigent parent. Others start much earlier by capitalizing on small opportunities to find a safe harbor away from the family storm. Without a clear destination in mind, many young resilient survivors begin the practice of straying, or making themselves scarce, when they first notice the storm clouds gathering. Straying is the earliest manifestation of independence in children of troubled families.

Resilient survivors typically remember rising to the challenge of their unhappiness by investigating the benefits of distance. As children, essentially limited to areas close to home, they were endlessly inventive in finding pleasant places to go. Anna, who eventually danced gracefully away from her overbearing, judgmental parents, set up shop in the basement, using scrap to make crude toys. Alan, the successful commercial realtor described in the last chapter, used the library as a private hideout for escaping his mother's wild mood swings. "I loved the quiet," he said.

When he was about seven years old, Alan began to visit the library daily instead of going home after school. After a while, he began to go on Saturday mornings also. He said:

> I went through every picture book, but I never took any out. I just hung around in the children's room and browsed. My favorite book was *Mike Mulligan and His Steam Shovel,* but I even got into books for girls, if you can imagine that! I really liked *Madeline,* probably because she lived in a convent without any parents. The librarian got to know me and would put new books on the side for me. She must have gotten my number, although I never said a word about my home life or my unhappiness. I sensed that people in the neighborhood knew about my mother.

Janet, the Atlanta schoolteacher whose poignantly honest letter I cited in Chapter One, strayed from her house to escape the oppressive burden of caring for her rapidly deteriorating psychotic mother. "The atmosphere inside was suffocating," she said. "I instinctively headed outside where I could breathe."

At first, alone on the rolling grounds surrounding the isolated estate where she grew up, Janet felt small and lost. Soon, however, her creativity, so prominent on her Resiliency Mandala, channeled her wanderlust and transformed Janet, the abandoned child, into her own fun-loving, adventuresome companion. She said:

> I liked the shadows and the dark. I would hide in the hayloft in the barn or in the orchards and act out great stories that I made up. I was a swashbuckling heroine, an intergalactic traveler, or Rapunzel escaping from the tower where I was imprisoned by my mother. My favorite was a game I played at night that I called "Spy." I was in a war and the enemies were in the house with the lights on watching for me. I was outside, behind their lines, evading them by dashing from tree to tree. The biggest feat was to get past the dog without having him bark. Once I accomplished that, I knew I was safe.

In the upside-down world of her troubled family, Janet found safety where other children might see danger. Playing in the dark, she felt protected. In the barn, which was home to a family of black snakes, she admired her own bravery and superiority. "Mother wouldn't dare go in there," she boasted to me. And alone on the grounds around her house, she ran free—invigorating herself to return inside and face the challenge that was always waiting for her.

A variation on Janet's outdoor getaway theme is seen in Barbara's story. As you will recall from her graduation photograph, Barbara rode her independence past her parents' chronic disparagement into a local college. Her capacity to follow her own compass was evident in her early childhood years. Barbara recalled her first episode of straying, which occurred when she was five years old:

> I'm sure I was five, because I wandered away for the first time at a birthday party. Before my friends arrived, my mother got angry at me for something I can't remember and told me that as soon as the party was over, she was going to punish me. My mother was a thief. She stole every milestone from me with her anger: by spanking me or pulling my hair or depriving me of something for a hundred years afterwards. For my fifth birthday, I had little heart for the party once she had issued her punishment decree. As soon as she got busy with the guests, I took off.

We lived near the water, and I walked toward the docks where I stood around watching. Eventually two older men, probably noticing my tear-stained face, asked me if I wanted to fish with them. One handed me his rod and baited it for me. Pretty soon, the pole jerked and I could feel a tug on the line. I puffed up my chest and reeled in a fish, thinking that its iridescent skin, dazzling in the sun, was the most beautiful thing I had ever seen in my whole life.

The next weekend, filled with hope, I went back to the docks. I wasn't disappointed. My two buddies were there and were just as willing to hand over a rod. I became a regular. They taught me how to bait a hook, to remove small fish carefully and throw them back, and to clean and cook the big ones. By the time I was nine, I was taking my catch home and making dinner.

Like these resilient survivors, you may have strayed away from agonizing scenes in your childhood. No doubt, remembering these times will bring back feelings of loneliness and despair. But these memories also hold traces of some of the skills you developed for protecting yourself and the self-assurance you gained by being independent.

Out of your parents' reach, you didn't have to be a

- messenger between warring parties
- maid cleaning up broken liquor bottles
- whipping post
- sexual object
- confidant for problems you'd rather not hear

Perched in a tree, closeted in an attic hideaway, nestled in a neighbor's house, or barricaded in their bedroom, resilient survivors think, "I look a whole lot better here than I do next to my parents, and I feel a lot better too." The idea feeds their confidence and instills the courage to begin disengaging emotionally.

DISENGAGING

In her ground-breaking work on how children cope with their parents' divorce, Dr. Judith Wallerstein identified emotional disengagement as a principal challenge.[2] She states:

At a time of family disequilibrium, when one or both parents may be troubled, depressed, or very angry, when the household is likely to be in disarray, the child needs to find, establish, and maintain some measure of psychological distance and separation from the adults.[3]

In my work on resilience, I have discovered that children feel the effects of their parents' troubles—insecurity, poor communication, conflict—more than they are concerned with the causes of family discord. Therefore, I believe that the task of disengagement, outlined by Wallerstein, is not limited to children of divorce. Disengagement, or the ability to hold yourself apart from your parents' crises, is a measure of resilience in most children beset by "family disequilibrium."

Dr. Wallerstein suggests that disengaging involves two related tasks. The first faces outward and requires the child to move physically out of the "parental orbit." We have already seen that resilient survivors stray away from home at a young age. With increasing skills to get around and take care of themselves, resilient children stray even more, expand the sphere of their independence, and become freer and freer of their parents' pernicious hold. For example, many of the resilient survivors I have interviewed took jobs as teenagers, as much to have a legitimate reason for getting out of the house as to earn money. Others joined every extracurricular activity at school or camped out regularly at friends' or relatives' houses. Later, in setting up their own homes, many of these survivors moved more than two hundred miles away from their parents and seldom visited. If you did any of the above, frame your actions as moving out of the "parental orbit"—the first half of disengagement.

According to Dr. Wallerstein, the second aspect of disengagement faces inward and involves mastering the anxiety and depression aroused by the troubled family. This task requires children to usurp their parents' power and take over the "commanding position" in their own inner lives. For most children of crisis, the revolt is feasible because dependence on parents normally declines with age. Resilient children are additionally fortified for the insurrection by pictures of themselves as independent, collected in early, successful experiments with straying. As teenagers, or later as adults, they ably remove themselves from the "parental orbit," take the "commanding position" in their inner lives, and overthrow the tyranny of their sick parents.

Some survivors I have known disengaged naturally, without much conscious effort. Describing themselves as "thick-skinned" or equipped with a "built-in shield," these survivors seem to be born with an easy-going temperament. A repeated refrain in discussions of their childhood is, "My family never really got to me." Dr. Anthony refers to these children as "buffered" from within.[4]

Other survivors remember drawing on every ounce of inner strength to ward off the intense negative feelings caused by their home lives. In achieving emotional distance from their parents, these survivors describe conscious strategies that I have grouped into four broad categories.

REGARDING ALIENATION AS A PLUS

For example, many survivors hold on to the belief that they were mixed up in the nursery, that they were adopted, or that nature made some grotesque mistake in delivering them to their parents' hands. "I thought I was a mutation," said Alan, recalling his childhood with a manic-depressive mother and a philandering father. "The thought was actually comforting."

Successful survivors find that being different from their family is a good thing. The greater the distance, the less susceptible you are to the same problems they have. Frame any solace you took in being unlike your parents as a sign of emotional disengagement.

MAINTAINING CALM

By reacting less and capitalizing on the knowledge that something was wrong with their parents, survivors are able to minimize the effects of the criticism, rejections, silence, and other strange and upsetting behaviors of troubled parents. For example, Alan relied on his intellectual under-standing of his mother's manic-depression to dismiss the cruel remarks she made about him. George, the boy with the schizophrenic father described by Dr. Anthony,[5] knew better than to put any stock in his father's psychotic outpourings. And with each of her mother's attacks, Janet was quick to tell herself, "This is not the truth; this is a sickness talking." Frame your successful efforts to dismiss your parents' unwar-ranted attacks as signs of your resilience.

STAYING REAL

Survivors protect themselves from repeated disappointments by giving up vain, self-defeating hopes for their parents' approval and love. For example, Barbara, who as a child was constantly criticized by her parents, said:

> I eventually came to see that my real problem was not my parents but a number I was doing on myself. Hope sprang eternal in my breast that they would change and be like normal, regular parents who cared about their kids. The more I hoped, the more disappointed I was. The cycle was a trap designed to exhaust me. Once I got my expectations down to the appropriate level, I felt a lot better.

Whenever you spotted and avoided the hope-springs-eternal trap, you were being resilient.

ORIENTING TOWARD THE FUTURE

When all else fails, resilient survivors keep hope alive by remembering that their days of dependence will eventually pass and they will then be able to leave home.[6] For example, Anna said:

> I kept myself going by plotting my getaway and putting my plan in motion as soon as possible. I decided to leave after high school, to work and support myself. When I was fourteen, I took my first job and opened a savings account. I picked the brains of every adult I could find about jobs and places that I could live that would not be expensive. And most of all I kept a picture of myself in mind as independent and self-supporting.

Similarly, Alan recalled:

> I was on my way out by the time I was ten or eleven. I knew that I was going to endure and that I would leave my family and the awful life they led. I was going to be someone they never dreamed of and all my energy was directed toward that goal.

If you kept yourself going by putting stock in your future rather than being dragged down by the present, you were resilient.

These four strategies of disengagement are not unique to survivors of troubled families. Most teenagers, to a greater or lesser extent, become disenchanted with their parents and aim to differentiate themselves in a process that continues through early adulthood. The difference for resilient survivors is that the push for independence:

- starts young
- proceeds consciously and deliberately
- reaches an early climax
- terminates in a fuller, clearer break
- requires vigilant enforcement efforts

Determined not to behold their parents' faces when they look in the mirror or to sing the same old songs of the past, resilient survivors make determined efforts to move out of the "parental orbit" and occupy the "commanding position" in their own inner life. Wanting freedom to become constructively involved with other people and to immerse themselves in satisfying, esteem-building activities, they disengage in earnest.

Take Anna. Well in command of her inner life and avoiding a cataclysmic fight, she left home, as planned, after graduating from high school. When I met Anna, she was twenty-one years old and living in rural Virginia. Her parents were located in Baltimore. Anna saw them a few times a year and phoned for birthdays, holidays, and their anniversary. She supported herself by working in a veterinarian's office. She was also applying to college. She had high hopes for her future, aiming to earn an animal-care certificate and believing that someday she would attend veterinary school. The initiative wedge on her Resiliency Mandala was bright.

Her relationships wedge was also strong. Anna was attached to a boyfriend whose parents loved and accepted her. The family had three sons and had always wanted a daughter. She basked in their affection.

To fully appreciate the deliberateness and care that Anna and other resilient survivors I have described put into achieving independence, listen to the contrasting story of Peter.[7] As a young man, Peter left home, not with insight but with his inner life sorely out of control. Pushed around by feelings he dimly understood, Peter bolted at seventeen when constant fighting among himself, his mother, and stepfather had become unbearable. Spinning in his own emotions, Peter fell flat on his face with his first step out the door. Drs. Richard Berlin and Ruth Davis, who reported the case of Peter, describe the consequences of his unresolved conflicts in vivid terms. They state:

> He [Peter] was living in cars and basements in the neighborhood. His arrogant and exploitative treatment of others was well-known and no one offered to take him in. Eventually, he sought out his older sister who lived on her own, and she was willing to let him stay with her. But after several incidents of stealing there, she threw him out. When seen at the clinic, he talked grandly about how he was going to make it big in California with the help of his father whom he had not seen in over ten years. He ridiculed the therapist for suggesting that he might be in any distress and said that all he needed was "some wine and weed." On his way out, he stole some money off the receptionist's desk."[8]

Peter failed to learn what resilient survivors know: Flight alone is not an answer to the survivor's painful dilemma of gaining independence from troubled parents. To leave without falling all over yourself, as Peter did, you need to settle your emotional score: to know yourself, why you're going, and how to choose a good destination. To the extent that you master your conflicting feelings toward your troubled parents and go gracefully, you are resilient.

SEPARATING

The challenge of maintaining independence from a troubled family does not end when survivors leave their parents' home. As I have seen countless times, the togetherness pull transcends the limits of physical space and the passage of time. Even if you are established in your own house, supporting yourself financially, and surrounded by friends, spouse, children, and colleagues, the task of managing your contact with troubled parents is not over. Separating, or relating to family out of freely chosen, rational beliefs, is a never-ending chore for survivors—with a few exceptions.

Among the resilient survivors I have known, a handful have reconciled with their parents as adults. Sometimes a gradual process of positive change begins when the proverbial shoe is on the other foot. As survivors demand the respect denied them as children, as parents age and become dependent, the rifts in troubled families can close. In other cases, a milestone—such as marriage, a career advance, having a baby, or renting an apartment—shakes up old, painful patterns and leads to satisfying realignments. A third route to positive change is the direct confrontation. Some survivors, drawing power from their adult successes, can return home without getting riled up, or falling back into the role of a despairing child, or yielding to the family's sick identity. By commanding themselves, they command the family, lay open the past, and present a blueprint for a better future. Chastened, amazed, and, upon occasion, deeply moved, troubled parents fall in line and try courageously, in their final years, to make amends.

Not surprisingly, adult survivors whose relationships with troubled parents change for the better report tremendous relief. Some even reach the point of forgiveness and experience a feeling of love for their parents that they never imagined possible. You may have the potential to do the same, and I would encourage you to make every effort to try.

But let me hasten to add that, in my experience, survivor stories with happy endings are more easily found on the fiction shelves in book stores and libraries than in the nonfiction sections. In real life, an agonizing denouement with troubled parents is, by far, more common than redemption in the final chapter. So, if you're in your late thirties, your parents are pushing their sixties, and the storm shows no sign of abating, understand this: Age is not renowned for improving the personalities of rigid, unhappy people. Don't hold your breath waiting for your family to undergo a magical transformation. Better to learn the rules of separating from those resilient survivors whose parents proved incapable of change to the bitter end.

I call the general principle of separating from troubled parents, used by resilient survivors, emotional pragmatism. Eminently practical, successful survivors stop looking to their families for satisfaction. Instead, they aim to do what hurts the least. Knowing their parents' unfailing capacity to inflict pain, yet aware of their own conscience, longing for family, and right to respectful treatment, resilient survivors steer a challenging course between a humane regard for their parents' suffering and their own wish to avoid further harm.

Like Anna, the young veterinary assistant who left home after high school and deliberately modulated her distance once she was gone, the resilient survivors I have known stoically accept their tie to troubled parents and the interminable debate between rage and sympathy that accompanies the thought of seeing them. Facing the cacophony head-on, they institute damage-control measures for visits or calls, which they commonly regard as "paying dues." For instance, they:

- think of contact as a challenge—planning and concentrating as they would for any demanding event
- rehearse the refrain "I am no longer a child. I don't have to let my parents affect me or control me the way they did in the past"
- explicitly decline the role they were assigned as children—for instance, "family doormat," "comforter," "go-between," or "scapegoat"
- choose the site where they are least likely to feel upset or anxious, and where their parents will be on their best behavior
- name their terms—laying down the law about drinking at dinner, bringing up incendiary subjects, being nasty, or making unreasonable demands
- call at selected times—for instance, when a troubled parent is at the office and is most likely to be civil, or late at night when the conversation can be short because everyone wants to go to sleep, or early in the morning before drinking starts
- write letters so they can pick the topic and stick to it; so they won't be interrupted, criticized or attacked; so they can avoid impulsive statements and sign off when they please

Barbara, an expert at several of these techniques, found that they served her well when she visited her parents alone. However, as her children matured, Barbara was beset by new worries. She felt guilty that she did not come supplied with two loving grandparents for her children, the way other mothers did. She was concerned that her parents, who were oblivious to the pain they caused, would cut away at their grandchildren just as they had belittled her. She dreaded that a family fracas might start in her children's presence. And deep down, Barbara wondered whether her kids would think less of her after learning about her background. Barbara's impulse was to shield her children from pain by keeping them away from her family. But insight stopped her. Barbara understood that the "iron curtain" approach could easily come back to haunt her.

"What do you mean?" I asked.

Her reply showed the typical farsighted vision of resilient survivors. "I'm far from perfect myself and I'm going to make plenty of mistakes as a parent. No doubt about it. If my children want to drop me off at a nursing home when I get old and never come to visit, they'll have plenty of reasons to justify themselves."

Barbara's resilience was seeing her power as a role model for her children, recognizing how anger can perpetuate a pattern of disrupted family relationships, and resolving not to be the "carrier of a historic curse." She armored her children against the harm her parents could do by explaining that "Grandma and Grandpa are very nervous people. Sometimes they say things they don't really mean." And when she visited, Barbara took the kids along, protecting herself and them with a long list of back-up plans for going to the zoo, riding the subway, and, if all else failed, going shopping for a new toy. She said:

> Ironically, having the kids with me was good, not bad. I had to remain the mother and not fall back into being the child. And even though the kids were disappointed in not having storybook grandparents, they were pretty hardy, and there was affirmation in that, also.

Other survivors subdue the influence of the past and reinforce their independence by aligning with siblings—people they may have gone to the mat with more than once, and not always playfully, in earlier days. For instance, one survivor recognized that his mother was dividing him and his brother by acting like a switchboard operator, a syndrome I described in Chapter Two. Rather than respecting the rights of family members to communicate, she insinuated herself into every conversation. At age thirty-seven, this survivor suggested to his brother that rather than "talking through Mom," they try, instead, to talk directly to each other. With that, the two began the work of building a relationship. He said:

My brother and I will never be best friends; we're very different. But we know each other's suffering better than anyone else and that holds us together. We've also seen that if we present a united front, she's a whole lot easier to handle.

Another survivor separated herself from the annual Christmas family free-for-all by joining with her two brothers and sister and refusing to go to their mother's house. Instead, she brought everyone to her house and excluded her mother. After dinner, all four siblings got on different phone extensions, called their mother, told her how much they missed having her, and said that they would love to have her next year if she dried out before the holiday and left the booze at home. Amazed by the confrontation, she agreed and actually met her children's requirement. The survivor relating this story reflected, "We didn't exactly qualify for one of those *Good Housekeeping* pictures with everyone sitting around a table cheerily smiling at each other and saying, 'Please pass the butter, dear,' but for us it was real progress."

Perhaps the greatest challenge to any survivor comes when you have to say good-bye to a troubled parent for the last time. Never easy under the best of circumstances, such partings raise thorny questions when you have suffered too much at your parents' hands. Many survivors whose parents are dead note that they felt little at the funeral or afterward and worry that they are emotionally deficient. Others with living parents anticipate being laid low by unresolved feelings of anger.

Probing the issue of a troubled parent's death with resilient survivors, I have found that many grow up feeling like orphans. Unlike loved and nurtured children, whose mourning begins when a mother or father falls ill and dies, many resilient children spend their youth grieving for the parents they wanted but never had. Often, by the time a troubled parent dies, the mourning period is over. The remaining challenge is not to uncover denied feelings of love or to resolve anger and disappointment, but to give yourself permission to express the relief mixed in with the grief.

Listen to a resilient survivor I treated struggle with her deepest, truest feelings about the untimely death of her young mother—an angry, self-centered alcoholic woman who drank herself and her children's wish for a loving mother into an early grave. Here she relates her response to a recurring dream of being chased by her mother:

> By the time my mother died, I was running as fast as I could. She almost outran me. I was wearing down and beginning to believe all the terrible things she said about me. If she had not died when she did, I would have lost the race. Her death freed me. I blossomed afterward. And that's the hardest thing for me to say, but it's the truth. If she had lived longer, I would have suffered more.

Not every survivor's "race" with a troubled parent ends as dramatically as this survivor's, but the challenge of facing the "end" is similar. Almost without exception, I've found that the greatest sadness comes not from the loss of something real but from knowing that "what might have been can never be."

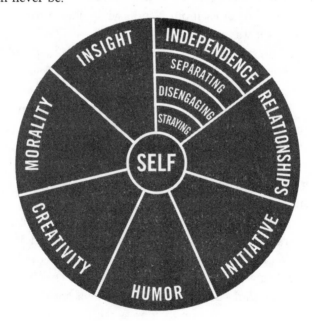

PATHS TO YOUR RESILIENCE

Look at the Resiliency Mandala above, focusing on the independence wedge. Remember an incident that pained you and made you feel that you wanted to get away from your family. Use the examples in this chapter to frame your memory around your resilience rather than around your pain. Recall the actions you took to remove yourself and to find protection either by being alone or by taking up with someone else. The questions about straying and disengaging will remind you of your early independence. The questions about separating can help you find greater independence now.

Straying

In early childhood:

1. did you distract yourself from your family's troubles by wandering off on your own?
2. were you inventive in finding more enjoyable places to go?
3. did you take solace in being alone?
4. did you compensate yourself for your troubled family by hooking up to people who liked you?

Disengaging

In middle childhood through adolescence:

1. did you stake out new territories of your own?
2. were you able to see the differences between yourself and your parents as a plus?
3. were you able to stay calm in your parents' presence, even when you felt provoked?
4. did you look forward with optimism to the future and your own independence?

Separating

As an adult:

1. are you able to balance your conflicting needs as you seek more effective ways of relating to your troubled parents?
2. can you be an adult with your parents rather than falling back into childhood patterns?

3. are you looking for opportunities to create a sense of family in the current generation?
4. are you mindful of the model you are setting for future generations?
5. are you able to express your true feelings about your parents even in the face of their death?

Chapter Six

RELATIONSHIPS:
THE SEARCH FOR LOVE

DEFINITION: RELATIONSHIPS are intimate and fulfilling ties to other people. Proof that you can love and be loved, relationships are a direct compensation for the affirmation that troubled families deny their children. Early on, resilient children search out love by *connecting* or attracting the attention of available adults. Though the pleasures of connections are fleeting and often less than ideal, these early contacts seem enough to give resilient survivors a sense of their own appeal. Infused with confidence, they later branch out into active *recruiting*—enlisting a friend, neighbor, teacher, policeman, or minister as a parent substitute. Over time, recruiting rounds out to *attaching*, an ability to form and to keep mutually gratifying relationships. Attaching involves a balanced give and take and a mature regard for the well-being of others as well as oneself.

"Isn't it true that for every resilient survivor, there's at least one caring, strong adult who makes a critical difference?"[1] Whenever I speak on the topic of resilience, I am invariably asked this question, in one form or another, about the role of supportive relationships in the lives of successful survivors. As many times as I've heard it, the inquiry always makes me uncomfortable. Usually, I have to pause and gather myself together before responding.

On the surface, the question is fair and relevant. The assumption that a child's resilience frequently turns on the involvement of at least one concerned person either in or outside the immediate family also happens to be true. Probably, the better times in your childhood bring to mind someone who was "there for you," gave you a shoulder to cry on, put salve on your wounds, or boosted you with a vital dose of hope or confidence when your prospects for happiness seemed dim at best.

My problem with the relationship question is not with the content; it's the emphasis that makes me uneasy. The subtle distinction between content and emphasis makes answering the question feel like walking a tightrope. I have learned, after many workshops and lectures on the topic of resilience, that the best way to keep my balance is to respond by saying, "Yes, but . . ." Then I take great pains, as I will do now, to do full justice to the "Yes" part of my answer, so that you will be receptive to hearing the "but."

Yes, resilient survivors often fondly remember a nurturing relationship with a parent substitute who provided praise, attention, sympathy, and the companionship missing at home. In interviews and in therapy sessions, again and again, I have heard resilient survivors attribute their endurance and determination to a "life-saving" figure who came to their aid. The remarks of Sandra, a successful, loving adult from a troubled home, are typical. With her permission, I've named her statement "The Rescue of Sandra."

> My savior was an old man who lived next door, in a row house attached to mine. His name was Mr. Berkowitz. I think he felt the vibrations of my unhappiness coming through the common wall between our apartments. Mr. Berkowitz felt sorry for me, and during the warm months, when he sat on the front porch reading the newspaper, he befriended me. I sat on his lap, and he told me stories that I could listen to for hours. If he didn't see me for a few days, because I was sick or something like that, he came to look for me. In the winter, when he "got some air" by walking instead of sitting on the front porch, he took me along. My regular afternoon stroll with Mr. Berkowitz was the high point of my life as a young child.

Yes, as "The Rescue of Sandra" suggests, survivors who "make it" have a special fan rooting for them—someone who was regularly available, served as a model, or gave encouragement at a crucial crossroad. Yes, as "The Rescue of Sandra" also suggests, well-meaning, generous adults often notice kids in trouble and become dedicated allies. Their positive influence is not to be underestimated. Indeed, many projects aimed at fostering resilience, especially in inner-city children, have been successful in developing and offering the services of adult mentors.

But, like all stories, the one about the caring grownup and the hurt child can be told from different perspectives, and some slants are better for survivors than others. The version I prefer least revolves on the theme of generosity. The leading player is an adult (in Sandra's case, Mr. Berkowitz) with unusual humanity and a talent for relating to children. I call this telling "The Save-the-Child Drama," a sentimental semitruth hatched from the same egg as Damage Model thinking. Just as the Damage Model portrays children as the unfortunate, passive victims of their parents' poisonous secretions, "The Save-the-Child Drama" sees survivors as the fortunate recipients of some benevolent adult's interest and attention. The added implication of "Save-the-Child" is that relationships are chance events, as likely to occur as not.

Don't buy it. Regard the generosity rendition of your survival story with caution. Yes, if you endured a troubled family and emerged in good mental health, some crucial person probably played a role, but etching a rescued-waif image on your expression of gratitude is not in your best interest. Consider another angle first.

A reframed version of "Save-the-Child," consistent with the Challenge Model, emphasizes the theme of resilience. I've named the rejuvenated scenario "The Appealing Child Meets the Potentially Interested Adult." This script depicts relationships as the fruits of your own labor, a rich yield carefully and deliberately cultivated in the soil of despair. "The Appealing Child" does not change the facts of your story. Instead, the revival imposes a refreshing perspective, highlighting incidents either ignored or eclipsed in the earlier script. "The Appealing Child" encourages you to see yourself as the active agent of your success and to shift your primary emotion from gratitude to pride.

For example, reconsider "The Rescue of Sandra." Intrigued by the pursuit of her own resilience, Sandra easily entertained the "Appealing Child" slant on her relationship with Mr. Berkowitz. After she had finished talking, I replied, "Yes, Mr. Berkowitz gave you a lot. But, tell me, how did you arrange for him to save you?"

A faint smile crept across Sandra's lips. I had seen it before—the half-suppressed acknowledgment of Survivor's Pride. After a thoughtful pause, the story of her courage, shrewdness, and sensitivity tumbled out. Together, we easily hit upon a name for her narrative: Listen to "The Wooing of Mr. Berkowitz":

Mr. Berkowitz's house was attached to mine by a common wall. I guess the noise from his apartment came through to my side of the wall just as the vibrations of my unhappiness crossed to his side. From the time I was about five or six, I was aware of the yelling that was going on. Mr. Berkowitz's son was always shouting at the top of his lungs. "Goddamn it, Pa, can't you even get a fucking phone message right?" Or, "Why don't you mind your own fucking business about how I'm raising my kids."

I'm not sure what I thought at the time, but I can remember wanting desperately to talk to Mr. Berkowitz. I thought, "How could I?" Can you imagine a six-year-old knocking on that family's door and saying, "I'm here to talk to Mr. Berkowitz"? I wasn't even sure that Mr. Berkowitz knew I existed or what I would say.

One Sunday morning in the spring, I saw Mr. Berkowitz sitting on a milk crate on his front porch as usual. But he wasn't reading the newspaper. It was just folded on his lap, and he looked sad and distracted. I ran inside and got my jump rope, positioned myself right in front of the porch, and started jumping like crazy. "My mother, your mother lives across the street; your mother, my mother gives us nothing sweet," I chanted. I could see out of the corner of my eye that I had caught his attention and that he was smiling.

I repeated the same ritual a couple of days after school and on the weekend. Each time, Mr. Berkowitz watched and smiled at me. I could tell he liked my routine. When the weather turned cold Mr. Berkowitz disappeared. He didn't sit on the porch and read his newspaper anymore. I missed our little ritual, and I didn't see him except for a chance passing on the street.

In the spring, Mr. Berkowitz reappeared, like the birds. I got back to the jump-rope routine, and he got back to smiling, but we never talked. And that's where Mr. Berkowitz and I stood for a long time. When I was around ten, I tried for more. Mr. Berkowitz was reading his newspaper on the porch, and I went out minus the jump rope. I just sat down on the top step so I was level with his feet. He was wearing those funny kind of shoes that were molded to your feet and looked like they were made for spacemen. I ran my hand around the heel and then across the toes. Then I started asking Mr. Berkowitz questions. "Where did you get these shoes? Are they comfortable? Do they come in different colors? I have brown shoes, too."

The questions started Mr. Berkowitz talking. Pretty soon, we got into regular conversations. He told me about his boyhood in Russia, his wife who had died, and his job as an engraver. I gobbled up everything he said and all the attention he was giving me. He could have talked about anything at all, and I would have listened.

That year, when winter was coming, I knew I didn't want to lose Mr. Berkowitz. So I asked what he did when the weather turned cold. He told me about his daily walks, and I sort of invited myself along. He waited till three-fifteen when I came home from school and we went out together. Our daily stroll was a reliable event. Mr. Berkowitz told me all about the old country and Jewish holidays and customs that my family didn't observe. Sometimes, on Saturday mornings and on holidays, I went to synagogue with him. My parents didn't like the idea very much and made a lot of snide remarks about why I was hanging out with "old farts" when I could be playing. But I didn't care. I went with Mr. Berkowitz anyway and loved sitting next to him joining in the prayers.

Listening to Sandra, I knew the "Yes, but" response was no longer necessary to structure our discussion of her relationship with Mr. Berkowitz. She had gotten the point and saw her own active role in soliciting the old man's affections. I responded by simply confirming what she already saw herself.

"You and Mr. Berkowitz did a lot for each other. You were a wonderful companion for him and filled as big a void in his life as he did in yours. And you matched his willingness, concern, and empathy with your admiration, persistence, and tenderness, gift for gift."

In relationships of their own making, resilient survivors earn the opportunity to see images of themselves as loving and lovable. These pictures substitute for the distorted reflections collected at home from troubled parents. I choose the word *earn* to emphasize the point that relationships do not merely happen to young survivors lucky enough to be in the right place at the right time. Relationships are an active, constructive response to the challenge of a troubled family. Propelled by an interplay of distress and a "knack for people," resilient survivors begin the search for love early in life. Learning the balance of give and take in relationships out of necessity, many forge deep and enduring personal bonds, as adults, to their own children, spouses, friends, and colleagues who fill the void and heal the wounds left by a disruptive and hurtful past.

CONNECTING

The search for love in resilient survivors begins with connecting, the initial, tentative attempts to reach out and engage with others. Connecting happens when a young, love-deprived child such as:

- Sandra positions herself next to an elderly man and jumps rope to the chant of a telling message.
- Alan attracts the librarian at the local children's reading room, who learns his tastes and sets aside books especially for him.
- Barbara lures a pair of guys who fish together on weekends to lend her a rod, teach her how to bait a hook, and expand a twosome into a threesome.

Connecting happens when children rise to the challenge of their loveless homes by endearing themselves to others.

The magnetic appeal of resilient children has been observed repeatedly in research. For example, Dr. Anthony, the psychiatrist who interviewed a young boy with the courage to defy his mother's food-poisoning delusion, described a resilient girl growing up in an overcrowded dirty apartment.[2] Her father was unemployed and beat her when he was drunk. He had been hauled into court on child-abuse charges. Her mother was chronically depressed. The girl, born with a hip dislocation, limped.

The girl's history, which Anthony read before meeting her, gave him good reason to anticipate that she would be either withdrawn or hostile. Instead she put him at ease and captivated him with her "warm, comfortable, and trustful" manner. Shortly after he began to talk to her, Anthony found himself conversing much more openly than he usually did at a first interview.

Carol Kaufman, another child researcher, described a similar encounter with a resilient child.[3] Visiting the home of a psychiatrically disabled couple, Kaufmann was greeted at the door by their young daughter, Susan. The girl was engaging and proudly invited Kaufmann into her room to see her projects, including a device for taking infrared photographs. Commenting on Susan and other resilient children she had known, Kaufmann said, "These kids approach, rather than avoid, adults. And they don't smother you as overdependent kids will, but act in socially appropriate ways."

The draw of resilient children originates in the same quality as their knack for disappearing at painful times. The common link is insight. Let's backtrack briefly. Recall that sensing—the early stage of insight—is an intuitive, psychological bent that endows survivors with a "nose for trouble." Although sensing is aimed at avoiding the dangerous moods and expressions of troubled parents, survivors also harness their emotional awareness to achieve closeness whenever possible. Thus insight gives children in disturbed homes an edge on a pair of complementary talents: getting away when trouble is brewing and staying close when calm sets in.

On the one hand, you may have been alert and quick to sniff danger in the air and to shield yourself by straying or removing yourself from harm's way. On the other hand, you may have been equally good at spotting safe openings, sizing up likely prospects, poising for an approach, and evoking a warm response. If insight was the coin of your realm, then straying was on one face and connecting was on the other.

In a research report called "Hard Growing: Children Who Survive," Dr. Marian Radke-Yarrow of the National Institutes of Mental Health details how some resilient children alternate between connecting and straying.[4] Her example is an intriguing portrait of Dominique Adams, the second daughter in a family of four children.

Dominique's father was unreliable, suffered from a major depression, and had a serious marijuana problem, typically smoking two to four reefers a day. His role in Dominique's life was only sporadic.

Dominique's mother also suffered from major depression. She supported herself by prostitution and drawing minimal benefits from various social agencies. By Yarrow's assessment, Mrs. Adams was the angriest mother in the research project and the most difficult to get along with. Yet Dominique, like the other resilient survivors in Yarrow's study, could connect and establish a warm rapport with her mother. The boost she got from the relationship with her mother was striking.

Dr. Yarrow and her staff assessed Dominique when she was two and found her to be creative, curious, outgoing, and charming. Seen again three years later, when she was in first grade, Dominique was still progressing along healthy lines. She described herself as happy and unafraid. The researchers who interviewed and observed her agreed.

Dominique's standard behavior at home was to engage with her mother selectively, shifting between asserting her own independence and striving for a relationship. Attentive to her own needs, Dominique answered the call to be alone for her own enjoyment. She also could sense when to stay out of her mother's way for the purpose of protecting herself. Asked what she was most proud of, Dominique pointed to her self-reliance. She answered, "I can do things for myself." Unlike her sister, who set the table for two and served meals only to herself and her mother, Dominique ate alone. As a toddler in Yarrow's laboratory, Dominique explored the new environment and chose the toys she wanted to play with, seeking support from no one.

Ironically, doing things for herself, the capacity that most enabled Dominique to keep her distance from her mother, was also her means of maintaining a relationship. By demonstrating her competence and her emotional and physical stamina, traits that appealed to Mrs. Adams, Dominique was able to connect and wring recogntion from a mother with scant emotional resources. Dr. Yarrow illustrates:

> An especially informative episode was provided when Mrs. Adams was asked to have Dominique open a tightly sealed and relatively large Plexi-glas container with a toy inside. Dominique, like most of the children [in the study], declared that she could not open it. Mrs. Adams absolutely rejected the idea. By barking instructions with some physical assistance and many loud angry statements, she informed Dominique that she could do it and how to do it. Dominique did succeed in opening the container by herself before Mrs. Adams would allow her to do anything else.[5]

"Hard Growing: Children Who Survive" suggests that resilient children like Dominique, who connect, get the best their troubled parents have to offer. Though Dominique's relationship with her mother was less than ideal, Yarrow concludes that something between the two of them was working. Dominique was undoubtedly paying a price for life with her mother, but her early history gives good reason to believe that by connecting, she also opened wellsprings of strength that could conceivably nourish her throughout her life.

In her final touches on the portrait of Dominique, Dr. Yarrow notes that at age five, this brave and hardy young child was leaving her family and searching out her own kind. On the street and in school, Dominique was associating with other children like herself, who were taking charge of their own lives. Dominique's early movement from home to friends suggests that connecting to a parent—even a troubled parent—provides a vital push to seek richer stores of support and affection outside a disturbed or incompetent family. Sandra's story, which takes us fifty years farther down the road from Dominique's, leads to the same hopeful conclusion.

Looking back into her past, Sandra recalled that her capacity to form a relationship with Mr. Berkowitz did not appear magically but also had roots in her family life. Like Dominique, Sandra widened her circle of contacts only after trying her charms at home. Her first "audience" was her mother, a woman so depressed and withdrawn that she often did not take her children to school or feed them. Sandra recalled:

> Aside from being physically hungry, I was starved for my mother's affection. I desperately wanted her to notice me, and after many tries, I finally found a way in. The trick with my mother was to get up real close to her face, put my head right up against her, and tell her a joke. The first time I tried, she was sitting at the kitchen table in silence, staring into space. I pulled up a chair and climbed up on the table so I could get my face right into hers. And then I started talking. I told her a joke I heard in school. I can't remember the joke now, but I do recall vividly that my mother roused, laughed, and actually got up and put dinner together.

On the basis of her success, Sandra repeated her experiment several more times. By objective standards, her results were good. With each successive trial, Sandra got dinner. She and I agreed that, by subjective measures, the outcome of her experiment was positive also. In her internal mirror, Sandra could watch herself perched on a table bringing her mother to life. The pleasing reflection gave Sandra the heart to expand her sphere of operations to Mr. Berkowitz and then to others, setting the relationships wedge on her Resiliency Mandala firmly in place. Defying the Damage Model prophets of doom, Sandra did not succumb to the effects of her mother's illness. On the contrary, her initiative pushed her into making relationships with healthy, caring adults.

As a child, your early attempts to make connections may not have always been as successful as Sandra's and Dominique's. But if you tried, even intermittently, you were resilient. Just as Sandra followed her hunch to a front porch where a distracted old man sat with a newspaper opened on his lap but unread, you may have appealed to a potentially interested adult, and you may have strengthened yourself in the process.

RECRUITING

"On my trips to the town dock, I began to see that relationships and catching a fish have a lot in common," said Barbara who went to college after she had become the mother of three children.

> You need to have a "feel" for both, a rhythm. When you get a fish on the line—especially one that you prize and don't want to lose—you need to give a little, lean forward, pull back, and wait. You need to repeat the cycle and respect the power and the will of the fish. If you err on the side of pulling too hard or not hard enough, the fish will get away. So you need to be sure and patient and work with the fish. It's just the same with people—knowing when to give a little, lean forward, and pull back.

When Barbara applied the lessons she learned at the town dock to other people and situations, she advanced from the connecting stage of relationships to the recruiting stage. When Sandra decided to leave her jump rope inside and approach Mr. Berkowitz directly, without props, she made the same leap.

Recruiting, the second stage in building relationships, happens when:

- sensing trouble in your house clarifies into knowing exactly what's wrong
- identifying the problem in your family translates into a conviction to be different
- straying away at painful times extends into staying away for longer and longer periods
- physical distance evolves into emotional disengagement
- the passing attention that someone gives you deepens into steady companionship
- a vision of a hopeful future with other people rises out of your pain and disappointment in your family

Recruiting can heal a survivor's wounds. Resilient children of parents who cannot give love and affirmation make families of their own. While having to search for love can make you feel like a rejected orphan, the undertaking also has rewards. Many people—not just survivors—prefer company they freely choose to their biologically determined relatives.

Take Sandra. Starting with Mr. Berkowitz, she built a social-support network that she described as an extended family, spanning the generations. Emboldened by her success, she began the practice of regularly visiting neighbors to see who was around and, as she said, "to get a look at how the other half lived." Some junk mail mistakenly delivered to her house one day turned out to be a perfect opportunity for her to satisfy her curiosity and recruit a "mother." Clutching the packet of coupons and catalogs, Sandra eagerly trotted down the two blocks to the home of Mrs. Simmons, the correct addressee. When Mrs. Simmons answered the door, Sandra pegged her as the receptive type. "She had two toddlers pulling themselves up on her legs and she was still smiling," Sandra recalled. "She had to have something going for her, I figured."

Knowing that the responsibility she showed by delivering the mail had struck the right chord, Sandra offered herself to Mrs. Simmons as a baby-sitter and left her name and phone number. A call came two days later. Just as Sandra had worked her way into Mr. Berkowitz's heart, she won over Mrs. Simmons. Over a few months, Sandra's child-care services revolved 180 degrees, turning an employer-employee arrangement into a mother-daughter relationship. In exchange for making herself useful, Sandra got the chance to pour out her worries. She talked with

Mrs. Simmons about getting her period, her tiffs with friends, her boy-friend problems, and, eventually, her family. Sandra said, "I always had to go home, and the comparison between Mrs. Simmons and my mother never stopped hurting. But the pain faded in the sunshine of that outside relationship. If anyone can truly substitute for a troubled mother, Mrs. Simmons came pretty close."

In school, Sandra recruited younger siblings. She explained:

> I volunteered to give up recess each day and act as an assistant reading stories to the kindergarten class. I also tied shoes, took care of kids who wet their pants, and wiped lots of snotty noses—all the stuff the teacher was disgusted by. I was like a big sister because I could see that the kids distinguished me from the teacher, who was scary. I soaked up their admiration.

Sandra's capacity to create a family of her own making culminated in college. The campus was an ideal milieu, filled with new people, all on the lookout for relationships. Seizing on the potential immediately in her freshman year, Sandra decided not to return home for Thanksgiving. Instead, she stayed at school and banded together with a few classmates, some "strays" like herself and others who lived too far away to go home for just a few days. The group celebrated the holiday together.

> It was probably the first happy Thanksgiving in my life. Even though I had to fight off the feeling that "normal" people were with their families and that I was doing something weird, my main feeling was relief.

In her sophomore year, Sandra moved out of the dorm. She and several of the same friends who had spent Thanksgiving with her rented a house where they lived year-round. She said:

> In the spring, we planted a garden. We plowed and sowed the seeds and nurtured them. And we had an abundance of flowers and vegetables. After the harvest, we put the garden to bed for the winter, and I felt at one with myself and with the world.

The pain of Sandra's past never completely disappears from her con-scious mind, but her enviable achievement has proved beyond the reach of others with far more fortunate backgrounds than hers. Sandra is at one with herself and the world. And I am sure that the relationships she has cultivated and those she is yet to seed will sustain her throughout her life. When I interviewed Sandra, she was fifty-five, married, and part of an active friendship network. Aside from the usual petty annoyances of raising children, she was a gratified parent. She was loved and respected by both her adult son and daughter. About to become a grandmother, Sandra could barely speak about the joy of her daughter's pregnancy without choking up.

Like Sandra, many children rise to the challenge of a troubled family by actively recruiting love. Many days, you can read in the newspaper about such children—outstanding students, entrepreneurs, and peer leaders—who seek out and live with families and friends when life at home becomes impossible.

While I was writing this book, a recruiting story even made the cover of *National Geographic* magazine.[6] The lead article of the May 1990 issue, "Growing Up in East Harlem," profiled a fifteen-year-old Hispanic youth named Pedro who rejects the despair and a destructive value system that surround and threaten to engulf him. Pedro's older brother, Falco, was shot to death over an alleged theft of stereo speakers. By contrast, Pedro knows how to take care of himself. "Guys who used to be my friends," he said, "got me to skip school. But I don't do that no more."

Now Pedro is an ardent student, studying wherever he can, usually on the living-room floor. In eighth grade, Pedro attends the Harbor School for the Performing Arts, one of several special schools in his neighborhood. He takes gymnastics and circus arts. His favorite academic subject is math. "I love probabilities," he said.

The *National Geographic* profile of Pedro portrays a child with a stubborn streak of optimism, a clear idea of his goals, and the wisdom and skills to get what he needs. Pedro successfully crossed racial, cultural, and economic lines, recruiting a "big brother," Barry Greene. The relationship got started when an attractive child caught the attention of a potentially interested adult. According to Barry, Pedro persisted until he won Barry over. At the local pool where Barry worked as a lifeguard, Pedro became an attractive nuisance. Barry said, "He pestered me to show him my flippers and mask."

In the eight years that Pedro and Barry have been together, one-sided pestering has developed into mutual respect. To Pedro, Barry has been a teacher, companion, confidant, and role model. To Barry, Pedro has given a spark, a cause, and the gratification of watching someone else grow. Barry and Pedro go caving and study animals and fossils together. The *National Geographic* article pictures the two striding down a path, wearing caving helmets fully outfitted with headlights. Barry is now helping Pedro through secondary school and intends to steer him through college as well. Pedro wants to be just like Barry. Their relationship shows that, when emotional support in a child's immediate surroundings are thin, health and well-being can be sustained on recruited backing. You were not crippled for life if you had to hunt for affirmation because the attention and care you wanted was not spontaneously offered at home.

ATTACHING

Children in troubled families see all the reasons why relationships can go sour. Taking their observations to heart, resilient survivors refuse to be discouraged and vow to live by different rules. Many form lasting attachments to friends, spouses, and children that are a reliable source of comfort and pride. Their formula for success—hard work, commitment, and a driving need to be different from their troubled parents—remains unchanged from childhood to adulthood. As one resilient survivor remarked on the subject of marriage:

> My parents had a deal. "You stay out of my way, and I'll stay out of yours." They weren't fighters, but I could tell there was something terribly wrong because the feeling between them was like a deep freeze. I'd rather live alone than live like that.

Talking about his twenty-one- and twenty-three-year-old children, another survivor expressed the same determination to avoid the mistakes of the past:

> My father could not accept me the way I was. I think he wanted some kind of replica of himself. It's really hard to hold back with my kids and let them make their own mistakes. I have to work at it constantly, but I'm bent on letting them live their own lives.

Survivors who grow healthy on the elixir of earned love emerge from childhood having mastered a valuable lesson: Anything worth having is hard to find and even harder to keep. Resilient survivors attend to the quality of their attachments. In both my clinical practice and my research, I have found that most learn to:

- choose relationships wisely
- control damage from the past that blocks intimacy
- bond relationships together by establishing and observing healthy rituals

WISE CHOICES

The same insight that guides resilient survivors to *separate* artfully from troubled parents guides their attempts to attach wisely. My research has shown that adult children of alcoholic families who do not repeat their parents' self-destructive behavior find protection by marrying strong spouses from healthy families.[7] Wanting to get away from their own heritage, these survivors welcome the opportunity to be "adopted" by their in-laws. They spend holidays and keep up regular contact with their spouse's family, and often develop deep personal relationships with a mother-, father-, sister-, or brother-in-law. Survivors describe the feeling sparked by attaching to welcoming in-laws as "coming home at last." Even after the proverbial honeymoon is over and the illusion of having found ideal parents begins to evaporate, resilient survivors like the sense of being rooted that results from "marrying family." I have heard about the feeling not only from the adult children of alcoholics but from resilient survivors who grew up in other kinds of troubled homes as well.

For instance, Sandra, who had adopted Mr. Berkowitz as a grandfather and Mrs. Simmons as a mother, told me:

> I think I married my husband's family as much as I married my husband. When we were going out we had very little money, so we went to his parents' house and played hearts. I always lost because I wasn't counting cards; I was keeping track of how people treated each other. I soaked up the respect that I saw, and before long I was in love with the whole scene and wanted in. It's no surprise that, after a while, I began to see my in-laws'

warts and some of them were U-G-L-Y. But their faults were nothing compared to my parents' flaws, and even at their worst, my in-laws had basic decency and solid love for their children. So while I pulled back a little, and my husband and I renegotiated a little, I still have a family that I know I can count on. Where I come from, that's more important than I can ever say.

The care that resilient survivors put into selecting the right spouse extends to other important relationships. Knowing the potential for healing by forming attachments, they band together with friends, neighbors, colleagues, and relatives to form a surrogate family—sharing tragedies and joys, supporting its members, satisfying the need to belong, and saying explicitly how much they mean to each other.

For instance, Alan, whose family lived isolated in its own chaos, says he has a network of friends that includes each other's children. He described the strength of their attachments to me:

It's typical for one of my friend's kids to come just to hang out. But more important the kids come around when something's bothering them. My friends and I—we have common values. And it's a tremendous relief to know that they have someplace that you can trust to go when they're too angry or embarrassed to come to you. I even had my friend Lester's son living with me during his junior year of high school when he just wasn't making it at home. I know that Lester was upset—very upset—but he never worried that I would turn the kid against him or care for him any less than I did for my own.

The pleasure of replacing a troubled, biologically determined family with a healthy, self-selected one appears also in Barbara's comments about her friends:

When I stand at the door at our annual Christmas party and watch all the people who I love and who love me file in, I know I've made a family where there was none, that I've broken a hex that could have followed me for life.

The healing that can result from positive relationships is the subject of *Psychological Resilience and the Capacity for Intimacy: How the Wounded*

Might "Love Well" a research report by psychologist Dr. Regina O'Connell Higgins.[8] The study consisted of extensive interviews with twenty-three resilient survivors who, as children, all felt rejected by their parents and who had sustained themselves by consciously enlisting love and support wherever they could. O'Connell Higgins concluded that the interpersonal skills these survivors cultivated early on eventually flowered into healthy adult relationships, essentially unmarred by too much giving, too little offering, power struggles, or unfulfilled dependency. She states:

> For those who are adept at sowing their seeds outside the gardens into which they were born, recruited love certainly seems to have the capacity to flourish and thereby restore.[9]

One of the resilient survivors O'Connell Higgins interviewed was André. Like Alan and Barbara, André is aware that positive relationships can reverse psychological damage. Guided by his insight, he attaches to people who bolster his efforts to be honest with himself. André compares his idea of a constructive relationship to a special kind of mirror. Rather than passively casting his reflection, the mirror André envisions asks what only a good friend could: "Are you authentic?" The confrontation forces André to review what he really thinks and feels deep down inside himself. In interpreting the mirror analogy, André said, "I put enough trust and confidence in that [kind of relationship] to allow it to be part of my life."[10]

Resilient survivors like André form relationships rooted in a clear understanding of their needs. Knowing his tendency to lose sight of his true feelings, André seeks out people who don't mince words and who challenge his expressed views. Janet, the schoolteacher who grew up in the shadow of her mother's illness, told me that she wants to tone down the "grim" side of her personality. She is attracted to people with a "wicked" sense of humor. "The friends I like best are the ones I laugh with the most," she said. Anna, the young veterinary assistant whose critical parents "were never wrong," fell in love with her boyfriend when he said and truly meant, "I'm sorry. I didn't realize I hurt your feelings." And Alan, who was on the run from the wild fluctuations in his mother's moods and the isolation that her illness caused, longed for a sense of community. He bought a house in a "real neighborhood," where people have roots, celebrate July Fourth together, and, while respecting privacy, will help each other out.

> Once my younger son wandered out of the yard into a gully behind our house. A neighbor saw him and called to ask if I knew where he was. That was a small thing, but it touched something deep inside me—knowing that she would notice and bother to call. No one knew where I was when I was a kid.

DAMAGE CONTROL

As children, survivors witness their parents' troubles every day—the fighting, hostile silences, pettiness, sadness, and loneliness. Well schooled in the methods for doing harm, resilient survivors resolve to "love well." In defiance of their experience, resilient survivors cling to the hope that attaching to others is possible and can be safe. At the same time, they know a dark truth—that relationships can just as easily shrivel up or explode as become a source of comfort and security. Their insight drives home the necessity of attending to lingering problems from the past that destroy a capacity for intimacy.

For instance, many survivors who were deprived or neglected as children try to fill themselves up vicariously by giving to others— sometimes too much. Like bazaar vendors, they hawk the generosity and attention they craved but didn't get as children to every passerby:

- listening endlessly to friends' problems
- volunteering for every community job that needs doing
- staying up all night to do the family budget while their spouse is comfortably asleep
- doing theirs and everybody else's work on the job
- trying to provide the perfect psychological environment for their children

Resilient survivors who are driven to endless giving and the "taking-care-of-it-all" syndrome have the insight to spot their weakness and understand just how self-defeating it can be. Knowing that uncontrollable generosity can exhaust you or make others feel engulfed, resilient survivors take deliberate steps to curb their "generosity." Barbara, for instance, tried to make up for her sense of deprivation as a child by being a perfect wife. The tactic backfired. Rather than filling up on her husband's gratitude, she sank into emptiness. As Barbara felt worse and worse, her insight penetrated to the futility of her nonstop giving and her initiative prodded her to change. She said:

> I decided that the way to haul myself out of the hole I was in was to do something that was strictly for me—something really important like getting the college education my parents thought I was too stupid to finish. Two years passed between the time I first had that thought and actually applied to school. One of the biggest stumbling blocks was breaking the news to my husband, telling him that he would have to learn to cook and market and maybe even drive some carpools. I spent hours talking to my friends, reading books on the women's movement, and running over the issue in my head until I really believed that I was doing the right thing. Then I did it.

The same awareness that giving has gone haywire may prompt you, as it did Barbara, to consider your own needs as well as others'. If, on the other hand, you do not fit the description of a bazaar vendor hawking the wares you lacked in childhood, you may need to address the opposite problem—being an emotional Scrooge. Feeling deprived and depleted by the past, many survivors lament insightfully that it's hard to give what you never got.

- Wanting to reclaim their lost childhood and be taken care of themselves, some survivors feel taxed by the demands of raising children.
- Eager for evidence that the family curse has been lifted, they are crushed by their children's imperfections.
- Confusing healthy dependency with helplessness or loss of control, they build walls to "keep out" friends, lovers, and spouses.
- Quick to feel abandoned, they are easily angered and have trouble tolerating disappointment or forgiving mistakes.
- Alert to abuse, they keep a running tally, always calculating whether or not they're getting their fair share.

Just as insight bails out the resilient survivor with the "I-can-do-it-all" syndrome, asking hard questions and answering honestly is the saving grace for survivors struggling with emotional stinginess. With the same methodical determination that resilient survivors use to remove other stumbling blocks in their life, they tackle the goal of becoming more generous. For instance, Noreen took herself into therapy when she realized that she was "piling up the corpses of people who had tried to get close." Sandra did the same when she found herself shouting at her teenage daughter once too often. "The last thing I could tolerate was feeling that I was turning into my mother. I knew I needed help," she said.

Alan, on the other hand, put himself on a self-designed "relationship program." Listen to his commitment to controlling the anger he felt toward women after shouldering the burden of his mother's manic-depressive illness:

> I was full of anger when I left my home, but I knew that love mattered and that I wanted caring and affection to be part of my life. But believe me, it didn't come naturally. I was great with men, but I had a lot of shit with women. I was having a lot of sex and then dumping women faster than I could screw them. It was like a compulsion that I couldn't stop but I was terribly ashamed of. When my friends started to get serious with women and get married, I started to see how abusive I was being. I was looking at the part of me that was like my family. "No way. Fuck this. You'll never get the love you want this way." So I made an effort to stay close with my men friends, which wasn't easy because they were into socializing as couples. But I kept calling and I developed a couple of regular running partners. And a five-mile run with a guy with a good marriage became like a therapy session. I actually got a few good men friends to teach me how to act around a woman, how to be tender in sex and satisfy a woman, and little by little I plowed out.

Despite an early history of poor sexual relationships, Alan made a successful marriage. When I met him, he and his wife, Sally, were about to celebrate their eighteenth anniversary. He had chosen a spouse wisely, realizing that Sally's dependability and steady affection would offset his mistrust for women. He said: "With Sally, I'm certain that things will never careen out of control. She's steady and regular. And most of all she makes me fell safe."

Survivors like Barbara, Alan, Sandra, and Noreen know all too well the pain that others as well as they, themselves, can inflict. Their resilience is the will to resist the bitterness and cynicism they have every right to feel and to live stubbornly by the belief that love is worthwhile. Even-handed, moral, insightful people who understand that relationships involve responsibility as well as entitlement, they invest themselves in getting the balance right.

RITUALS

More than any other topic, the subject of holidays and milestones revives survivors' worst memories. Fights. Tension. Drunkenness. Missing relatives, long alienated by family feuds. Forgetting or refusing to celebrate at all. Grotesquely inappropriate gifts. Cold, hollow interchanges. Forced smiles. And a beeline to the door right after dessert. For many survivors, holidays are a vivid symbol of everything they want that is missing in their troubled families. While television, magazines, and storefronts are broadcasting sentimental images of family togetherness, survivors can feel most alone.

Childhood recollections of holiday rituals can cause visceral upheavals in many survivors. "Thinking of weddings, baptisms, and birthdays in my family gives me hives," says Barbara, who now has a family of her own. And Alan, recalling the same events, notes, "Just mentioning Christmas in my parents' house makes me shiver." Of all the comments survivors make about family celebrations, the most hopeful mingle sadness with resilience. "My family didn't have a Passover Seder," Sandra sighed. "Once, Mr. Berkowitz gave me some chocolate-covered matzohs that I used to make a Seder for my dolls."

In the same research project[11] that demonstrated the protective value of maintaining a distance from troubled parents and attaching wisely to others, I found that resilient survivors ensure that the nightmare holidays of the past do not recur. Knowing how celebrations tore their families apart, they take full advantage of the same occasions for:

- knitting relationships together
- conveying a healthy family identity
- creating a sense of belonging to a unit with a past, a present, and a future
- connecting to a larger culture, community, religion, or ethnic group

Barbara remembered her fifth birthday, her mother's threats, and her first experience of straying away. She also recalled subsequent birthdays when her parents typically recited her failures from the previous year. Deliberately attempting to "rework" the past, Barbara has established birthday rituals with her husband and children that are events of affirmation.

> We make a big point of everyone's birthday. Our tradition is that the person whose birthday it is gets to do whatever they want and the rest of the family goes along—happily! One year my son ate on top of a ladder. My husband got his shoes shined, including his cruddy walking boots that are about twenty years old. I got the bedroom furniture rearranged.

Barbara's remarks about Christmas were flavored with the same respect for personal preference and concern for the individuality of every family member:

> There are five of us and five different-colored tissue papers. We each picked our favorite color. Every year all your presents under the tree and all the little things in your stocking were wrapped in that color. Everybody outside the family who sent presents—cousins, friends, neighbors—used our colors, too. I got goose bumps when I realized how much this whole thing meant to my daughter. My color is bright, emerald green; when my daughter was twelve, she asked me, "Mommy, what will happen if one of my children wants green?"

While Barbara's satisfaction lay in putting a personal stamp on her rituals, Alan found comfort by joining with a glorious, ancient tradition that overshadowed his tarnished, more immediate past. He said:

I remember the moment I embraced Catholicism. It was Easter Sunday and I was in college. I didn't have any strong religious feelings at the time, but somehow I felt that I ought to go to church. In the middle of mass, I started to feel that I was soaring. Probably the music set me off. I began to see that even though I had no history to be proud of, no family to go to, I did have something to hang on to. I had a tradition that was almost two thousand years old and that no matter where I was in the world, I could go to church and say mass and feel that I had a place—no questions asked. I've become a religious person, and I really believe in God, but what I like most about religion is the feeling that I'm not floating around unconnected, bare-assed in the universe.

Some of the most animated discussions I've had with resilient survivors have revolved around the renewal they feel from planning and participating in successful celebrations. Many are so gratified by the experience that they do not limit rituals to holidays and milestones but leap on any occasion to start a new tradition. Sandra, for instance, took special pride in transforming her daughter's weekly shampoo from an ordinary routine into a bonding event. She said:

Hair washing, from the time my daughter was about five, was not hair washing. It was a "beautiful treatment." We made a big deal of going to the store and picking out shampoo, conditioners, sprays—the whole works. We soaped up together in the kitchen sink and twisted and pushed each other's hair into fantastic shapes. Then we rinsed each other out, towel-dried, and combed. We always started exactly at seven-thirty and it was always Tuesday night.

For everyone, celebrations weave the web of group and family identity. For successful survivors, rituals in the new generation have the added significance of making up for the past, reinforcing a positive self-image in the present, and reaching out toward a hopeful future. Therefore, from religious holidays and birthdays to mundane events like hair washing, resilient survivors value rituals. Spurred on by ghastly memories of celebrations with mom and dad, they resolve that rituals become a living testimony to a past that is over.

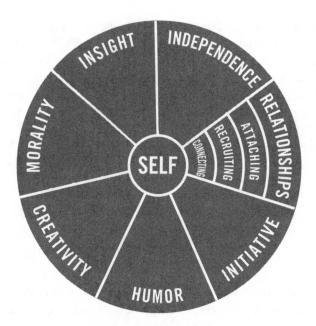

PATHS TO YOUR RESILIENCE

Look at the Resiliency Mandala above, focusing on the relationships wedge. Recall the fighting, silences, and animosities that disrupted your family life. Recall also your own wishes for something better and the times you actually went out to find the company of others. Use the examples in this chapter to help you use those memories to reframe your story around your resilience rather than your pain. The questions below on connecting and recruiting will remind you of your early skill at forming relationships. The questions about attaching can help to strengthen your relationships now.

Connecting

In early childhood:

1. were you on the lookout for chances to earn positive attention from your parents?
2. did you also seek positive attention from other adults who passed through your house or who were available nearby?

3. did you have a winning personality, and did an awareness of your social skills boost your self-esteem?

Recruiting

In middle childhood through adolescence:

1. did you put out your antennae for people who could serve as substitute family members?
2. when you spotted a likely candidate, could you easily initiate a relationship?
3. were you able to sustain relationships once they got started?
4. did the relationships you established help release you from some of the pain and disappointment you felt in your family?

Attaching

As an adult:

1. do you value your relationships and view them as a way of compensating for the healthy family you never had?
2. do you choose relationships carefully, knowing what you need from others in order to stay attached?
3. are you aware of lingering damage from your past that could interfere with your capacity for intimacy?
4. are you aware of the bonding value of rituals, and do you use celebrations, traditions, and heritage as a way of holding relationships together and affirming their value?

Chapter Seven

INITIATIVE:
THE PLEASURE
IN PROBLEMS

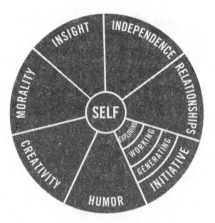

DEFINITION: INITIATIVE is the determination to assert yourself and master your environment. Resilient survivors prevail by carving out a part of life they can control amid the swirling confusion and upheavals of the troubled family. As pieces of the world bend to their will, successful survivors build competence and a sense of power. Initiative is seen initially when resilient children turn away from the frustration of their troubled parents and follow the call of their curiosity to go *exploring*. Opening and closing drawers, poking around, and conducting trial-and-error experiments that often succeed, resilient children find tangible rewards and achieve a sense of effectiveness. By school age, exploring evolves into *working*. Though not all resilient children become outstanding students, the random activities of their earlier years become focused, organized, and goal-directed over a wide range of activities. In adults, the gratifications and self-esteem associated with completing jobs become a lifelong attraction to *generating* projects that stretch the self and promote a cycle of growth.

In an article titled "Children Who Will Not Break,"[1] psychologists Julius Segal and Herbert Yahres define resilience as the capacity of children to conquer the "psychological Everests" that loom in their developmental paths. Contemplating the analogy took me back many years to a slide show and lecture[2] given by Barry Bishop, a member of the first United States team to climb Mount Everest and one of three to reach the summit. At the time of the talk, I was just beginning to work on the Challenge Model.

In anticipating the evening, I had expected Bishop to discuss the majesty of the mountain and his exhilaration at standing on top of the world. I thought the "survival" part of his story, which I was more eager to hear, would come out only in passing. I was surprised. The talk went the other way around. After showing a few magnificent slides of the summit, Bishop devoted the rest of the evening to his contest with one of the world's most forbidding environments.

Starting with the fierce weather and treacherous terrain, Bishop riveted his audience with a vivid account of the daily ordeals of the climb. "It's a never-never land up there," he said. Then Bishop described, in intimate detail, the effects of the severe mountain conditions—losing his ten toes to frostbite, the nausea, the sleeplessness, and the dehydration and weight loss at high altitudes. Most compelling for me was Bishop's description of his difficulty breathing, a function I tend to take for granted.

> At twenty-four thousand feet we were forced to pant with our mouths wide open. The sun's rays were bouncing off the snow and the insides of our mouths were burning and blistering. It was time for Merle Norman's makeup powder base. I broke out a tube, squeezed a generous glop on my index finger, smeared up my palate, and passed the rest along. Climbing in Alaska earlier, I had discovered that the dark shade is great sun block. The taste leaves something to be desired, but being able to breathe at twenty-four thousand feet without frying the roof your mouth is nothing to take for granted.

Bishop's description made me gag; minutes later, he had me gasping for air.

> In the final assault on the summit, I was carrying thirty extra pounds of gear and a camera. We had run out of oxygen, and I had developed a high-altitude cough that interrupted the alternating pattern of panting and walking I thought I had firmly in place. Suddenly, I felt two sharp pops in

my side, like gun-shot wounds. I knew instantly I had broken some ribs, probably as a result of a misstep. The pain of coughing was excruciating, but I could keep going by working the cough into my regular rhythm of walking and panting. Step, pant, cough. Step, pant, cough.

He stopped talking and started demonstrating.

Bishop's narration of agony invited the obvious question of how people manage the unmanageable. The climber explained how he and his teammates had overcome their physical problems, but he only hinted at how he had survived emotionally. "It's ninety percent mental and ten percent physical," he said. "Succeeding and reaching the summit is a matter of a mind-set."

What the required mind-set for a successful Mount Everest climb is, Bishop didn't say, and I was left wondering how he had sustained his spirit. Why didn't he turn back, overwhelmed by despair? How did he control his fear? What held him to the challenge of the mountain? I speculated that the secret of his endurance was hidden in the tilt of his talk—away from the triumph of the summit and toward the individual crises the expedition had faced and mastered day by day. The emphasis hinted that the achievement of solving each problem as it arose pulled him through.

Years later, in my conversations with survivors of troubled families, I was given the chance to ask the kinds of questions that I hadn't posed to Bishop: "How did you rise to the challenge of the 'psychological Everests' that your parents put in your way? What was your mind-set?"

Many survivors pointed to an abiding belief that they could influence the course of their lives, no matter what. Noreen, the medical student who survived her alcoholic parent by immersing herself in a whole array of activities, gave an answer that is typical of survivors. Along with the emotional distance she had put between herself and her family came a deep self-trust. She said:

I always saw myself as separate, different, and resistant to my family's troubles. Not that they didn't hurt me. They did; I certainly had my share of misery, but I tried to validate myself by finding something that I could control. No matter what the problems were, there was always some small part that I could chip away and manage to solve. I wasn't overcome by the feat of reaching the summit—which was for me getting out, being on my own, and having a different kind of life. I just closed out the chaos and focused on one thing at a time, and I believed that I would eventually get there.

I use the term initiative to name the assertiveness, capacity for problem solving, optimism, and belief in personal control that combine in Noreen's reflections on herself. Initiative is the resilience forged when survivors take charge of their lives and witness the tangible evidence of their competence. I suspect initiative fortified Noreen against a debilitating sense of her powerlessness no less than the same resilience shielded Bishop against despair at the heights of Mount Everest.

I have a mental picture of Noreen planting her flag in the snow, smiling and exhausted, every inch of her body layered and protected against the bitter cold by state-of-the-art insulated gear.

"Does my picture suit?" I asked her.

She beamed.

The protective power of initiative is a key concept in the work of Dr. Herbert J. Lefcourt.[3] An experimental psychologist, Lefcourt maintains that even extended extreme stress can be reduced by a mind-set he calls an "internal locus of control." Believing that the ability to influence your life resides inside you, Lefcourt says, can defeat the forces outside that threaten to bring you down. Lefcourt has illustrated his point in experiments with both humans and animals, among his own patients, and in a survey of nonfiction survival stories.

For example, Lefcourt cites the case of a patient who flew a plane and survived a disastrous crash with aplomb.[4] The injured man never relinquished his own role in the recovery process, secretly doing rehabilitative exercises the medical staff had explicitly discouraged. His value system revolved around a sense of personal responsibility. "Moreover," states Lefcourt, "he did not simply dwell upon his recovery but was already engaged in a pursuit of new plans and adventures, including the purchase of a new plane to replace the one that had been destroyed in the crash."

Turning to nonfiction, Lefcourt summarizes *Lost,* the story of three people shipwrecked in the Pacific Ocean.[5] One was the ship's owner; the other two were a couple—the owner's brother-in-law and his wife.

139

Together, the three lived in an overturned trimaran for seventy-three days.

The woman died at sea. The owner, who firmly believed that his fate was in the hands of God, gradually succumbed to helplessness as divine intervention failed to materialize. He died shortly after being rescued. The brother-in-law, by contrast, ardently believed that God helps those who help themselves. From the moment the group was struck, he took the initiative, organizing their resources and planning social and intellectual activities. Reflecting on his endurance, he stated:

> I proved that if a man husbands his energy and uses his powers resourcefully, then the man can pass marked but basically unharmed through the most excruciating of ordeals.[6]

The notion of "marked but basically unharmed" expressed here should be a familiar theme to you by now. The identical paradox is the core of the Challenge Model, which says that although you were scarred by the troubles in your family, you may also be strong. Resilience is the mind-set that says, "When your mouth is scorched, break out Merle Norman's makeup base and stop railing at the sun."

EXPLORING

"The incident was small," said Lena, "compared to the other indignities I suffered as a kid. But somehow it's etched in my memory as a symbol of my childhood."

"What kind of symbol?" I asked.

"A symbol of my pain and a symbol . . ."

Lena broke off, turning red. She seemed to be groping for words.

I had spoken with enough resilient survivors by then to feel safe filling in where she left off. "A symbol of your shrewdness?" I asked. My tone fell somewhere between a question and a statement.

Her embarrassment lifted.

"You said it first," she continued. "Now it's easier to admit that I do feel pretty shrewd. I have a genius for surviving."

Minutes into our interview, Lena and I had hit upon her Survivor's

Pride, that affirming-unsettling-embarrassing mix of vanity tempered by pain that churns inside all resilient survivors.

When Lena was seven years old, her buddies in school were abuzz about going to the circus over Easter vacation. At first, Lena was surprised; she hadn't even heard the circus was coming to town. Then her envy and sense of betrayal set in. Why was she being left out? Why were her parents always doing things that made her feel so different from regular kids?

Lena's parents, second-generation Polish immigrants, lived in an extended family beset by communication chaos and the mysterious comings and goings of various members. She described the family scene with a mixture of recollected anguish and humor:

> It was the kind of house where you would ask a question like, "What time is it?" and get an answer like, "The steak is burning." The only connected form of conversation was backbiting. They listened very carefully to one another's insults and always tried to do each other one better. I never felt there was any room in their minds for me. So in looking back, I was really naïve to think that something I might like would ever enter their minds. Besides, they were totally inept at dealing with the world outside the walls of their four-room apartment. Even if they heard of the circus, they would probably think that going was dangerous—that they would contract a disease there or something like that.

Despite the risk of being swirled up in a Mad Tea Party–like free-for-all, Lena decided to broach the subject of the big top. She rummaged through a neighbor's trash can in the alley behind her house to find a circus ad in the newspaper, which she recognized by the picture of a clown. Lena tore the ad out and flew into the house waving it, full of anticipation.

This incident in Lena's life does not have the happy ending you want to hear. Her initiative did not get her to the circus; sadly, it paved the way to a twofold defeat. For starters, her curiosity, excitement, and wish to be like her peers were thwarted, one and all. On top of that, she was confronted brutally with her own ineffectiveness.

"Stop bothering me," her father barked. "I have enough to take care of around here without wasting my time with nonsense."

Lena's face dropped as she watched her hopes go down the drain. But she didn't go down with them. Though she was flooded by grief and anger, she rallied quickly, warded off her disappointment, and branched out to explore her options. Pushed on by her parents' inattention, Lena became a ceaseless investigator for opportunities to make herself count.

Exploring, the first sign of initiative, is experimenting and manipulating your environment. Exploring, backed up by insight, was Lena's strong suit. Despite bitter defeats, she remained constantly on the look-out for situations in which her actions would matter, and she entered each one with gusto. In the process, Lena piled up undeniable evidence that she was someone who could make things happen.

Lena's first explorations were flavored by the same intrepid style that would come to characterize her adult personality. She began studying her family, sizing up its interactions, and figuring out how to be heard above the din of constant bickering.

Days after the circus episode, the family received an excessive phone bill that sent them into a tizzy. The ensuing fracas was replete with cursing, threats to put each other out on the street, and hysterically expressed fears that the family would be deported if they complained.

Lena sat back and watched, having less to lose than in the circus encounter. Relieved of the threat of disappointment, she was willing to experiment and be more brazen. During a lull in the storm, Lena piped up, "Why doesn't someone call the phone company?" No one paid any attention to her or even seemed to hear. Unnoticed amid the yelling and screaming, she picked up the disputed bill, marched off to the kitchen, and dialed the phone number at the top of the page. Feeling as clear-headed as she had when scanning the newspaper for the circus ad, Lena reasoned that she had the correct number for complaints and inquiries.

TRIUMPH 1: She guessed correctly and got to the place she wanted to be.

TRIUMPH 2: The person who answered listened to Lena explain that a mistake had probably been made and offered to help.

TRIUMPH 3: Lena made a grand display of her achievement. She asked the person on the other end to hold on. Then she put her uncle on the phone and listened as the problem evaporated. Puff!

Then Lena returned to the living room and presided over the family cease-fire.

TRIUMPH 4: Lena's experiment succeeded. She learned that she could move into the vacuum of her family's incompetence and throw her weight around. She also saw the first opening out of the four-room apartment in which she was being held captive.

"Pretty good for a little kid," she said, now unabashed by her Survivor's Pride.

"You bet," I answered.

Psychologist Robert W. White suggests that part of our in-born psychological apparatus is the motivation to be competent and make our influence felt.[7] The drive to be effective, which White calls effectance motivation, explains why babies like to clatter, throw toys around, and splash in puddles. The same motivation explains why older children like art projects, construction toys, and cooking.

Achievements are their own reward, and then some. Our accomplishments also serve as mirrors where we can see ourselves as a cause and a mover, an agent in our own lives, and someone who can bring matters to a successful conclusion. When you thread a needle and sew on a torn-off button or reattach the wheel to your broken wagon, you know your worth before anyone offers an opinion on the subject. For resilient survivors like Lena, achievements can heal the wounds that troubled parents inflict. By exploring and molding the environment to their will, resilient children consolidate confidence and hope for themselves.

The self-repair that results from demonstrating competence runs through the early memories of the resilient survivors I have interviewed. Alan, who grew up with a psychotic mother and a father who denied reality, recalled his behavior when his mother was really "out of it" and he and his sister were not fed:

One day when I was hungry, I remember wandering around opening and closing cabinet drawers that had nothing in them. At first, the activity was an aimless distraction from the dull roar in my stomach and the loud roar of desperation in my head. But then I saw that I could arrange the drawers like steps and climb up to the cupboard, which is exactly what I did. I guess I was a pretty agile kid. At any rate, there were some crackers and even some peanut butter and jam up there. To an outsider, I might have looked like I was standing on a counter, but with my fingers in the jar of peanut butter, I was, for a few seconds, on top of the world.

If Alan's mother was a double injury, his ascent to the cupboard was a twofold success. He not only found something to eat but also got a healthy taste of his own competence. Unlike the hollow praise that adults can shower on children for relatively minor accomplishments, the pride Alan felt was real and deep.

The same surety can be seen in Noreen's account of her early explorations outside her troubled household. The fragmentation in Noreen's family gave her a craving for "wholeness." Picking through the broken, discarded machines that littered the empty lot next to her house, she discovered a way to satisfy her hunger. On top of the heap was an old typewriter. She recalled:

> The roller was stuck, but the keys were in working order. I tried them one at a time, and as each one worked, I got more and more excited. I dusted the typewriter off with my skirt and took it inside, feeling like I had found a treasure. I spent hours fiddling with the roller until I got it unjammed. As I worked, I became totally absorbed. The typewriter became my world, and my family faded out into one big blur. By the time I finished, I understood the construction of the whole apparatus. I went from typewriters to radios to television sets. Knowing how something works gave me a special kind of power that was especially sweet. You know, my father was such an impotent fool. When something like a vacuum cleaner broke, he would actually stand in the middle of the room, kicking it and yelling at it.

In Noreen's story we see how fixing things can help you "fix" yourself. Psychologist Seima Fraiberg, author of *The Magic Years*, demonstrates the point dramatically in the case study of Tony, a child who mastered his fears by developing an investigative approach to his world.[8]

Tony's favorite toy at the age of two was a pocket-sized screwdriver that he always kept with him and used to unhinge doors, tables, and chairs. He was particularly afraid of the vacuum cleaner until he took it to pieces and found out where the frightening noise came from. As Tony grew up, his urge to take things apart was supplemented by a need to put them back together.

When Tony was four, he had an emergency appendectomy that left a wound on his body and bruised his inner self. Tony's body healed naturally; his inner self was another matter. The frightened boy could not tolerate the idea of being knocked out, cut open, and sewn back together—all in a procedure beyond his control.

After his operation, Tony rejected the toys his relatives brought and asked, instead, for an old, broken alarm clock. Over the next few days, Tony symbolically reenacted his traumatic operation, putting himself in charge. He dismantled the clock and put it back together. The activity restored his sense of control and repaired his injured self. As Fraiberg suggests, Tony's anxiety about his operation provided powerful motivation to surpass the normal capacities of a child his age. As an adult, Tony became a physicist, turning his childhood drive for mastery into a life-long career.

For Janet, the Atlanta schoolteacher who felt trapped by her mentally ill mother, the motivation for exploring was an awful feeling of emptiness. When other children confidently displayed the tangible signs of their parents' love and attention, she felt the sting of her loneliness most.

In first grade, Janet's teacher announced a Halloween costume contest, the kind of event that sends shivers down the spines of children in troubled families. Expect your parents to help you, and you're set up for a big disappointment. Be required to appear in school with something your parent should buy or make, and you're an open target for humiliation. You probably remember the feeling well. Janet said:

> I felt guilty about ever asking my mother to do anything because of her sickness, so I reconciled myself to something totally inadequate like putting a hanky on my face and being a bandit. Two days before Halloween, I went into the kitchen to throw something away, and I spotted an empty cereal box in the trash. I took it out and started to do the puzzle on the back. Slowly, I got an idea.

Exploring, channeled by creativity, transformed Janet from a lonely, disappointed child into a well-appointed breakfast table. Enjoying every word, Janet explained how she constructed her costume. She said:

> I found a carton, draped a plastic table cloth over it and cut a hole so I could stick my head through. Then I pasted the cereal box, a napkin, a

spoon, and a light plastic bowl on the top surface. Eureka! I was a table. To top it off, I tied a basket to my head with a ribbon and stuck a banana in it. I won first prize for the most original costume.

Janet showed me a photograph of herself, fully outfitted, taken by a friend's mother. Her expansive smile tells the story of her resilience. By refusing to halt, by actively exploring, by putting her finds to good use, by pushing the limits of her ingenuity, even a young child like Janet can rebound from hardship.

Survivors' memories of exploring could easily be framed as deprivations. Alan and Janet could have emphasized their parents' neglect, and Noreen could have decried her poverty. But to what end? While sadness mingled with smiles as these survivors spoke, they also saw that exploring allowed them to:

- fill in the gaps left by troubled parents
- master and relate to the world of physical things
- practice and build skills that last for life
- consolidate feelings of self-worth
- look in the mirror and see an image that says, "You can make things happen"

WORKING

The experiment I am about to recount, and several others like it, was conducted at the University of Illinois psychology department.[9] The purpose was to describe the mind-set of children who continue to work toward a goal despite poor odds. Working, or picking your way up a psychological Everest in the face of daunting obstacles, is the second stage in the development of initiative. An intellectual notch above trial-and-error experimentation, working adds the elements of purpose, planning, organization, and concentrated effort to the random exploring of younger resilient children.

Imagine yourself as a child in this experiment on working. You are in fifth grade. You and nineteen other boys and girls in your class have been asked to help some scientists who are doing research. You are not told that the scientists' agenda is to see why some children plow through frustration while others are stopped in their tracks. Instead, you are led to believe that the researchers, requesting your participation, want to know more about how children learn. This bland explanation is the kind of legitimate semitruth typically used to recruit volunteers for psychological experiments.

As an eager volunteer, you go by school bus to the university where the research is being conducted. There you are greeted by an energetic, friendly-looking woman who introduces herself as Dr. Diener. At first glance, Dr. Diener seems about a thousand times nicer than your mom. She escorts your group into a room and seats each of you at an individual table. Then she distributes a set of block-design puzzles and asks you to figure them out. She compliments you when you discover the right solution, and, like the nice woman she seems to be, helps you when you bog down. Under her gentle guidance, you attack each new puzzle with zest. The blocks fall into place. You think you've learned the game easily, and you sit back when you're done, feeling very smart.

When everyone else has finished, Dr. Diener commends the group for its effort and distributes a new set of puzzles. She tells you to think aloud so that she can hear how your minds work. You get back to work, but this time, no matter how you arrange the puzzles, Dr. Diener breezes by your desk and says, "That's wrong." Unbeknownst to you, the situation she is creating is a little like home. There's no obvious way to win. The idea is to see how you respond to defeat.

Oblivious to the trick, you are heartened by your earlier success and continue to work as hard as you can, expecting that you will eventually find the right answer. But you don't. With each manipulation you make, Dr. Diener reappears and, albeit with a reassuring smile, repeats the words, "That's wrong." You still think she's nicer than your mom (after all, she does smile instead of yell, berate you, or threaten to tell your father), but the contrast is beginning to fade, and your heart is starting to sink.

What do you do, think, and feel? Do you lapse into helplessness or do you persevere? Do you attribute your failure to your own inadequacy, give up any hope of success, and work halfheartedly? Or do you rebound? Are you pushed on by your curiosity and self-assurance to take charge of your discouragement? Do you plunge in and give the discouraging task your best shot? Do you stay on the mountain or do you go home?

If you keep working, even though your family drops one frustrating puzzle after another on your table, you are resilient.

To understand the resilient mind-set, Diener analyzed the transcripts of the comments her research participants made while working on insoluble puzzles. She found that the children who held up best—she called them failure-resistant—were noticeably unconcerned with the cause of their predicament. Predisposed to action, they did not discourage themselves with self-blame or paralyze themselves with belittling comments such as, "I'm not smart enough for this." Nor did the failure-resistant group dodge personal responsibility. None resorted to the familiar ploy of calling the puzzle "stupid" in order to justify quitting. In the picture of the resilient mind-set revealed by this experiment, the elements of fault-finding and feelings of victimization were absent.

Instead of assigning blame or dwelling on the reasons for their frustration, Diener's resilient children searched for solutions to their predicament. Their typical comments were aimed at staying on track. For instance, "I should slow down and try harder to figure this out," or, "The harder it gets, the more I need to try."

Influenced by their own constructive feedback, the failure-resistant, or resilient, children continued to work the impossible puzzles, systematically trying out and altering strategies with the hope that one would eventually turn out right. Even when their best efforts failed, they did not lose heart. In contrast to the youngsters who gave up, saying, "This is not fun anymore," the resilient children seemed to enjoy stretching and testing themselves. Many commented, "I love a challenge."

At this point, you could justifiably question the relevance of this experiment to your real plight in a troubled family. You might ask: Can a child's enthusiasm for frustrating puzzles, presented by a smiling experimenter during a morning off from school, actually tell you anything about your own response to difficult and demoralizing parents? I am convinced the answer to your question is yes.

While resilient survivors who confronted impossible puzzles as children do not exactly recommend the experience, they do acknowledge that pursuing solutions to family mind-benders brought a special form of satisfaction. As Lena, who transcended her family's dizziness by asserting her own competence, said:

> Don't get me wrong. Managing in my family was no joy ride. Asserting myself was not like the fun you have by buying something new, going to a movie, spending time with someone you like, or taking a luxurious vacation. Those pleasures are simple—relatively easy to come by. The kind of satisfaction I got from handling problems in my family was far more complicated and mixed with pain. There was always a build-up and release of tension. It was a matter of seeing what I could do for myself.

In keeping with Diener's research findings and Lena's remarks, resilient children in real-life situations do not deplete themselves by looking behind problems for causes that cannot be changed. Neither do they blame themselves. Instead, successful survivors remain active on their own behalf.

We have already seen how Noreen combatted the misery in her alcoholic family by taking the initiative and anchoring herself in Girl Scouts, school achievement, and household responsibilities. Noreen said:

> At home, the rules were always changing. I never knew what would be praised and what would be punished. Working in school brought a reliable result. Finishing assignments, the Scouts, and the babies were a sure thing. I could always say to myself when my parents went on the rampage against me, "Say what you like, folks. The truth of the tale is in the pile of finished workbooks, the A's, the badges on my Scout sash, and the babies fed, quiet and sleeping in their cribs."

While she was bitter about being abandoned along with the younger children, Noreen was equally boastful about stepping into the breach and upstaging her mother. "I was a better caretaker than my mother could ever hope to be," she announced with conviction and only a slight tinge of resentment for being pushed into adulthood too soon.

Bent on finding solutions to life's problems, resilient children go from random experimentation to planning, organizing, and mobilizing their best efforts to help themselves. Evidence that an active, solution-oriented mind-set can override the debilitating effects of a troubled family comes from many cultures.

GENEVA, SWITZERLAND

In 1903, seven-year-old Jean Piaget struggled to free himself from his mother's psychotic delusions. He planted himself firmly in reality by studying mechanical devices. He also became deeply involved in collecting fossils and seashells, and he invented an automobile equipped with a steam engine. Yet, after eight years, the pressure of his mother's psychosis became too much for him.

At fifteen, Piaget "broke" temporarily and was hospitalized. He was jarred. But taking control of his illness, he began a novel that symbolized his inner conflicts and integrated the warring elements of rationality and irrationality inside his self. On finishing, he was well enough to leave the hospital.

Years later, Piaget wrote:

> One of the direct consequences of my mother's poor mental health was that I started to forego playing for serious work very early in childhood in order to take refuge in a private and non-fictitious world. I have always detested any departure from reality, an attitude which I related to this important influential factor of my early life, namely my mother's poor mental state.[10]

Currently, Jean Piaget is considered the world's most prominent theory builder on the development of rational thinking in children. He was a resilient survivor. By his own observation, Piaget saved himself by working. The solutions he found to the puzzle of his mother's illness produced a lasting contribution to the world of thought.

BOSTON, MASSACHUSETTS

As a teenager, Lena worked all the time. Completely taking over the management of her family's practical affairs, she found them an apartment when they needed to move, filled out insurance information, paid the monthly bills, and located a decent low-cost medical clinic for them to use. She recalled:

> One night, I was doing homework and my uncle came to me with some tax forms. I looked them over and said, "Go upstairs. In the bottom drawer

of my desk, you'll find a folder labeled 'Taxes.' Just get it for me, and I'll take care of this. And ask your boss for your W2 tomorrow. He should be able to get you a copy if you lost it."

Lena turned the same skills she honed in the process of running her family's affairs to her personal advantage. She said:

In high school, I became a serious photographer. I built a darkroom in a closet by following directions from a library book. I bought supplies with the money I saved from working. Since I was expert enough to know the junk from the good stuff, I bought my equipment in pawnshops, from secondhand dealers, and at garage sales. The dealers got to know me. They called me when something came in that they knew I wanted.

Sitting in my office at the age of thirty-two, Lena wavered between her satisfaction with her own accomplishments and her resentment at losing her childhood to her family's incompetence. I spoke to her Survivor's Pride.

"You came from a family that was afraid of its shadow, and as far back as you can remember, you got to work and learned your way around your world. That's resilience."

MARIN COUNTY, CALIFORNIA

Like many resilient survivors, Jeffrey, the teenage boy who cared for his younger sisters after his mother died, found a sense of self-sufficiency by turning to nature. He recalled that he came home from school on a fall afternoon in his senior year and tried to tell his father that he had a date for Homecoming.

"You know what his answer was?" Jeffrey asked me. " 'The house-keeper wants another raise. The bitch is trying to bleed me because she knows I can't get along without her. What should I do? Should I let her go or give her what she's asking for?' "

Jeffrey told me that he snapped at that point and had to get away. He headed into the hills and took a twelve-mile hike, jogging for part of the time and walking at a good clip for the rest. Jeffrey was no athlete, and he hadn't been exercising. But his physical stamina amazed him and seeped into his inner self, where a plan began to take shape.

That same week, Jeffrey signed up for a three-day backpacking and rock-climbing trip in the high country of Yosemite. Paying for the trip and equipment wasn't a problem since Jeffrey's father considered cash a substitute for affection and was free with money.

On the morning of the trip, Jeffrey, five others, and an instructor backpacked for five miles. Arriving at the Merced River, they camped overnight. Although his shoulders ached—Jeffrey had never carried a pack before—he liked the feeling of working out his body. He pitched his tent and had the best sleep he could remember, feeling far away from his father's pitiful dependency.

In the morning, at the west face of Half Dome, Jeffrey put on a pair of crampons and looped a rope around his waist. As he edged up the rock, conquering his own fear, he saw a solution to being engulfed in his father's weakness. He would pit himself against nature, working himself to his limits, gathering strength, and proving his will to prevail. Jeffrey said:

For the rest of high school, I headed outdoors at every opportunity, looking for bigger and better challenges. It was on a Mount Rainier climb—my most challenging venture—that I resolved to backburner my father and leave home. We started from jump-off camp at three A.M. in the dark with headlights so we could reach the summit by eleven and begin down before the sun was strong and the snow began to soften and avalanche. About five hours out, we hit a narrow crevasse that we had to jump over. The distance was short—about a foot—but the crevasse was so deep, you couldn't see the bottom. Three guys freaked out. I was one of them.

"Here's your choice," the leader said. "You can go up, or you can stay here. If you want to stay here, get into a sleeping bag. I'll tie you in and stake it to the ground with your ice ax. You'll be warm and safe, and we'll pick you up on the way down in about five hours." The two other guys took the sleeping bag option. I got hold of my terror and went up. I never worked as hard in my life—to fight back my fear and to fight my fatigue. When I got down, I had few doubts that I would be able to tell my father, when the time came, that I intended to leave.

In school, Jeffrey sloughed off but did all right. At home in his father's eyes, he saw the reflection of a timid, frightened little boy. Out in nature,

Jeffrey demanded the best of himself. Decked out with his ropes, crampons, and an ice ax slung across his hips, he looked in the mirror and saw a man.

CALI, COLOMBIA

Today, hundreds, perhaps thousands, of boys ranging from age six through adolescence roam the streets in small groups. They live without adult supervision and eke out subsistence earnings doing menial labor and begging. UNICEF has officially categorized these boys as abandoned.

Young street dwellers like the Cali boys are found throughout Colombia, other Latin American, European, African, and Asian countries, as well as in poor urban centers of the United States. The countries of their birth consider street children social discards and hold them in contempt. In Spanish-speaking cultures, they are pejoratively labeled *chinches* (bedbugs) and gamins (urchins). In truth, they are the essence of resilience, working with everything they have to overcome their lot. Many succeed.

In defiance of society's standards, street children proudly call themselves "El Hijo de Nadie" (The Child of No One). The phrase is also the title of a favorite collective song. The words, which refer to "brothers" who will uphold each other through a "pact," are testimony to the determination of street children to take responsibility into their own hands.

In a period of six months, Dr. J. Kirk Felsman interviewed more than three hundred of Cali's street boys.[11] The activities he observed and the stories he heard show that children living at the most extreme end of hardship and those tackling a contrived set of puzzles in a university laboratory share the same basic elements of the resilient mind-set.

Street children, Felsman observed, did not blame themselves for being homeless. While acknowledging society's injustices, the boys focused on solutions to their poverty rather than immobilizing themselves in the Victim's Trap. Few reported running away from home impulsively after a dramatic incident such as a severe beating. On the contrary, they strategized, making decisions that were neither haphazard nor purposeless. Most of their stories told of conscious problem solving, a desire for something better, careful planning, deliberate action, and a gradual drifting away. Before leaving their parents, street children typically tested the waters, established a firm system of peer supports, and consolidated a means of earning a wage. Once on their own, they banded together in small groups to furnish themselves with food, clothing, and shelter. Their competent behavior ensured the group's physical survival while working against a crushing emotional sense of helplessness.

For example, an entire group secured pride and provisions as one member hatched the idea of using suspended political banners for bedding material. Another scaled a building to claim the colorful cloth. And two more scavenged needle and thread to sew the prize into crude but efficient sleeping bags.

Overall, the three hundred boys Felsman interviewed were physically healthier than the equivalent children remaining at home with their parents in squatter settlements. Felsman stated, "While they were not free of psychological problems, the gamins' lack of severe, overt pathology was striking." He attributed the superior condition of the street children to their ability to take charge, work cooperatively, and engage each other emotionally.

At the end of his stay in Cali, Felsman shared the street children's view of themselves as proud conquerors. His attitude was far closer to awe than to the establishment's typical contempt. Felsman's deep respect for the dignity of the children's struggle and their determination to keep working on life's toughest puzzles comes through clearly in his writing:

> Darting in and out of traffic, begging in open-air restaurants, singing for change in city buses, bathing in public fountains, or sleeping together curled up amongst stray dogs, these young ragamuffins manage the often-tangled course of human growth and development with little or no support from the traditional institutions of family, school, church, or state.
>
> Amidst such environmental adversity, the gamins represent a self-selecting group of children standing at the intersection of human strength and vulnerability. Much of their daily life is a display of endurance, resiliency, and adaptation as it is witnessed in childhood.[12]

Working is a practical, down-to-earth approach to solving the problems of a troubled family while tending to your own needs. By setting goals, by persisting despite frustration, and by claiming successes where they can, resilient survivors forge lasting strength.

You can measure your resilience by the efforts you made, the strategies you tried, and the goals you set for yourself and reached despite the counterpull of your troubled family. To the extent that you take hold of life rather than letting life take hold of you, you are resilient.

GENERATING

Dr. J. Kirk Felsman went to Cali, Colombia, with one question in mind and left with another. He set out wanting to know how the earth's forgotten children manage the "tangled course of growth and development." He left wondering what would become of the shrewd and durable street children who had so openly shared their lives with him.

Groping for an answer, Felsman tracked down an older Colombian who had been a street child himself. The gentleman responded indulgently. "Well, it depends. What becomes of any man? You're right, the gamins are smart and strong; they survive. But it still depends on where you go, what you find, and who you meet."[13]

Ask a psychologist or a psychiatrist a question, and you're bound to get a question in reply. The wily Colombian gentleman, burnished by years on the street, beat Dr. Felsman at his own game. As if to say, "Isn't my simple presence here with you a good enough answer?" he returned a single question with three. When you've grown up in unspeakable hardship, where can you go? What can you find? And who is there for you to meet?

In a study intended to learn where resilient chidlren go, what they find, and who they meet, Dr. Felsman and Dr. George Vaillant followed the lives of seventy-five American inner-city males.[14] Similar to the Cali children, all of them grew up in poverty-stricken, socially disadvantaged families. As children, they were left largely on their own. Their family lives were complicated by alcoholism, mental illness, or a history of arrests in at least one parent. The seventy-five were called the Core City High Risk Group. Many did well. According to Felsman and Vaillant, the men's success demonstrates that "the things that go right in our lives do predict future successes and the things that go wrong do not damn us forever."

Felsman and Vaillant found that, as a group, the resilient Core City Men progressed from working to generating, the culminating phase of initiative. Generating is a zest for seemingly impossible puzzles. More than solving the puzzles that fall on your table, generating is an attraction to problems—an enthusiasm for planning, acting, and bringing sticky matters to a successful conclusion. Generating is stretching yourself, achieving, and becoming a model for others to follow.

One Core City man was Bill. At fourteen, he was neither a genius nor a superkid, though a work ethic was well-ingrained in his inner self. As Felsman and Vaillant describe him, Bill had a competent, methodical involvement with his environment, a capacity to make the most of a difficult and disorganized home, and an expectation that he could and would succeed. In a discussion of his family's poverty and the rampant delinquency in his neighborhood, Bill was asked why he didn't steal. His answer was an emphatic display of personal gratification and Survivor's Pride. "I don't have to," he said. "I can earn what I need."[15] Indeed, Bill was working and earning money and had been for some time.

At forty-seven, Bill was typical of the successful Core City men. Balancing initiative and relationships, the entire group was productive, showed a capacity for caring and empathy, and had assumed sustained responsibility for the growth, well-being, and leadership of others. Most were married, genuinely enjoyed their children, and had friendships that extended beyond the immediate family. Courageous individuals, their lives demonstrated a pattern of mastery and competence despite occasional setbacks and multiple factors that conspired against them. Like you, they were indelibly marked by a destructive past. Yet, standing back and taking the broad view, the resilient Core City Men gained by framing their life stories around their achievements and their resilience. In accounting for the stamina of the group, Felsman and Vaillant state:

> Our preliminary indications are that the successful men in our high-risk group are . . . not free of their difficult early memories. We would speculate that it is their style of remembering *and* feeling that is important. . . . Most do have access to their pasts and are able to bear that pain and sorrow, and in so doing, to draw upon it as a source of strength. . . . [This perspective] seems to inform that "generative" quality in the way they live.[16]

Like Bill, many resilient survivors turn adversity to advantage by taking an active role in shaping their lives. Used to handling problems alone, they have well-developed practical skills, a tolerance for frustration, and a well-cultivated talent for picking their way through psychological mine fields. Many are gamblers. Having little to lose, they take risks, have no expectations that life should be easy, and thrive on tackling obstacles that test their competence.

Take Congressman Steven Solarz, whose personal story appeared in the press at the time I was collecting case studies of resilient survivors.[17] Still showing his childhood pain, Solarz's face went blank as he described his early memories. When Solarz was ten, his father's second marriage broke up, and his stepmother, who had raised him since infancy, left abruptly. Young Solarz was sent to live with an aunt in Brooklyn. "I loved my stepmother very much," he said. "I never saw her again." At the time, he did not know that his biological mother was alive and had also abandoned him.

Solarz had good cause to break or rage or become permanently embittered, but he didn't. Instead he protected himself, imposing strategy on misfortune by setting and reaching one goal after another.

First, Solarz armored himself socially, making friends who served as an emotional substitute for the family he did not have. In the summer twilight, they pounded their Spaldeen balls on concrete stoops and spun out their dreams. Combatting the loneliness of his aunt Beattie's house, Solarz also turned to books. He devoured biographies, history, and the encyclopedia. He poked his nose into politics, and in 1956, he armed his buddies with Adlai Stevenson placards. Teaching himself how to campaign, he won virtually every top school office. He became president of his junior high class, "mayor" of his high school, and vice-president of the student body of his college, setting one image of his competence next to the other in a vibrant collage of his self.

All went well until Solarz was nineteen and was hit, for the second time in his life, by a puzzle that seemed impossible to crack. On a break from college, he stumbled upon a letter that his father had written to an uncle. It revealed that Solarz's birth mother was still alive. Up to that point, Solarz had assumed that she was dead. He had not pressed for information from his father, who had communicated that the subject was taboo. "Once when I was very young," Solarz recalled, "a little girl on my aunt's block said, 'Where's your mother?' I said, 'I don't have a mother.' She said, 'Everybody has a mother.' I said, 'I don't.' "

Faced with the painful realization of abandonment yet again, Solarz mobilized his energy, brains, and courage and generated a daring scheme. He contacted an uncle, who referred him to his maternal grandfather. Solarz said, "When I phoned my grandfather, he told me that everybody had to go through life with a cross to bear and my cross would be that I would never know my mother. So that ended the conversation." But it didn't end Solarz's determination; the remark became high-energy fuel that propelled his plan.

Solarz found the name of his mother's second husband, a lawyer working in a storefront office in Brooklyn. Taking a friend, Solarz went to the address he had been given. From a phone booth across the street, the friend called and asked for the lawyer while Solarz peered through the window to see who would answer and lead him to his mother. Then Solarz and his friend followed the man home.

His destination was just a few miles away from where Solarz had been living with his aunt. Solarz stood and stared at the house. Unable to knock on the door, he phoned instead. When he was asked about the call, Solarz replied, "I asked her if she wanted to meet me. She said, 'Yes.' We met at a coffee shop. I asked her what happened, why she left. She told me. That will remain between us."

Talking about the impact of the boy's heartache on the man, Solarz's shows his pain, but it does not dominate his thoughts. He said:

> It perhaps created a need on my part to enhance my own self-esteem . . . and to win the confidence of my peers both on the block and also in school by succeeding. Clearly I was always running for some office or other. But at a certain point, you must know, the truth of this hypothesis has been superseded by other motivations which have more to do with what I feel obligated to do with my life—to leave the world a better place.[18]

Resilient survivors treat their pain as a problem to be solved—not a fate to be endlessly lamented. Many survivors who once felt helpless achieve a sense of effectiveness by generating projects that stretch the self, produce growth, and instill feelings of competence and effectiveness.

Not to be confused with workaholism, generating lends pleasure, affirmation, and quality to life. Workaholism detracts, monopolizes your energy, and pulls your life out of balance. The difference is not caused by the issues or tasks that occupy the workaholic and the generative individual. The two part ways on the basis of style.

Audrey, for instance, was a workaholic. Coming from an abusive family, she strove to correct childhood insults by redressing the land-right grievances of Native Americans. A rising star in a law firm known for its commitment to pro bono cases, Audrey arrived at her office at seven A.M. and often left around nine P.M. When she was writing a brief or preparing for a trial, all-nighters were common. In tending to Native Americans, Audrey forgot all about herself.

Audrey had many colleagues, but few friends. Her marriage was on the rocks, and her children saw little of her. To assuage her guilt over her mothering, she had a third child when her two older ones were in elementary school. She went back to work weeks after delivery, taking a breast pump with her. A taxi diver drove her pumped milk home at noon and at four P.M. to a waiting nanny. Pulled in every direction, Audrey was anxious and unhappy most of the time.

Resilient survivors also throw themselves into worthy causes—such as returning the stolen lands of Native Americans—in order to reverse their own helplessness in the past. But generating reduces the pain of childhood rather than trading it up, as workaholism does, for a different brand of agony. Lena, for example, shared Audrey's zeal for fighting injustice, but she was careful to strike a balance between her need to be productive and her right to a personal life. Like the Core City Men, Lena was a caring person, successfully married and actively involved with her two adolescent daughters. At the same time, she had a taste for daunting projects.

After leaving home, Lena expanded her knack for photography into filmmaking. The fearlessness that she honed in her family—she called it constructive defiance; I called it generating—was her hallmark. "Push-overs bore me," she said. "When something gets too easy, I lose interest."

When I met Lena, she was involved in a venture that suited her generative style perfectly—a muckraking film on a suburban high school that was hiding its racial tensions behind a public image of being well integrated. The school administration, fearful of exposure, flatly refused Lena access. "That really got me going," she said.

The rejection unleashed the intrepid survival style Lena had used in her family. She stopped pursuing permission for the project and pulled directly into action, taking matters into her own hands. Knowing how to turn chaos to advantage, she submerged herself in the community's confusion and kept a low profile.

Lena started going to a local hangout, a diner near the school. With her salty style, she fit in easily, gaining the confidence of kids she interviewed. She also ingratiated herself with the school custodians, who allowed her in the halls, the lunchroom, and the school restrooms. When she was arrested for trespassing, she paid her fine, lay low for a few days, and then returned. If a guard turned her away at the front door, she went to the back door. And if that was locked, she tried the windows. Lena also enlisted parents who agreed with her agenda. And she recruited the help of two school-board members.

Six months into the project, Lena was actually able to cajole her way into several classrooms. After a year of pushing, prying, coaxing, and simply refusing to take no for an answer, she completed the project. Aired on public TV, her film received rave reviews and was responsible for some significant changes in the school it featured.

Brimming with Survivor's Pride, Lena gave me a videotape. I could see the stamp of her generativity on every frame. Despite the avalanches, ice slides, and pummeling winds, she had stayed on the mountain and continued to climb. I am happy to say that she reached the summit.

PATHS TO YOUR RESILIENCE

Look at the Resiliency Mandala on the next page, focusing on the initiative wedge. Recall the times you felt helpless and ineffective as a child and some of the attempts you made to assert yourself. Use the information and examples in this chapter to frame your memories around your resilience rather than your damage. The questions below on exploring and working will help you recall the early signs of your initiative. The questions on generating may propel you to take greater initiative now.

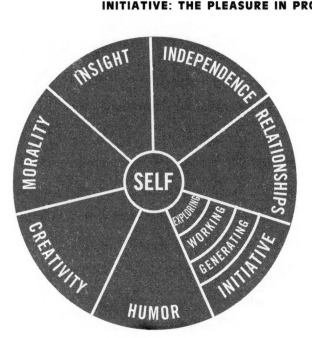

Exploring

In early childhood:

1. did you enjoy nosing around and getting involved in constructive activities outside your parents' sphere?
2. did you experiment with objects and mechanical things that you could find?
3. were you successful in taking care of some of your own physical needs or in tending to your younger siblings?
4. can you remember an early sense of yourself as someone who could get things done?

Working

In middle childhood, adolescence, and young adulthood:

1. did you take a paying job or do volunteer work that took you out of the house regularly?
2. were you an achiever in school?

3. did you have hobbies or other activities that you took seriously?
4. when hit with problems, did you think about solutions or get bogged down in frustration?

Generating

As an adult:

1. do you consider yourself a political or social activist?
2. do you participate in community projects that aim for positive change?
3. does your career give meaning or a guiding purpose to your life?
4. are you a leader?
5. do you achieve a balance between the projects you take on and your personal needs?

Chapter Eight

CREATIVITY: NOTHING INTO SOMETHING HUMOR: SOMETHING INTO NOTHING

DEFINITION: CREATIVITY and HUMOR are safe harbors of the imagination where you can take refuge and rearrange the details of your life to your own pleasing. In contrast to the resiliencies that keep the wheels of reality rolling, creativity and humor turn reality inside out. Both originate with *playing* or pretending to be a superhero, princess, space explorer, or ferocious beast when you were actually under siege. With time, the imaginative energy that drives playing is channeled into *shaping* or making art. In adolescence, many resilient survivors dabble in writing, music, painting, or dance to break the constraints of their troubled families and their own hurt feelings. In some adult survivors, shaping evolves into *composing* or skilled creative activity. However, most resilient survivors direct the urge to play into humor, mixing the absurd and the awful and *laughing* at the combination. Related resiliencies, creativity and humor are tangible proof that you have stopped the course of destruction and have emerged whole from shattering experiences.

To deal honestly when you were deceived, to have empathy when you were often hurt, to speak straight when you heard mostly double talk, to risk intimacy when you were rejected, to separate when you were needy, to produce when nothing you ever did was good enough, to live well when you've been brought up badly require imagination. You need to see beyond life as it actually is and envision how it could possibly be. Imagination backlights each section of your Resiliency Mandala. On the humor and creativity wedges, your imagination beams directly, revealing the comic in the tragic and the order in chaos.

Freudian analysts were among the first to recognize humor and creativity as related resiliencies with the magical power to invert reality. Freud himself noted the power of humor to reduce something to nothing. He regarded a joke as a mirror in which you can see your hardships shrink and your self become larger than life.

In his essay on "Humour,"[1] Freud illustrates the power of a joke by describing the rogue who, on the way to his Monday morning execution, sticks out his chin and defiantly proclaims that the week is beginning nicely. Faced with death, the rogue cleverly dismisses his plight and refuses to suffer. "[His ego] insists," says Freud, "that it cannot be affected by the traumas of the external world; it shows, in fact, that such traumas are no more than occasions for it to gain pleasure. . . . 'Look! here is the world, which seems so dangerous! It is nothing but a game for children—just worth making a jest about.' "[2]

Jack McDuffy is a resilient survivor who uses humor to transform bitter realities into mere games for children. Jack was born an accident and raised a burden. His mother was a prostitute. One night she got sloppy and conceived. Not wanting to risk an abortion, she took a "sabbatical" and carried the baby. Shortly after leaving the hospital, Jack's mother dropped him off with his grandfather, a widower who "didn't know the first thing about taking care of a child." And Jack knew it.

> He wanted me about as much as an advanced-stage cancer. At least once a day he would bemoan how he was put on earth to suffer. "Jesus had only one cross to bear. I have two," he'd mumble. The first cross was my mother. The second was me.

Jack prevailed by learning to deflate despair. He told me about the day he decided to get serious about being funny. Locked up with his grandfather and seeing that he was in an awful jam, Jack said to himself, "This is ridiculous. I think I'll become a comedian."

Jack's first experiments with being funny were conducted in school. In second grade, he began putting on plays. He recalled:

Bobby's Brains: written by Jack McDuffy, starring Jack McDuffy, directed by Jack McDuffy, and produced by Jack McDuffy. The kids were in stitches. And the teacher liked me too. When I saw that, I thought, "I don't have to stick up grocery stores. I can do something else."

Jack has been the official winner of the Funniest Consultant in Washington contest for two years running. A couple of times a year, he attends open-mike night at Garvin's Comedy Club and brings the house down. He told me:

It's like conducting the biggest symphony orchestra in the world. I'm standing on the stage and telling a joke, and everyone is laughing. And they're all following me. I could actually say, "Let's go to Saudi Arabia," and the whole group would get up and go.

Resilience is the capacity to channel your pain rather than exploding. Resilience is getting up in the morning, looking in the mirror, and seeing the Pied Piper, not Jesse James. The choice is real; you do not have to win contests or be Woody Allen to reap the psychological rewards of humor. Resilient survivors regularly defeat despair with a good laugh.

Since Freud first advanced a psychological perspective on humor, his followers have recognized the same transforming magic in creativity that he saw in a joke. According to the Freudians, both resiliencies have the power to reverse a harsh reality by turning inward to the imagination. Whereas humor reduces something to nothing, creativity enlarges nothing into something. Word by word, stroke by stroke, note by note; the artist fills a void. The finished work is a mirror in which you can see evidence that you have stopped the course of destruction and can breathe life into dust. As psychoanalyst Dr. Hanna Segal said:

All creation is really a recreation of a once loved and once whole, but now lost and ruined object, a ruined internal world and self. It is when the world within us is destroyed, when it is dead and loveless, when our loved ones are in fragments and we ourselves in helpless despair, it is then that we must recreate our world anew, reassemble the pieces, infuse life into dead fragments, recreate life.[3]

Tanya Stemple created a world from flimsy scraps of paper. When Tanya was three, she had a tonsillectomy. Her father, who "flew the coop" when her mother first became pregnant, was not available. Her mother, though never formally diagnosed as mentally ill, was too disturbed to take care of herself, let alone a child. Tanya's tonsillectomy depleted her mother's scant resources. Instead of taking her child home from the hospital, Mrs. Stemple placed her in the County Home for Children.

Tanya's story appeared in *The Washington Post*[4] in 1950 as part of a feature on the home, a facility for chronically sick and abandoned children. A compelling picture of her, leaning on the metal bar of her crib, her hand reaching toward the camera, appeared in the *Post* with the story. Tanya was a strikingly beautiful child with dark, beseeching eyes.

Sitting in my office years later, Tanya related that she didn't remember being in the home. An older cousin, who visited her there, directed her to the article in the *Post*. Seeing the picture was a shock, but the caption underneath did not surprise Tanya at all. It told how she filled her days by creating a world of cutout paper dolls. The description confirmed Tanya's memory of the period of time in her life between five and seven years old, just after she left the home and went back to live with her mother. She said:

> Living with my mother, I felt terribly alone. I peopled my empty world by making elaborate cutouts—dolls, dollhouses, furniture and clothing—and by using them to play out stories. Some of them would go on for days. And then, of course, I had favorites that I repeated over and over.

Now Tanya Stemple is an aspiring poet and short-story writer. The rhythms of her language and the unlikely elements that combine in her metaphors are mirrors in which she can see the goodness in herself. She said:

> One of the greatest highs I can have is reading something I've written that really sings. Sometimes I read the same passage over and over, just relishing the idea that I wrote it. I figure, if I can do something this beautiful, there must be a lot of good inside me.

As Tanya talked, her voice cracked and she began to cry. But her tears did not blur the connections in her mind between her early pain, the first signs of her emerging creativity, and the restorative powers of her writing. She explained:

> For me, writing is like the love affair between a caring, sensitive mother and her very young baby. When I sit down to write, I cry out into the dark, where words are waiting to answer. They come at my will, bringing delights and comfort and form for my unshaped thoughts. Writing is hard, sometimes excruciatingly hard, but it is the elixir of my life.

Resilience is soaring on your own juices rather than crashing on alcohol or drugs. You do not need extraordinary talent to get a thrill from writing, painting, music, or dance. You need only to experiment with expressing yourself in a creative medium. Many resilient survivors are closet artists, seeking no public recognition, maybe even avoiding notice. Working for their own pleasure, they mix words, paints, notes, and pirouettes into a magical healing brew.

Creativity and humor are cousin resiliencies that can reverse a bitter reality and turn:

- struggles into strengths
- pain into pleasure
- defeat into triumph
- irrelevance into significance
- something into nothing and nothing into something

As an old Japanese proverb says, "The reverse side also has a reverse side."[5]

PLAYING

Caught in a troubled family, you may have filled up large blocks of intolerable time by playing. That choice was resilient. Your early imaginative activities probably represent your first attempts to overcome adversity.

Before reading any further, get out a poem you wrote as a child or a story that compelled your attention. Dust off a picture you drew or a construction you assembled from a cereal box, odd buttons, and some string. Recall a favorite game or a fantasy. The purpose here is to peel back your young imagination and uncover the restorative powers beneath the surface of the games you played.

Playing is the common ancestor of humor and creativity. Our language preserves the tie and traces a connection to the Resiliency Mandala. Recreation, a synonym for play, has the related meaning of giving new life—refreshing the mind or body. Humor is wordplay. A drama is a play; an actor is a player; and a dramatist is, of course, a playwright.

In his *Creative Writers and Daydreaming*,[6] Freud noted that in German, where "play" translates as *Spiel,* a *Lustspiel,* or comedy, literally means "pleasure play," and *Trauerspiel,* or tragedy, is a "mourning play." Elaborating further on the links between play, humor, and creativity, Freud poses this rhetorical question:

> Might we not say that every child at play behaves like a creative writer, in that he creates a world of his own or rather re-arranges the things of his world in a new way which pleases him?[7]

I use the word *playing* in the Freudian sense to include all the imaginative activities in which you consciously or unconsciously liquidated your real-life hardships. A magic mirror, playing reverses time and circumstance, turning big into little and little into big and sad waifs into kings, queens, superheroes, master builders, and ferocious beasts.

For most children, playing is a natural method for achieving emotional repair. Go to any playground or preschool, and you can see imagination in action, healing bumps and bruises, speaking out against the pressure to remain silent, and making the self whole again after a shattering experience. For children in troubled families, the importance of playing is heightened and the capacity for playing can be highly developed. In myriad settings, roles, and disguises, successful survivors test their skills for battling adversity.

Take Janet, for example. Trapped on an isolated estate with her decaying mother, Janet spent hours acting out dramas of escape. She drew countless pictures of a little girl with supernatural speed outrunning ogres, secret police, and supervillains. She galloped her horse from the top of a hill across an open field and climbed the highest trees and the tallest fences on the grounds surrounding her house. At night, she ran between the trees, playing a spy behind enemy lines. And during the day, while her mother slept in a bedroom closed off by double doors, Janet acted out the tale of "Rapunzel."

The stairway in the "great front hall" was the tower where Rapunzel was imprisoned by her jealous mother. A doll became Rapunzel, and a rope suspended from the top of the bannister to the floor below was her long golden braid. And for herself, Janet reserved the role of the prince who rescued the forlorn, isolated maiden. Reaching the top of the stairwell by climbing the rope braid hand over foot, she flung herself over the rail in a burst of pride and confidence and carried her Rapunzel doll away.

Janet's miniature dolls came to life as Harry Houdini and the Great Santini. She carefully sealed them up inside her father's discarded wooden cigar boxes, submerged them in the bathtub, and then engineered escapes more fantastic than anyone would believe. And her stuffed animals were a revolutionary brigade, storming the dungeons of a wicked king and releasing his innocent prisoners. Sometimes Janet's escape games dangerously crossed the line between fantasy and reality. She said with more than a little glee:

> Mother raised rabbits that she kept locked in cages in the barn. Once I sneaked in there and let whole families of them out. They ran all over and ate up mother's roses.

You can see the magic of play wherever resilient survivors reverse loneliness, fear, rage, confusion, and despair by:

- joining the devoted circle of Winnie the Pooh, Tigger, Eeyore, Kanga and Roo
- swinging on jungle vines with Tarzan
- slaying the fearsome seven-headed, fire-breathing dragon
- setting the table with fine china and serving their dolls high tea daily at four

- stalking the elusive white tiger across the world's highest mountains
- pampering a beloved doll
- plundering the seas with Bluebeard's dreaded band of pirates
- dancing out of the ghetto and into the stars

In his study of children with psychotic parents, Dr. Anthony took advantage of the telling quality of play to watch resilience in action.[8] His research staff gave children arts-and-crafts materials and asked them to construct how living at home felt. Ellen, one of the most creative survivors in Anthony's study, came up with the castle that was the key to her resilience.

One of six sisters, Ellen was subjected to the relentless and vicious verbal attacks of a manic-depressive mother. Her father, a psychopath with a sadistic streak, was equally disagreeable. According to Anthony, Ellen maintained composure despite her parents' wildest accusations. She also thrived academically, socially, and emotionally.

Asked about her castle construction, Ellen revealed how she managed to stay healthy despite the unbearable pressure, crowding, hostility, and confusion in her home. By conjuring an image, Ellen enclosed herself in privacy, exerted control, and imposed order on utter chaos. She described her castle as the "little space" that she had arranged to which she could retreat when things outside got "rough." The most important part of the castle was an iron gate that she could lift to let herself inside and escape her "enemies" and drop so that no one could penetrate her defenses. Inside the castle, Ellen envisioned a smoothly functioning world where cooperation was balanced by respect for personal boundaries. She laughingly said:

> It was like being in a world in which everything worked and everyone worked together and where you had a job to do that you wanted to do and no one could stop you from doing it.[9]

Ellen concluded her interview with an unabashed statement of her Survivor's Pride:

> I am the queen of this castle, and I do not want anyone to enter who can spoil my life.[10]

Playing is a resilience because the order that Ellen enforced in her imaginary castle, the freedom that Janet achieved in her make-believe games, and the powers you found in your fantasies can stick in reality. As psychoanalyst Dr. Albert Solnit noted:

> Play enlarges the child's sense of himself, his capacities and his effectiveness in altering the reality in which he lives. In that sense play enables the child to explore safely how he can become active in shaping his world and not feel helpless or dependent on it any more than he prefers.[11]

SHAPING

In Barbara Hudson's short story "The Arabesque," a resilient survivor, Kate, teaches her younger sister, Arden, how to chase away the ghost of their bizarre and frenzied mother. The technique that Kate demonstrates is shaping, the second stage of creativity and humor. Shaping is a refinement of playing that adds discipline and effort to your imagination and strives to produce art.

"The Arabesque" opens by contrasting Kate's sense of responsibility and knack for knowing trouble when she sees it with her mother's blindness and reckless abandon:

> Sometimes Arden's mother would get them up in the middle of the night to clean house. The first time Arden was four. The room was dark and her mother stood in the light from the hall.
>
> "It's time to get up," she said and turned on the overhead light, and Arden saw the crack that began above the door and ran across the ceiling. Her sister Kate rose from the other bed. The ceiling was blue and their beds were white. Her mother wore an old print dress and tennis shoes. "We're going to clean. Before your father gets home." She turned and moved away, her feet soft on the carpet, heavy against the stairs. Soon *The Firebird* by Stravinsky filled the house.
>
> "Come on," said Kate, pulling at her arm. "Get out of bed. Get out."
>
> "What is Mommy doing?" Arden asked.
>
> "Hell," said Kate, who was nine. "I don't know."
>
> Arden had never heard her say that word, and she was scared.
>
> Later when the beds were made and the baseboards dusted, they sat at the kitchen table eating cornflakes; their mother was talking. "I'm going to

paint the living room today. Kate, when you get home from school, Arden and I will have painted the entire living room. What color shall we paint it?" She turned to Arden. "My little angel, what color shall we paint it?"

Arden was worried. She had no idea how to paint. "I don't know," she whispered. . . .

"This is terrible." Kate twisted a piece of her long blond hair tighter and tighter. "Maybe you should go with me. Maybe I should take you to school."[12]

As the story unfolds, Kate becomes the voice of sanity in an otherwise insane family. She stands up for herself, says what she sees, confronts her father about her mother's destructive behavior, and keeps Arden out of harm's way. Both girls benefit from Kate's strength and especially from their mutual closeness.

Finally, one night after Kate has gone away to college, her mother puts her head down on the kitchen table and dies. Returning home for summer break, Kate finds Arden in terrible shape, sitting in a bathtub, clothed and dry, but soaked in agony. With the same compassion and wisdom that has characterized Kate since age nine, she reaches out, helps Arden out of the tub, and teaches her how shaping can keep you sane.

"This is what you do," she [Kate] said, and Arden followed her into the living room, where Kate stood in the middle of the Oriental rug, in first position, her shoulders back, her chin lifted, her heels, calves, and finger-tips meeting. "This is what you do. You take your mother," and she pushed onto her toes and turned, stepping with the leg that would become her base, one arm moving forward, lifting her upper body, the other leg and the other arm rising slowly behind her. "You take your mother and you turn her into something else."

It was the most beautiful arabesque Arden had ever seen: one long smooth arc stretching from Kate's fingertips to her pointed toe, and the leg on the carpet straight and sure. "Do you see?" Kate asked.

"Yes," Arden whispered. "I think I do."[13]

Resilience is the capacity to shape your awful experiences at home into art and convert a victim's posture into a proud and beautiful stance. In adolescence, many survivors turn to writing, music, art, sports, or dance to express their inner turmoil and to bring order out of confusion. By imposing the discipline of creativity on their despair, resilient survivors heal an injured self.

While I was conducting the interviews for writing this book, many survivors who had been creative adolescents brought me samples of their work. Some had written stories and poems or painted pictures that were undisguised expressions of grief. For example:

> *Iter Vitarium*
> I wander in a black lagoon
> through life's temptatious waters.
> I search through tears dried by the moon,
> "Pray, what becomes Thy daughter?"
> I stalk through swampy drudgery
> a clue to my despair.
> A life of solitude to be
> the answer to my prayer.[14]

"Where's the Survivor's Pride here?" the poet asked half-skeptically, half-hopefully during her interview.

"Covered over," I answered, "but in there, anyway."

She dared me to show her.

"You could have handled your pain by going in for promiscuous sex, but you didn't. You could have beaten up your younger sister, but you didn't. You could have kept your silence and shriveled up inside yourself, but you didn't. You handled your pain in a way that wouldn't come back to haunt you—by creating a poem. And no matter how badly you felt, that poem and all the others you wrote are a source of pride for you. Didn't some hidden pride motivate you to bring your poems here today?"

"That's a different point of view," she said, wondering whether to buy it.

Other resilient survivors are more like Kate in "The Arabesque," transforming grief in their art rather than expressing it in an undisguised form.

Take Janet, who as a bereaved teenager withstood her mother's illness and eventual death by channeling her loss into music and soaring away on her own notes. She said:

Music made my world beautiful and gave me peace. My cello sang out my grief and the full strength of my will to be alive. I loved walking out on the stage for a recital, taking my bow in hand, and saying, "I am more than a victim with a mother to whisper about. I am a real person and a musician worthy of your attention."

Take Micah Gaines, who paints strength and grace into his broken body. The child of a fragmented, impoverished family, he was thrown thirty feet in a hit-and-run car accident at the age of eight and left severely palsied. Before his injury, Micah was interested in drawing and had ably copied some great artists. "I liked Michelangelo," he said. "Especially that ceiling painting where God and Adam touch fingers."

Micah's accident was the impetus for moving from art as a pastime to immersing himself in painting and developing his own style. He attributes his daily refusal to pity himself to the sense of power that wells up in him as he begins to fill an empty canvas. "I just paint those feelings away. They don't get the better of me."

I met Micah when he was eighteen at his makeshift home studio, where he demonstrated his painting technique for me. Micah's hands both shake uncontrollably. He wields his brush with his left hand, supported at the elbow and guided to the canvas by his right. Imposing figures, laid down in bold strokes and brilliant colors, dominate his canvases. His natural backgrounds, while not overwhelming, often threaten. Walking me around his studio, Micah stopped at "Journey," where he pictures himself under a fiery orange sun rowing across a vast expanse of water. Micah judges "Journey" to be his best canvas. Pointing to it, he explained how he realizes his resilience in the creative process:

> My paintbrush represents "able to do." The paint is my lifeblood, and the canvas is my own world, my universe, my dream feelings of taking charge of my whole being.

Take Jack McDuffy, who, in high school, expanded his humorous repertoire from spontaneous one-act plays like *Bobby's Brains* to more sophisticated productions that laughed in the face of his miserable situation at home. Jack spent hours making joke books that he covered, bound, and sold to his classmates for a penny each. "Every one was autographed," he said with an ear-to-ear grin. "They went like hotcakes."

Looking through the pages of Jack's comics, we both could see how the strokes of his pen expressed and reversed his plight at the same time. One series that we interpreted together featured a muscular twosome, Pete and his unnamed buddy.

CARTOON	OUR INTERPRETATION
Pete and his buddy, drawn naked to the waist, meet on a beach. They greet each other with a strong, manly handshake.	Jack, feeling alone and weak living with his grandfather, gives himself a pal and a powerful body he's proud to display.
Pete and pal liquidate their enemies and travel to an island to bury the bodies.	Jack, who keeps his own counsel at home, vents his rage and wish to break his personal captivity.
Having completed their task, the terrible twosome take off their helmets and shin guards and strip down to their underwear.	Jack finds relief by expressing his rage. He can now unload some protective emotional armor, relax a little, and enjoy that light feeling.
After a while, the two decide that it's time to go home. They plunge into the water and swim back to the mainland.	Jack cleanses the little guilt he feels over his anger. He is now ready to return to reality, more in charge of his life.

"Everything was set"—Jack's final blurb—smacks of healthy defiance and Survivor's Pride.

Resilience is not a suit of armor or a magical ability to walk between the raindrops. Nor is it the capacity to bounce back from every blow. Resilience is the will to accept the discipline of an art form in order to shape your pain into "something else." Resilience is expressing your feelings in flights of fancy and returning to earth in control of yourself and better for the trip.

LAUGHING AND COMPOSING

When patients get locked into a fixed point of view, a respected colleague recommends the ultimate reframing. Breaking out of English and laying claim to the authority of Freud's Germanic tradition, he declares, *"Mann tracht und Gott lacht.* Man strains and God enjoys. *Play God!"* he commands his patients.

Creativity and humor are related resiliencies that pit God's cosmic perspective against your troubled past.[15] Both begin with playing and cycle back to playing. As you progress from one arc to the next on the Resiliency Mandala, you go from dressing up in high-heeled shoes, Viking helmets, Superman's cape, and Her Majesty's royal robes to trying on God's glasses and taking a fresh look at yourself.

Composing, the adult phase of creativity, and laughing, the adult phase of humor, are imaginative leaps that permit you to stand above yourself and record what you see. At a distance, you can observe patterns and possibilities that are not visible from closer up. Laughing is spotting the absurd in the deadly serious and telling about it in a good joke. Composing is seeing the potential for growth and strength in your pain and reporting about it in art.

"I Go Back to May, 1937"[16] is a poem composed from the cosmic perspective. Playing God, the poet Sharon Olds breaks down the barriers of time and space. Her words transport her backward in years to a college campus where her parents are young lovers, childless and blind to the harm they will do. The surreal view jogs Olds's awareness and brings her face-to-face with a soul-searching question—one that many survivors have entertained: "If I had the power to decide, knowing what I now know, would I choose to live or never to be born?"

> "I Go Back to May, 1937"
> I see them standing at the formal gates of their colleges,
> I see my father strolling out
> under the ochre sandstone arch, the
> red tiles glinting like bent
> plates of blood behind his head, I
> see my mother with a few light books at her hip
> standing at the pillar made of tiny bricks with the
> wrought-iron gate still open behind her, its
> sword-tips black in the May air,
> they are about to graduate, they are about to get married,
> they are kids, they are dumb, all they know is they are
> innocent, they would never hurt anybody.
> I want to go up to them and say Stop,

don't do it—she's the wrong woman,
he's the wrong man, you are going to do things
you cannot imagine you would ever do,
you are going to do bad things to children,
you are going to suffer in ways you never heard of,
you are going to want to die. I want to go
up to them there in late May sunlight and say it,
her hungry pretty blank face turning to me,
his pitiful beautiful untouched body,
but I don't do it. I want to live. I
take them up like the male and female
paper dolls and bang them together
at the hips like chips of flint as if to
strike sparks from them, I say
Do what you are going to do, and I will tell about it.

Olds's poem records her journey away from anger toward a commitment to life, from the Victim's Trap to an appreciation of her own resilience. Like the other survivors I have known with a strong creativity wedge on the Resiliency Mandala, she converts her pain into a serious artistic purpose. "I want to live. . . . Do what you are going to do, and I will tell about it."

"Creativity," says psychoanalyst Dr. John Rickman, "is building a New World on the ruins of the old."[17] The promise of renewal pushes many resilient survivors in creative directions. Of the resilient survivors I have seen as patients and have interviewed for my research, only one was a professional artist. Most were pursuing writing, painting, dance, or music as a serious hobby. They were working at night, on the weekends, and on vacations.

"Why?" I asked, feeling the agony of writing this book.

They replied without hesitation. Their answers all echoed the theme of "building a New World on the ruins of the old."

AUTHENTICITY IN THE SELF: In a creative state, I get down to the bare essentials. There's no dodging myself. I am who I am. The word that comes to mind is *wholeness*. I feel whole and I feel real when I paint. It's the opposite of the fractured feeling of living in my family.

FREEDOM: Dancing, learning new movements, I leave the familiar behind and give over my body—no, myself—to uncertainty. And it feels good; not scary the way uncertainty used to be. To know that I've achieved enough trust in myself to try the unknown is to be sure that I'm not looking for my parents' approval anymore.

BEAUTY: I came from ugliness. I'm horrified by ugliness. I feel compelled to make beauty.

POWER: I make my own world and know my own power. That's a far cry from the way I grew up.

CONNECTEDNESS: When you tell your story in art, you touch other people, and you know that you're not alone. You know that what you feel other people feel too.

CONTROL: When I fit my problems into a canvas limited by four edges, I know that the hurt will never get big enough to overtake me.

MORALITY: I feel the obligation to be all that I can be. Creating is the ultimate stretch. Living at home with my parents was like shriveling up.

JOY: It's an out-of-body experience, the closest I can come to ecstacy. And that's one emotion I never thought I could achieve.

The history of humor suggests that laughing has the same renewing qualities as composing art. Biblical sages advised, "A merry heart doeth like good medicine." In the early part of this century doctors recommended laughter to stimulate the heart, lungs, and respiratory system and to blow away the cobwebs in every nook and cranny of the body.[18] More recently, in *Anatomy of an Illness,*[19] Norman Cousins documented how he cured himself of a deadly collagen disease with large doses of old Marx brothers films and reruns of *Candid Camera.* And on the research front, psychologists are turning up more and more evidence of the connection between resilience and getting up there, playing God, and laughing as you watch yourself strain.

In a study of professional comedy writers, Drs. William Fry, Jr. and Melanie Allen concluded that humorists incorporate situations that pain them most into their work.[20] Their talent is tilting our awareness toward the funniest moments in the midst of sadness. Fry and Allen state that humor is more than an escape. Laughing at your troubles, they say, "is a means for establishing a firm identity, one more secure than it might have been, in the midst of constant explosions and instability."

From their study, Fry and Allen offer a portrait of Nathan, a professional comedy writer. During his interview, Nathan slapsticked, turning his eyelids inside out and playing, just as he did as a child. His antics clearly distracted him from the traumas he was relating.

Nathan grew up in a "state of suspended tension." His family had little money. His father was a "prolific dreamer, waiting for his ship to come in." His mother gave up waiting and went in for worrying. The couple's common ground was fighting. Nathan described the connection between his humor and his parents' feuds this way:

> I was always funny, they tell me, when I was a kid. I started off being funny physically, not wanting to write but *being* funny. I think I was in pain; I think most of it comes out of pain. I came from a family who yelled a great deal. They lived at the top of their lungs always. The only defense against that was to laugh at it, find what was funny in it.[21]

Nathan went on to describe the details of the humorous defense:

> I used to sit in the kitchen in full view of them, and have a pad and pencil, and I would be scoring them. What *could* I do after all? They paid no attention to me. I became largely an observer.[22]

In therapy, resilient survivors frequently take the first step in breaking out of the Victim's Trap by seeing the humor in their situation. "Look at me," a successful survivor said with tears streaming down her face as she described the miseries of her family. "You would think I was the world's greatest sufferer." Asked to write about the role of humor in her resilience, she said this:

> As a direct result of living with one of the great undiscovered tragedians of our age, I have refused all my life to take anyone or anything too seriously, sometimes to my own detriment. From where I stand, the Final Judgment has lots of comic potential, and I'll probably end up in big trouble with God by the time it's over.

I chose writing to impose order on the chaos that was life with Mother, and humor was the only way to offset her determinedly bleak outlook. The brain is cunning in looking for ways to live when you're ready to give up. On paper, I get to choose what happens, and I get to try to make it lighthearted even if I have to wrestle every word to the ground with brute force. It's her perspective I'm fighting with every word, and when I win, the victory is sweeter than any other I can imagine.

In therapy groups, resilient survivors are comics par excellence. Usually by the third therapy session of a newly formed therapy group, a spirited game of "Can You Top This?" gets going, with members engaging each other in a competition for the most absurd and painful family story. They laugh in order not to cry.

During manic episodes, my mother ran around the street in her nightgown. I lived in terror, never knowing what would come next. When she was finally hospitalized, I felt tremendous relief. I never thought there was anything wrong with mental hospitals. I thought they were places that were set up so families could have a vacation.

Recently, I went out to Arizona to visit my mother. It was my birthday, and she made a big deal out of giving me a present—a gift certificate for a massage. We went down together to the health club in the basement of her building, so she could charge it. When the guy behind the desk told her the price, she turned to me and asked, "Do you think this would be so expensive if you weren't so fat?"

My mother is the queen of broken promises. I couldn't count the number of times I was expecting to get a new dress, go ice skating, go to a party, get help with my homework, that she was not feeling up to it. It was like she was equipped with a specially designed retractable nipple. It would stand up on her breast, full and promising, inviting, and just as I was about to close my lips around it, bam, she'd snap it in.

Here's a letter from my loving mother. "My Dearest Daughter, It's going to be so much easier for me to write—I can say exactly what I want without your 'Mother, I refuse to listen.' So listen, my dear. You my darling daughter are a complete slob. Your house is a shit house. Disorder everywhere! I threw out more junk from your fridge—rotten peaches, tomatoes, lettuce, spoiled cans of food. Organization, my dear, plus baking soda opened to remove odors. Try it. I could go on and on. You were so horrified at my using hair spray. What about the germs in your home? And the disorder? Your handbag hanging on the stair rail! What a lovely entrance picture it makes. I remember, years ago you told me that you had a fight with a young man you were dating who had taken a nap in his clothes. You refused to go out with him unless he changed. What ever happened to my daughter with her beautiful sensitivities?"

In some respects, laughing is like a primitive magical formula for getting rid of your enemies, suggests psychologist Albert Rapp.[23] You make a miniature wax or rag doll in the image of your enemy. Then, with a certain amount of abracadabra and mumbo jumbo, you stick pins into it. While the chances that such a ceremony will defeat the foe is unlikely, it might very well work off your anger and relieve your tension, leaving you feeling that you have won a victory.

Humor is resilience that stands somewhere between the absurd and the awful, that is both and neither at the same time. In the words of the novelist Hermann Hesse, humor is a third kingdom where the spirit becomes tough and elastic. You should not take things too seriously, for seriousness puts too high a value on time. "In eternity, however, there is no time. Eternity is a mere moment, just long enough for a joke."[24] I can think of no better advice to fortify survivors of troubled families.

PATHS TO YOUR RESILIENCE

Look at the Resiliency Mandala pictured on the next page, focusing on the humor and creativity wedge. Recall the times you felt stifled or hurt and turned inward to your imagination. Use your memories to frame a picture of yourself around your resilience rather than your damage. The questions below on playing and shaping will remind you of the early signs of your resilience. The questions on composing and laughing may encourage you to add more humor to your life or to try your hand at creative activities now.

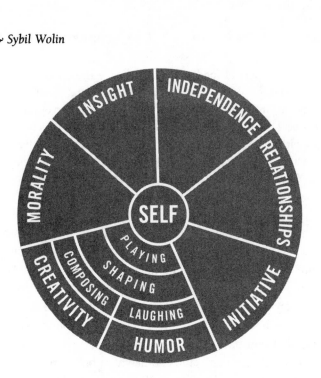

Playing

In early childhood:

1. did you spend much of your time in imaginative play?
2. did the games and roles you played most often help restore your confidence and courage to face reality?

Shaping

In middle childhood through adolescence:

1. did you seriously pursue or just dabble in art?
2. did your art express your hurt feelings in an undisguised form?
3. were you aware of using art and humor to transform your family situation and your own difficult feelings into something better?

Composing and Laughing

As an adult:

1. are you involved in an artistic hobby or profession?
2. do the positive feelings you get from creating compensate you for the pain of your past?
3. can you laugh at your own pain?
4. can you see the absurdity in your troubled family?
5. can you use humor to pull yourself out of a bad mood or to diffuse tension between yourself and others?

Chapter Nine

MORALITY:
HOLINESS IN AN
UNHOLY WORLD

DEFINITION: MORALITY, the activity of an informed conscience,[1] is your wish for a good personal life grown large and inclusive. The seeds of morality are sown early when strong children in troubled families feel hurt, want to know why, and begin *judging* the rights and the wrongs of their daily lot. In adolescents, judging branches out into *valuing* principles such as decency, compassion, honesty, and fair play. Restoring themselves by responding to suffering in others, resilient survivors champion the underdog, dedicate themselves to causes, and try to impose order at home. In successful adult survivors, morality becomes more a matter of obligation than of private satisfaction or personal repair. By *serving,* or devoting time and energy to institutions, community, and the world, resilient survivors join their individual selves to the selfhood of humanity.

I have reserved the discussion of morality for last because this resiliency resembles but surpasses all the others. Each of the other resiliencies keeps the past in its place. Morality keeps the past in its place and leans into a better future. Each of the other resiliencies aims to repair an injured self. Morality aims to repair an injured self and to improve the world as well. Each of the other resiliencies is a mirror in which survivors can see a pleasing self-image. Morality is a mirror in which survivors can see a pleasing self-image and catch a glimpse of humanity perfected.

Morality first emerged as a resilience not in the context of troubled families but against the background of a crumbling society. During the political and social turmoil that overtook this country in the sixties, child psychiatrist Robert Coles and his wife, Jane, joined the civil rights effort in the South.[2] More students of human nature than politicians, the Coleses saw the school segregation crisis brewing around them as an opportunity to document how stress causes psychological wear and tear in children. They went to New Orleans to observe the unfolding drama of black children entering a previously all-white school for the first time. Instead of finding emotional damage in the students who were involved, the Coleses uncovered the steeling power of morality.

For Jane Coles, the discovery was no surprise. An English teacher who had spent years discussing the secrets of human nature revealed in great literature, she knew the wellsprings of strength and courage. She also knew that her young students were more than capable of grappling with serious moral questions.

Her husband, on the other hand, was stopped in his tracks by the resilience he saw during those tumultuous days in the South. A physician, Robert Coles had concentrated on seeing disease processes in action. In order to recognize the dynamics of resilience, he first needed to shed the orientation toward damage that was ingrained during his medical training. I know the painful experience of his conversion from the inside, down to the well-deserved jabs he took from his wife.

In his latest book, *The Spiritual Life of Children,* Coles describes his medical school, pediatric, and psychiatric education. In a passage laced with wry humor, he recalls how readily his seniors dispensed diagnoses such as "serious trouble" and "major emotional difficulties," how quick they were to prescribe "prolonged treatment," and how grudgingly they would acknowledge that a patient was well, using such quaint terms as having "good mental hygiene."[3] Once when a supervisor used the phrase "mental health," one of Coles's fellow psychiatric residents requested a definition. "Good question," the usually talkative teacher returned. Then, becoming uncharacteristically short of words, he lapsed into naming the features of illness that were absent in a mentally healthy individual—"no serious acting out," "no character disorder," "no neurosis." Coles concludes, "By then we had come to know that everyone has a neurosis, large or small."

Despite his misgivings about its emphasis on damage, Coles's training took hold, just as mine did. By the time he had finished his work in child psychiatry, he considered himself "savvy" about all known forms of mental affliction. He had successfully pushed his earlier reservations about pathology to the back of his mind, and he strode out of Boston Children's Hospital eager to embrace the task of diagnosing children's psychiatric ills. When a wise senior colleague, Dr. Marian Putnam, warned him to be wary of labels, Coles was impressed, but he was just as reluctant to surrender his damage perspective.

"Since we've all got our problems," Putnam said, "it's what we do with them that distinguishes us."

Describing the scene, Coles turns the same wry humor on himself that he had earlier directed at his mentors. He labels his response "the plaintive cry of someone who was just finishing a five-year stint of struggling with those 'problems' and was beginning to feel like an expert."

"Yes," he objected, "but some 'problems' are much worse than others."

"True," replied Putnam, "but some people are so much better able to deal with their problems, however severe, than others; and some people whose problems don't seem all that serious get quite undone by them."

Coles still remembers his overwhelming anxiety as he listened to Putnam. "If some were troubled badly, yes, but had the knack of living well with those troubles," he wondered, "what, then, should I think or do? I began to feel the ground under me giving way. I fell silent."

Responding to Coles's stunned expression, Putnam said, "Maybe, at a certain moment, it's best to think differently about people. Maybe we shouldn't be emphasizing so strongly what 'problems' they have, but how they get through their lives."[4]

Shortly after their conversation, Coles went to New Orleans to observe the school segregation crisis with all the confidence of a novice and his training in pathology firmly in hand. In *The Moral Life of Children,* he tells the story of the children he met there and his own moral awakening.

The focus of Coles's attention in New Orleans was Ruby Bridges, a six-year-old black child who led the city's integration lines. Going to school and coming home each day accompanied by federal marshals, she passed through murderously heckling mobs. Her trial continued for months.

As Ruby walked her treacherous path, Coles scrutinized her from the sidelines with all the scientific objectivity he could muster. While his wife marveled, he interviewed Ruby and those who knew her. He tracked her eating habits and her sleeping patterns. And he smugly waited for her to break. Ruby looked strong, but Coles assured himself and those around him that all was not as it seemed. Sooner or later, she would crumble. Ruby's calm was a defense that could last for just so long. She was denying her fears and anxieties. Perhaps her strange composure in the face of such obvious danger represented a reaction formation or a repression.

The longer Coles waited for Ruby to crack, the stronger she became.

Enter Jane Coles in a style of marital interaction I have become quite accustomed to myself. The more Coles tried to dissect Ruby's underlying motivations and conflicts, the more his wife emphasized the young girl's competence to manage under stress. The more he resorted to developmental theories that consigned children of her age to the bottom of the developmental ladder, the more Jane pointed out how Ruby's morality elevated her above the mob. One day as Coles was muttering the dogma of some psychiatric theory, she broke in:

> You are making her sound as if she ought to be on her way to a child guidance clinic, but she is walking into a school building—and no matter the threats, she is holding her head up high, even smiling at her obscene hecklers. Last night she even prayed for them![5]

Jane Coles's well-intentioned dig opened her husband's mind to new possibilities. Coming around to her opinion that "six-year-old Ruby Bridges was demonstrating character to all the world," Coles stopped waiting for signs of her distress to emerge. Instead, he began to look for the source of her strength. His search identified the regenerating power of morality, the final wedge on the Resiliency Mandala.

In order to live, Coles states, we need a sense of purpose. We need to know why we are getting up in the morning and why we go through each day. The clearer your answer, the more resilient you are. Coles slowly came to see that Ruby would not break because her sense of purpose was like a rock. Duty-bound, this young child was trying her level best to right the upside-down world where she had been thrust. And day after painful day, she was protected against the slurs hurled at her from the outside and the fears threatening her from within by her deep sense of morality.

Coles coined a phrase—"moral energy"—to name Ruby's source of courage.[6] Moral energy is a life-sustaining force that can lift survivors above the downward tug of hardship.

When Ruby was nine, Coles went back and interviewed her about her triumph and her ordeal in New Orleans. Wiser for his experience, he was not suspicious of her sturdy appearance this time around. Ruby showed no signs of a delayed reaction to stress. Her conviction was unchanged, and her words glowed with the same moral energy that had flowed through her actions three years earlier. Reflecting on her experience, she said, "We inched a little closer to God, and because we did we became a little better ourselves."[7]

The story Coles tells of his stay in New Orleans is as much about his own moral struggle and progress as about the crisis he went to observe. "Go easy on the labels," a wise colleague had warned. After months of frustration, Coles finally acceded to Marian Putnam's advice and his wife's good sense. Pushing the security of diagnostic categories aside, Coles took a risk and walked with Ruby across the unknown territory of childhood resilience.

JUDGING

Do abused children feel that they deserve to be hit or that severe physical punishment is an acceptable form of discipline? Dr. Sharon Herzberger, a professor of psychology, put this question to children who had been abused by their parents.[8] "Please be honest," she said. "I will not tell anyone your answers."

According to Herzberger, every child participating in her research answered willingly. In fact, many were eager to be interviewed. Here is a sample of what they said:

I don't think other families whoop their kids with extension cords. I don't think they would put their children outside with no shoes on.

I think I should be treated like a normal person.

Child abuse isn't a good thing to do to a person when they just do something little.[9]

These statements display the capacity for judging in young children. Judging, the first arc on the morality wedge of your Resiliency Mandala, is telling right from wrong even when it comes to your loved ones. Painful and frightening as this resiliency can be, it also provides protection from the ravages of troubled parents by placing responsibility for wrongdoing where it belongs. Judging puts the badness in your family outside you and helps you hang on to the goodness inside. As Noreen, whose father was especially brutal around the dinner table, told me:

I always knew my father was a mean machine. I can never remember thinking otherwise. Nor did I ever think that I or anyone else in the family deserved his violence. I had my own standards, and I knew when I had misstepped. My father's brutality was his problem, and I saw that it had nothing to do with me. In fact, that was one of the worst parts of growing up in my family. There was no rhyme or reason to him. What he did was so unconnected to what we did.

Other survivors recall a similar early awareness that their parents were often out of bounds. Their concerns and hopes were expressed with reference to the guardians of justice the young know best:

- The police: I was worried all the time that my parents would be arrested.
- God: I thought God would punish them, and that St. Francis would save me. I had a special alcove in my room that I made into a shrine, and I prayed to St. Francis for hours.
- The school: I believed the principal or my teacher would find out what was going on in my house and would report my parents.
- Fairyland: I thought my mother was a wicked witch and that she would be punished the way all the witches were in the fairy tales I knew.

Dan, a resilient survivor interviewed by Dr. O'Connell Higgins in her research on resilient adults who "love well,"[10] recalled how a story, *The Wizard of Oz*, became a vehicle for clarifying his own moral rights. The week he saw the movie, his mother had mistreated him so badly that he tried to run away to his grandmother's house. He said:

> In thinking about *The Wizard of Oz* I realized that the really powerful thing was . . . good triumphed over evil, which was wonderful to see . . . and secondly was that Dorothy had on ruby slippers all along. She just didn't know that was the case, and I can remember saying to myself . . . "It's the same with me. . . . I have on [something] like ruby slippers. If I want to make things right in my life, *I can do it!* It was a very clear sense . . . the power was always there, you just had to *know* it was there.

The capacity to make accurate moral judgments like Dan's also appeared among the young survivors in Herzberger's study. She found that harmed children are capable of sizing up their own raw deal and of talking about it as well. Nobody's fools, survivors are deeply aware that being hurt by a mother or father is wrong, unusual, and unwarranted. Many recognize that they are punished more frequently and severely than other children. When Herzberger asked why, they echoed the sentiments of Noreen and Dan. The most common answer was, "My mother [or father] is mean."[11]

Herzberger's study on judging is part of a growing research effort to understand early moral development in children. For instance, in an intriguing series of experiments to determine when you first began to form standards of right and wrong, psychologist Dr. Jerome Kagan brought a group of toddlers into a laboratory playroom full of toys.[12] Many of the toys were perfect, but some had been purposely damaged. For instance, one doll's face was marked with black crayon. The head of one stuffed animal had been removed, and the buttons were torn off its shirt. Despite the full stock of good toys, the toddlers who had reached nineteen months of age were preoccupied with the broken objects. "They would bring a damaged toy to their mother," Kagan observed, "point to the broken part, stick a finger in the place where the animal's head had been removed, and indicate that something was wrong by saying, 'Fix,' or, 'Yukky.' "

Kagan concluded from his experiments that children seem to develop standards early. Somewhere around two years of age, they appear to form an internal image of the way objects, people, and events should be. Animals should have heads. Dolls should have clean faces. Shirts should have buttons.

And parents should be good, adds Dr. Robert Selman,[13] who also does research on the development of morality in young children. Selman has found that by the age of seven, boys and girls have clear ideas about the basic qualities of a good parent. He says that sensitivity is the child's number-one concern. Parents should notice and take their children's feelings into account. Their number-two concern is generosity. Parents, say seven-year-olds, should be willing to give up something important for their children—for instance, time.

After extensive interviews, Selman has concluded that young children are not apt to fool themselves. Seven-year-olds know that mothers and fathers are fallible and can punish a child unjustly. They also defend the idea that being uncaring, emotionally stingy, or insensitive to a child is wrong.

You can find a textbook case for illustrating the early capacity for judging in John Cheever's short story "The Sorrows of Gin."[14] The main character is Amy Lawton, a nine-year-old poor little rich girl. Her parents are pretentious, neglectful, and hypocritical. They also drink too much. Amy is resilient, and she has their number.

Shooed away by her parents and regularly cooped up with disinterested baby-sitters, Amy, a creative child, keeps herself happy by reading voraciously and playing the piano. She is also a moral child, easily able to see through the thin veil of her parents' hypocrisy. When her father, tipsy from gin, self-righteously fires Mrs. Heinlein, a housekeeper, for drinking, Amy recoils. Because the woman was Amy's one adult confidante and friend in the household, she also feels enraged and begins the regular practice of pouring her father's liquor down the drain. Before long, he discovers an empty fifth and accuses a baby-sitter of drinking it. The ensuing battle wakes Amy. Listening to the shouting voices rising through the floor of her room, she vaguely sees

the pitiful corruption of the adult world; how crude and frail it was, like pieces of worn burlap, patched with stupidities and mistakes, useless and ugly, and yet they never saw its worthlessness, and when you pointed it out to them, they were indignant.[15]

Alone in the dark, Amy's moral vision is crystal clear at first, but her judgment blurs momentarily when the accused baby-sitter starts calling for the police. Amy is terrified and sinks into guilt, thinking that she has set off a chain of events that will end in the fall of her father's house. Under the pressure, she lapses into recalling her father's small kindnesses, and she decides to run away. But in the morning, one dose of her father's cheerfulness and oblivious self-satisfaction with his treatment of Mrs. Heinlein restores Amy's clarity. Her returning judgment elevates her plan to run away from a decision made in fear to a moral choice. She will distance herself from her parents' corruption, leave home, and become independent.

Amy goes through the rest of the day with the calm deliberateness of a resilient child, deciding to attend her ballet lesson, to have lunch with a friend, and then to take a train to New York City, where she will try to stay with people she had known when she lived there. Through the eyes of an adult reader, Amy's escape scheme is both sad and hopeful at the same time. While we recognize in it all the elements of a doomed childish fantasy, we can see too Amy's assurance, methodical thinking, and staunch optimism.

Late in the afternoon, just as she had planned, Amy sets off for the train station, never looking back. Arriving there, she buys a one-way ticket to the city from Mr. Flanagan, the station master.

In a moment of consummate irony, Mr. Flanagan intervenes to "save" her. He alerts Mr. Lawton, who comes to take Amy home. Standing on the platform, pathetic and blind, he resolves to meet his fatherly responsibility by teaching her that "home sweet home" is the place that she belongs. Comparing father and daughter, we leave the story believing that Amy's integrity in childhood is a seedbed for a moral adult life and that her deliberateness and determination will eventually lead to the independence she craves.

VALUING

Following their encounter with Ruby Bridges in New Orleans, Jane and Robert Coles traveled around the world together to see if the same fortitude they witnessed in her could be found in other children of hardship. Their research took them to American ghettos and migrant camps, the Brazilian favelas, and the South African mandated homelands. Where corruption and brutality are the normal order of things, Coles found children who valued compassion, fairness, and decency. Valuing is the activity of a generous spirit, the capacity to give when you have gotten very little. The benefits of valuing are self-respect and being attached to something that matters.

In *The Moral Life of Children,* Coles describes his conversations with the spiritually generous, resilient survivors he met. One was Eduardo, a young boy from Rio. Another might have been you, a determined child in any city or town searching for moral integrity.

An entrepreneur on Copacabana Beach, Eduardo lived by his wits, selling shoelaces, suggesting to passersby that they stop at this vendor or that, asking to wash a car or to help one of the well-off with a package or a beach chair, or simply begging for a coin. Eduardo was on the run from a brutal stepfather and an unstable mother. A widow grasping for security, his mother lived with one man after another, drifters in and out of her children's lives.

Eduardo was not one to take pleasure in virtuous self-display or pious tirade. Yet the more time Coles spent with the boy, the more he could see the creative moral vision that shimmered in Eduardo's words. The boy spoke hopefully about wanting to distinguish himself from the gamblers, drug dealers, and sex peddlers who populated the tarnished world in which he lived. Even-handed and compassionate, he also held himself apart from the self-righteous clergy whose claims to purity came solely at the expense of others. "I do not like to hear the bad ones pushed around in church by the priest," he told Coles.

One night, sitting with Coles on a rooftop overlooking the slums of Rio, Eduardo revived a memory that shows the nature of his resilience. He told about the harrowing circumstances surrounding his aunt's death. As Eduardo speaks, we see his compassionate regard for others, frank condemnation of brutality, distaste for empty pieties, and, most of all, the power of his morality to defeat despair. Listen to Eduardo and try to find yourself.

> My mother had a sister, and she came with us to Rio. . . . She was very religious. She listened to every word of the priest and nuns, a mistake. . . . One day a gang of men saw her. . . . They took her and gave it to her, maybe one hundred times. Who will ever know? They found her near the church.
>
> Would you believe it, the priest didn't want to touch her! That's what his cleaning lady told us, later! . . . He must have called a nun on that phone he has. She came, and she nursed my aunt, and my aunt started talking, so they let her go. She got home . . . and she just started crying . . . and she never stopped, not really for the rest of her life. She didn't live long after that day. . . .[16]

On the final day of her life, Eduardo's aunt called for him. She told him that she was dying and that she feared for his soul. Afraid, merciful, responsible, and deeply moved by the spectacle of her suffering, Eduardo wanted to give what the church had denied. He succeeded in the way resilient children often do, making an inspired response that achieved the spiritual richness of last rites. Listen to Eduardo's pride as he describes the scene.

> On the last day of her life, she called to me. . . . She asked me if I knew what happened to her. I said I thought so, yes. She said the men were not good, but she wasn't worth much herself! I got angry, but she just smiled. She said she was glad to be dying, and she wasn't sure she'd go to heaven because the priest knew what he knew about her! I got angrier! . . . Then she said that Jesus could come back any day, and He could be anyone. . . .
>
> I didn't know what to say! I was scared. . . . I could see that she wasn't going to be with us too much longer! I wanted to say something good, something that would make her better, something she'd like to hear and she'd smile hearing it. I couldn't think of a thing to say—and then, I just came close to her and said it: "Jesus could be you." . . . I was scared for a minute I'd said the wrong thing. . . . Then she stared right at me, and she gave me the biggest smile I've ever seen on her face. She never spoke to anyone after that, and she died the next day. We got the priest, and he

wasn't very friendly to her body. I've seen him be nice to some dead bodies. He is a two-faced one . . . and if Jesus entered *his* body, He'd find out quick it was a big mistake and leave in five seconds!

The triumph in Eduardo's account is packed into the humor of his conclusion. I can picture him now as I write, laughing, then stopping short of one last flourish—a declaration of Survivor's Pride, the faith of a holy child in an unholy world. I think Eduardo would not mind at all if I put these words to his final unspoken thought. "If Jesus entered that priest's body, He'd find out quick it was a big mistake and leave in five seconds, but if he entered *mine,* He'd find out that he made a great choice, and He'd stay for a real long time."

As Eduardo's story shows, survivors capable of moral reasoning and action can lift themselves above the corrupt world they inhabit. For instance, in Noreen's alcoholic family, no less than on Copacabana Beach, an informed conscience was a saving grace.

Noreen could have been depleted by her plight and become incapable of giving anything to anyone. She could have tried to even her score by imitating her parents and treating her younger brothers and sisters according to the family style. Or she could have become a troublemaker in the neighborhood, a dropout in school, or a loner. But Noreen did none of this. Instead, she was impelled by her conscience and her compassion to impose moral order in a family where the difference between good and bad was lost and punishment was dealt out without rhyme or reason.

Noreen, like Eduardo, was not given to vain demonstrations of her virtues. As you know, she resisted seeing her strengths and dwelled on her anguish. But, in therapy, as she opened up to the idea of her resilience, she was able to take credit for her morality and see how she had gained by her generosity.

Listen to Noreen.

It was a matter of tolerance. I saw all the suffering and I couldn't abide it. The worst was the way my father would go after the younger kids, the little ones who couldn't defend themselves. He was a bully—a coward at heart—and once he saw that he wasn't getting to them, he went after me. I felt that I had to protect the little ones. It was a moral obligation, something I couldn't avoid, something any decent person would do.

"What exactly did you do?" I asked.

Lots of things. I taught them the tricks of the trade. I would tell them how to spot my father's bad mood or know when he was drunk so they could get away. Or I helped them avoid his temper about food. Like taking a half a slice of cheese from the middle of the package or watering down the juice so my father wouldn't notice his special foods missing from the icebox. If something got broken, I would make sure it got fixed or taken out of the way. If they did not do their chores exactly right, I helped them so they didn't get the full brunt of his anger, because they were so little. When there was a fight, I felt like it was my role to remove them from the violence and entertain them so they would forget what was happening. I would take them upstairs and read to them or get some puppets and we would do a play. I distracted them while the house rocked with my parents' fighting.

"You put a lot into your sibs, didn't you, and you missed a lot of your childhood not only parenting yourself but taking care of them. What was in it for you?"

I couldn't turn my back. I felt that making a difference was my duty. And when I could see that I had changed things, I felt important and strong and that fed all my hopes that I would eventually get away.

Many resilient survivors exercised their conscience as adolescents by taking the responsible role in an irresponsible family. For instance, you may have:

- taken over housekeeping chores such as cooking, cleaning, or shopping
- sent a birthday card to a relative estranged by your parents
- protected your sibs as Noreen did or helped them with homework
- worked and contributed money to the family budget

Although the burden may have been heavy, you should claim the self-respect you deserve for shouldering it.

Other survivors were less prone, in adolescence, to fill the gap left by troubled parents and more inclined to take a stand and fight for change.

One was Alan, who confronted his ineffective father on the topic of his mother's undiagnosed manic-depression and her wild behavior. Listen to the moral reasoning behind Alan's position.

> I knew my father had lovers and that he was running away rather than doing the right thing at home. I mean, if he wanted to have lovers, that was one thing, but he also had an obligation to us, and he wasn't meeting it. I think I had the courage to keep bucking him not only because of the pain in the house. I also knew I was right and I wouldn't back off. The night he finally took my mother to the hospital, I grabbed him by the throat and screamed at him. I used to feel terribly ashamed of that. Maybe there was some better way. But that was the turning point, and I can finally let myself feel the pride in that awful confrontation.

Valuing right action, motivated by mercy and charity, resilient children fight corruption on the home front. "Why do they bother?" Coles wondered, recalling the beleaguered children he met in his travels. One day, he shared his puzzlement with Eduardo. The boy's answer did not disappoint. Taking a characteristic leap of moral imagination, he reflected, "We are here to stay awhile, and if we're lucky we'll leave people behind who like us, and when our name is mentioned, they'll smile and clap."

SERVING

Planning a graduation party for her daughter, Sandra—the resilient survivor who thrived on recruited love—began to feel less excitement and more anxiety about the celebration than she had hoped. "I dreaded bringing my family together," she said. Sandra confided her fears to a friend, who, in turn, insisted on relieving the pressure by making dinner for everyone the evening before. Sandra said:

> My friend Alice knew my family; she had seen them in action. I couldn't believe that she would let herself in for them. I bet her that instead of thanking her they would criticize her cooking or find something wrong with her husband.

So moved by her friend's generosity and compassion, Sandra could think of no way to reciprocate. Eventually she came up with a moral act: "to give back to the world." When another friend's son was marrying, Sandra hosted a brunch the morning after the wedding, for out-of-town guests. Her gesture began a tradition of unselfish giving that has spread beyond Sandra's immediate circle and continues to this day. Now, people with ties to Sandra are rarely left on their own to handle an important family affair. Someone, touched by her example, usually helps with dinner the evening before, lunch that afternoon, or breakfast the day after.

Remembering the emotional deprivation of her childhood, Sandra, who had gotten so little, connected her need "to give back to the world" with a sense of gratitude. She said:

> Coming from the kind of home life I had, you never stop remembering that things could have been very different. I'm left with a deep awareness of just how fragile the good things in life are and how easily they could disappear or just not be. I certainly have my horrible days, but I also have an abiding sense of appreciation for what I have—a sense of indebtedness and the obligation to repay. It's like offering the gods a sacrifice in times of plenty.

As a child, Sandra witnessed how the poison of her parents' fighting infiltrated their whole existence and threatened to overtake hers. Whatever sweetness she had in life, she cultivated by herself. Like so many resilient survivors in her position, she exited her family's house committed to passing along the good she had achieved for herself to others. I call Sandra's personal ethic of giving back to the world serving, the final arc on the morality wedge of the Resiliency Mandala. Serving is trying to make the world you inhabit a better place by spreading around your emotional and material wealth. Serving is:

- including charitable contributions in your household budget
- picking up the litter as you walk through your neighborhood park
- volunteering to tutor the illiterate, work in a blood bank, support political reform
- looking out for friends who are alone at holiday times
- giving up your favorite exercise class to take a friend for her weekly radiotherapy treatment

- writing a letter to the editor about unfair, biased reporting
- searching for the parent of a lost child who crosses your path
- lending a friend money, if you can, to start up a business
- reducing your standard fee for a needy client

In *The Ministry of the Laity,* James Anderson suggests that serving can solve the problem of personal fragmentation brought about by living in a society run by faceless bureaucracies and beset by complicated and, often, incomprehensible problems. A resilient survivor and a minister by profession, Anderson cares passionately about morality. He writes for all people, urging each and every one of us to rise above our individual concerns and contribute to our common good. Without diminishing Anderson's intention to convey a universal message, I think it's fair to say that his topic—how to stop the destruction of our planet and our society—is the dilemma of the resilient child in the troubled family writ large.

Anderson proposes that the key to prevailing is moral literacy, or distinguishing what is right, proper, just, and fair from what is pleasurable, exciting, reassuring, or practical.[17] As an example of someone who knows the difference, he offers the story of Joan, a young woman who truly served (in contrast to participating) on the volunteer board of a nursing home for the elderly.[18]

Unlike her fellow board members, who were most concerned with insurance matters and meeting legal building requirements, Joan exercised her responsibilities as a board member by asking quality-of-life questions—moral questions: How can we help the people who live in this facility keep control of their own lives? How can we foster their ties to the larger community beyond the home? What activities can we provide that will encourage our residents to remain productive rather than sitting down and waiting for death, as so many do?

Although other board members thought Joan was overstepping her bounds, she read up on geriatric research and talked with the people in the home. She found that some residents organized shopping trips while others deferred to the professional staff for fear of being put out on the street. Bringing these and other observations back to the board, Joan did not dramatically change the tenor of the meetings, but she made a small difference that gave the residents a little more independence and raised the level of compassion and fairness in her corner of the world.

Using Anderson's standards, I can say that, without exception, the resilient survivors I have known are morally literate people like Joan. Having prevailed over hardship, they feel equipped—perhaps better than most—to deal with life's mean and petty sides. Many who grew up feeling they had little to lose are also gamblers, unafraid to risk themselves in order to do what's right.

Take Noreen, the young medical student who had protected the babies in her family against her brutal father. On her way to an anatomy exam, she passed an old woman who was being mugged. Three teenaged girls had backed the woman against the wall of a government building, while a security guard stood by watching. Noreen could no more have passed the scene than she could have ignored her younger siblings' dirty diapers, crying, or hunger. Taking the risk of missing her exam, she stepped into the fray, screamed, chased the girls away, and helped the dazed woman.

With characteristic humor, Noreen described the ironies of the scene:

> I pushed past the guard, who didn't want to let me in because I didn't have a security badge. Then I ran past the woman at the front desk, who wanted me to stop and sign in. Then I barged into the first office and had to give a protesting secretary a gentle push in order to use the phone. I damn near got charged with trespassing and assault.

She chuckled as she talked.

I laughed too, but I also needed to ask, "It's funny in the telling, but not so funny at the moment. What pushed you on?"

"I can't stand bullies," she said.

"You dislike them so much that you'll risk your personal safety and a full year of work in anatomy by missing an exam unannounced?"

"Yes," she said without a moment's hesitation.

Take Alan, who spent years pushing his father to acknowledge his mother's manic-depression and its awful consequences for the family. The same moral courage that drove him then is apparent now as he goes about the daily rounds of his commercial real estate business, consciously choosing between squeezing out every cent of profit and creating a dignifying workplace for his employees.

Alan is dedicated to democracy and egalitarian policies in his company. He stays in touch with employees up and down the career ladder. His office door is open and his home phone is accessible. Even the janitors call him Alan, in part because he insists, but also because he is a real friend. Alan knows their children's names, their personal problems, and their special occasions. He said:

> I know some people are grumbling that I'm inefficient and that we could be making bigger profits. I really don't mind. I don't need everyone to love me. I just do what I think is right, and I believe that the people who don't like it will eventually come around because I make sure that I do right by them also.

Take Barbara, the survivor you first met in Chapter One. She grew up feeling chronically unfairly accused by her parents. While in therapy, she was called for jury duty. She served in the fullest sense of the word.

On trial was a twenty-eight-year-old man charged with taking indecent liberties with his daughter. At first, Barbara worried that in light of her own experience with emotional abuse, she wouldn't be objective—that her sympathies would lie with the child. To her amazement, however, she became more and more convinced of the man's innocence as she listened to the testimony. Describing a particularly painful episode of unfairness toward him, she said:

> It was clearly established that this guy, the woman he had been living with for ten years, and their three children—were so poor that they had always slept in the same double bed. The prosecuting lawyer built her whole case on the fact that on the morning of the alleged crime, this guy was in bed with his daughter. There was not a single shred of evidence that he had done anything to her. Yet she—the lawyer who was dressed to the nines in her designer clothes—asked with a voice dripping with contempt how he could possibly justify being in the same bed as his child. The guy looked speechless. He finally muttered, "It wasn't ever any other way." I felt sick.

At the end of the trial, the judge announced that Barbara had been one of the two alternate jurors and dismissed her. "I had to leave the courtroom without saying a word!" Her voice was still full of indignation. Someone else might have heaved a sigh of relief to return to work.

Barbara was no saint; she was glad to get back to the pile of stuff that had accumulated on her desk too. By the same token, she could not put questions of duty, responsibility, and service out of her mind. She said:

> It was terrible, bearing witness to that sordid drama, thinking I could have an influence, and then being cut out—just like that! It was even worse thinking that some innocent guy might be convicted, and that I could have stopped that from happening.

Barbara called the judge's chambers each morning during jury deliberations to find out if a verdict had come in. When she learned, on the fourth day, that the defendant was found guilty, she fumed, she cried, and she acted by doing the only thing she could. She wrote a letter telling the judge and the lawyers how poorly she felt the family had been served by handling their dispute with accusations, cross-examination, and punishment, techniques she knew all too well from her parents. "Why wasn't this problem referred to a social-service agency instead of a court?" she asked. "And why didn't someone think of spending just a fraction of the money that went for the trial on buying this family a couple of beds?"

Starting out life essentially alone, successful survivors have compassion and concern for others. They also know the necessity of watching out for themselves. Their resilience is a never-ending search for answers to the fundamental human questions posed by the sage Hillel in the first century B.C.:

> If I am not for myself, then who will be for me?
> If I am only for myself, then what am I?
> If not now, when?

PATHS TO YOUR RESILIENCE

To complete your Resiliency Mandala, focus on the morality wedge. Recall the times you went out on a limb and stood up to your parents because you thought they were doing something wrong. Or remember an incident when you gave up something in order to help your siblings, another member of your family, or an outsider. Use the examples in this chapter to frame your memories around your morality rather than your

sense of deprivation or your fright. The questions about judging and valuing will remind you of your early resilience. The questions about serving can help lead you to greater resilience now.

Judging

In early childhood:

1. did you think that your parents' behavior toward you could be wrong?
2. did you have some standards for determining what "good" parents are like?
3. did you talk to anyone about being hurt by your parents?
4. did you resolve to be different as an adult?

Valuing

In middle childhood, adolescence, and young adulthood:

1. did you hold values such as compassion, justice, loyalty, and fair play?

2. did you identify with and stand up for underdogs?
3. did you fill in around the house when your parents were less than responsible?
4. when you saw your parents' hypocrisy, pettiness, and cruelty, did you stand up to them?
5. did you hold yourself to a standard of being "good"?

Serving

As an adult:

1. is service part of your daily activities?
2. do you think about giving your life meaning as well as having it run smoothly?
3. are you willing to risk your own pleasure or even security for the sake of doing what you think is right?

Epilogue

THE INTERNAL IMAGE
OF A SURVIVOR:
ONE WHO PREVAILS

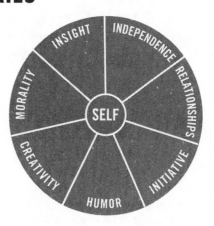

In the movie *City Slickers,*[1] a resilient survivor and two other New Yorkers verging on forty feel threatened by the middle-age blues. Wanting an "essential experience," they buy an adventure package—driving a herd of cattle across New Mexico into Colorado. On a slow ride across a plain, they reflect on the past by playing a question-and-answer game: What was the best day of your life? And the worst day? The first two, Mitch and Phil, answer easily. Ed, the survivor, holds back at first but then agrees to take his turn. From the struggle on his face, I gathered that he was giving in to group pressure and, perhaps, an urge to reveal the details of his shame-ridden but proud past for the first time. This is how the dialogue goes. "I'm fourteen," Ed tells them, "and my mother and father are fighting again. You know, because she caught him again."

"Caught him?" Mitch asks.

"This time," Ed continues, "the girl drove by the house to pick him up, and I finally realized he wasn't just cheating on my mother; he was cheating on us. So I told him, I said, 'You're bad to us. We don't love you. I'll take care of my mother and my sister. We don't need you anymore.'

And he made like he was gonna hit me, but I didn't budge. Then he turned around and he left. Never bothered us again. But I took care of my mother and my sister from that day on. That's my best day."

Stunned by Ed's unlikely answer, Phil blurts out, "What was your worst day?"

"Same day," says Ed. Then he rides off on his horse, leaving his friends to ponder the paradox of Survivor's Pride.

In this book, I have tried to trace the path of resilience in survivors of troubled families and to show how some of the worst moments in your life can also be framed as proud times. I've talked to you through:

- a vocabulary of research
- the words of my patients and other survivors who agreed to be interviewed
- my own clinical observations
- the experience of my colleagues
- the fictional truths of Louie Pollit, Adam Bede, Amy Lawton, and Arden and Kate
- and the literal truths of Cali's street children, Congressman Steven Solarz, Pedro, Jean Piaget, and others whom I have known only through my reading

I have not tried to persuade you that you can emerge from a troubled family unscathed, or that your problems are inconsequential. No person is immune to harm. Every survivor has vulnerabilities and is susceptible to the damage that troubled parents inflict.

Nor have I tried to profess that the pain of a troubled past can ever disappear completely. Adversity scars. And, at best, the memories you may have retrieved or reexamined while reading this book are a checkerboard of despair and hope, helplessness and determination, fear and courage. Like Ed in *City Slickers,* you may have found that the worst day and the best day of your life are the same.

Nevertheless, I have tried to encourage you with several optimistic claims and suggestions:

I have said that mental illness is not an inevitable result of growing up in a troubled family. You can also grow up resilient.

I have offered you the Challenge Model as a framework for reviewing your experiences as a survivor and have asked you to consider seriously the evidence that children who are vulnerable and hurt by troubled parents are also challenged by hardship to grow strong.

And finally, I have suggested that while you cannot change the past, you can change the way you understand it. For your past is more than a collection of cold facts. It is a living story that shifts with each telling, unsettling old connections to the present.

You can frame your story around themes of your resilience or themes of your damage. You can find reasons to be proud in some of your worst memories, or you can let yourself be overwhelmed by the horror of it all.

Much advice on the popular market today for survivors of troubled families encourages you to make a case for your damage, casting yourself as a helpless victim of your parents' hurtful behavior. I have argued that this image can perpetuate fear, passivity, and despair. The image I believe is needed is one that will make you proud, fortify you against your pain, and instill the belief that you can live well despite a troubled past. It is the image of a resilient survivor—one who has suffered and one who prevails.

I sincerely hope that these pages have inclined you toward the more liberating choice by serving as a mirror in which you can find reflections of a resilient self.

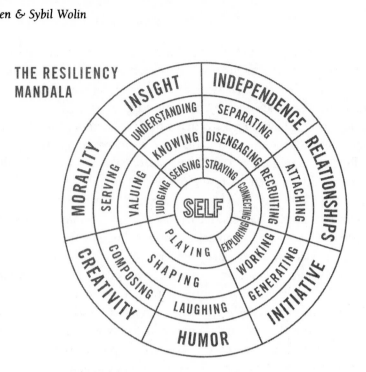

THE RESILIENCY MANDALA

Appendix

THE DAMAGE INVENTORY

The Damage Inventory[1] is an informal assessment. The overall inventory is divided into two parts. Part I covers your childhood and adolescence, and Part II covers your adult life. The questions evaluate how badly your self-image was hurt by the experience of growing up in a troubled family. Since evidence of a poor self-image extends beyond your mental picture of yourself, the Damage Inventory surveys signs of damage as they appear in your thoughts and feelings, your behavior, and your personal relationships.

PART I CHILDHOOD & ADOLESCENCE

Directions: The items below refer to your childhood and adolescence. Read all the items carefully, and decide how well each one describes you at the time you were growing up. To the left of each item, circle **4** if the description was *very often or always true* of you, **3** if it was *often true* of you, **2** if it was *sometimes true* of you, **1** if it was *seldom or never true* of you. When you have finished each section, calculate your subtotal for all the items, and enter it in the space provided. At the end of Part I, after you have completed all three sections, add together your subtotals, multiply by two, and enter your total childhood score in the space provided.

A. THOUGHTS AND FEELINGS

While I was growing up, I:

1 2 3 4   1. was generally anxious.
1 2 3 4   2. was frightened, panicked or phobic in specific situations.
1 2 3 4   3. was afraid of strangers, animals, new situations, or
                 unfamiliar places.

1 2 3 4   4. worried about myself or my family a lot.
1 2 3 4   5. was guilt-ridden.
1 2 3 4   6. blamed myself for my family's troubles.
1 2 3 4   7. worried that something was seriously wrong with me.
1 2 3 4   8. felt worthless or inferior.
1 2 3 4   9. couldn't tolerate making mistakes.
1 2 3 4   10. felt that I was not living up to my own expectations.
1 2 3 4   11. felt lonely and forgotten, as if I didn't belong.
1 2 3 4   12. thought I was a fake.
1 2 3 4   13. believed my body was ugly.
1 2 3 4   14. was self-conscious, easily embarrassed.
1 2 3 4   15. was uncertain of my ideas, unconfident.
1 2 3 4   16. thought the same thoughts over and over.
1 2 3 4   17. was shy, timid.
1 2 3 4   18. feared success or positive attention.
1 2 3 4   19. was unhappy, sad, or depressed.
1 2 3 4   20. was irritable, sullen, stubborn, or angry.

Section A: Subtotal _____

B. BEHAVIORS

While I was growing up, I:

1 2 3 4   1. acted young for my age.
1 2 3 4   2. clowned around excessively.
1 2 3 4   3. had temper tantrums.
1 2 3 4   4. was restless or hyperactive.
1 2 3 4   5. was impulsive, acting without thinking.
1 2 3 4   6. was cruel to people or animals.
1 2 3 4   7. destroyed property.
1 2 3 4   8. lied or cheated.
1 2 3 4   9. was reckless or accident-prone.
1 2 3 4   10. was physically self-destructive.
1 2 3 4   11. made suicide threats or gestures.
1 2 3 4   12. had serious school problems.
1 2 3 4   13. daydreamed or was inattentive.
1 2 3 4   14. had nightmares or sleep disturbances.
1 2 3 4   15. was overly neat or clean.
1 2 3 4   16. had an eating disturbance such as overeating, undereating, or binging.

1 2 3 4   17. abused alcohol or drugs.
1 2 3 4   18. had compulsive habits.
1 2 3 4   19. had psychosomatic problems, such as headaches or digestive problems.
1 2 3 4   20. had physical complaints with no known cause.
Section B: Subtotal _____

C. RELATIONSHIPS

While I was growing up, I:

1 2 3 4   1. preferred being alone.
1 2 3 4   2. was secretive.
1 2 3 4   3. had few friends.
1 2 3 4   4. couldn't get along with my age-mates.
1 2 3 4   5. fought or argued a lot.
1 2 3 4   6. was suspicious and did not trust others.
1 2 3 4   7. ended relationships at the first sign of trouble.
1 2 3 4   8. thought others were taking advantage of me.
1 2 3 4   9. was afraid of being abandoned or rejected by others.
1 2 3 4   10. couldn't stand up for myself.
1 2 3 4   11. was clinging or dependent.
1 2 3 4   12. tried too hard to please people.
1 2 3 4   13. demanded excessive attention.
1 2 3 4   14. was overinvolved in the problems of others.
1 2 3 4   15. became jealous easily.
1 2 3 4   16. boasted, acted like a show-off.
1 2 3 4   17. was sexually promiscuous.
1 2 3 4   18. was sexually inhibited.
1 2 3 4   19. couldn't express negative emotions such as anger, disappointment, or disagreement.
1 2 3 4   20. couldn't express positive emotions such as affection, optimism, enthusiasm, or praise.

Section C: Subtotal _____

Childhood & Adolescent Damage Inventory Score:
A + B + C Total _____ multiplied by 2 _____ = Total _____

PART II ADULTHOOD

Directions: The items below refer to your current life as an adult. Read all the items carefully, and decide how well each one describes you now. To the left of each item, circle **4** if the description is *always or very often true* of you, **3** if it is *often true* of you, **2** if is *sometimes true* of you, and **1** if it is *seldom or never true* of you. When you have finished each section, calculate your subtotal for all the items, and enter it in the space provided. At the end of the Inventory, add together your three adult subtotals and enter the sum in the space provided.

A. THOUGHTS AND FEELINGS

Currently, I:

1 2 3 4   1. am generally nervous, high strung, or tense.

1 2 3 4   2. get anxious in specific situations, such as open or closed spaces.

1 2 3 4   3. worry a lot.

1 2 3 4   4. easily feel guilty.

1 2 3 4   5. think the same thoughts over and over.

1 2 3 4   6. have unwanted thoughts.

1 2 3 4   7. become confused easily.

1 2 3 4   8. am suspicious, skeptical.

1 2 3 4   9. am vigilant, on the lookout for danger.

1 2 3 4   10. am irritable, touchy.

1 2 3 4   11. am quick to take offense.

1 2 3 4   12. think that I am the cause of others' problems.

1 2 3 4   13. am not living up to my expectations of myself.

1 2 3 4   14. am perfectionistic.

1 2 3 4   15. feel incompetent and unable to meet adult responsibilities.

1 2 3 4   16. see only the worst parts of myself.

1 2 3 4   17. feel weak or indecisive.

1 2 3 4   18. feel vague and unclear.

1 2 3 4   19. think something is seriously wrong with me.

1 2 3 4   20. feel alienated, like I don't belong.

1 2 3 4   21. feel inauthentic or fake.

1 2 3 4   22. feel constricted and unimaginative.

1 2 3 4   23. feel disillusioned by life.

1 2 3 4   24. am self-absorbed.

1 2 3 4   25. am afraid of success.

1 2 3 4   26. am self-conscious, easily embarrassed.

1 2 3 4   27. am ashamed of my body.

1 2 3 4   28. feel outside of my own body.

1 2 3 4   29. feel that I am watching situations from outside.

1 2 3 4   30. am unhappy, sad, or depressed.

1 2 3 4   31. have changing moods, from high to low.

1 2 3 4   32. have suicidal thoughts.

1 2 3 4   33. feel I am empty and without meaning.

1 2 3 4   34. am close-minded, inflexible, and intolerant.

1 2 3 4   35. am self-dramatizing, theatrical, or exhibitionistic.

1 2 3 4   36. am unable to experience deep feelings.

1 2 3 4   37. am solemn, joyless, unemotional.

1 2 3 4   38. fear losing power.

1 2 3 4   39. am nonchalant, overconfident, expansive.

1 2 3 4   40. am excessively hard-headed, competitive.

Section A: Subtotal _____

B. BEHAVIORS

Currently, I:

1 2 3 4   1. am restless.

1 2 3 4   2. have disturbed sleep.

1 2 3 4   3. am inactive, lethargic, sluggish.

1 2 3 4   4. am physically self-destructive.

1 2 3 4   5. do not allow myself pleasure.

1 2 3 4   6. have odd or peculiar mannerisms.

1 2 3 4   7. avoid people, places, or situations.

1 2 3 4   8. am wary, aloof.

1 2 3 4   9. am reluctant to assert my views.

1 2 3 4   10. am docile and passive.

1 2 3 4   11. place myself in inferior positions.

1 2 3 4   12. fail to complete projects and commitments.

1 2 3 4   13. procrastinate and, therefore, have problems at work.

1 2 3 4   14. am financially irresponsible.

1 2 3 4   15. have eating disturbances such as undereating, overeating, or binging.

1 2 3 4   16. am stubborn and contrary.

1 2 3 4   17. abuse alcohol or drugs.

1 2 3 4	18. am addicted to gambling or spending activities.
1 2 3 4	19. am sexually promiscuous.
1 2 3 4	20. am easily bored.
1 2 3 4	21. am in need of thrills.
1 2 3 4	22. am short-sighted.
1 2 3 4	23. am inefficient and erratic.
1 2 3 4	24. am easily frustrated.
1 2 3 4	25. am involved in illegal or antisocial activities.
1 2 3 4	26. use poor judgment.
1 2 3 4	27. behave impulsively or recklessly.
1 2 3 4	28. hold society's rules and conventions in contempt.
1 2 3 4	29. overvalue discipline, prudence, and loyalty.
1 2 3 4	30. have trouble limiting obligations or saying no.
1 2 3 4	31. am overly responsible in my work.
1 2 3 4	32. am overly disciplined or compulsively organized.
1 2 3 4	33. have compulsive habits, for example touching, counting, or washing things.
1 2 3 4	34. am compelled to keep things neat or clean.
1 2 3 4	35. have illnesses of no known physical origin.
1 2 3 4	36. talk excessively.
1 2 3 4	37. am boastful.
1 2 3 4	38. act like a clown.
1 2 3 4	39. do things for which I am later ashamed.
1 2 3 4	40. make promises that I do not keep.

Section B: Subtotal _____

C. PERSONAL RELATIONSHIPS

Currently, I:

1 2 3 4	1. am anxious in social settings.
1 2 3 4	2. am untrusting and suspicious of others.
1 2 3 4	3. have no close friends.
1 2 3 4	4. am overly concerned with my privacy.
1 2 3 4	5. keep relationships tentative.
1 2 3 4	6. end relationships at the first sign of trouble.
1 2 3 4	7. am independent to a fault.
1 2 3 4	8. prefer emotional distance to intimacy.
1 2 3 4	9. try to get my way through manipulation.
1 2 3 4	10. actively solicit praise or demand the attention of others.

1 2 3 4   11. expect people to do things for me.

1 2 3 4   12. make other people feel guilty about how they are treating me.

1 2 3 4   13. am unpredictable in my relationships with others.

1 2 3 4   14. enjoy intimidating and humiliating others.

1 2 3 4   15. am physically or emotionally brutal.

1 2 3 4   16. am minimally self-aware and surprised by others' views of me.

1 2 3 4   17. am overly polite, preferring formalized relationships.

1 2 3 4   18. invite blame and criticism.

1 2 3 4   19. am overinvolved in the problems of others.

1 2 3 4   20. fear separation or abandonment.

1 2 3 4   21. am sensitive to rejection.

1 2 3 4   22. expect too much from a partner.

1 2 3 4   23. try too hard to please people.

1 2 3 4   24. do things for other people and end up feeling unappreciated.

1 2 3 4   25. am overly concerned with how others view me.

1 2 3 4   26. am envious or jealous of what others have.

1 2 3 4   27. am unable to express anger or disappointment.

1 2 3 4   28. am timid or shy in social situations.

1 2 3 4   29. am sexually inhibited.

1 2 3 4   30. am overly dependent on others.

1 2 3 4   31. am passive with others and avoid asserting myself.

1 2 3 4   32. double-talk or say things that I don't really mean to other people.

1 2 3 4   33. assume responsibility for others.

1 2 3 4   34. try too hard to please.

1 2 3 4   35. brag or show off.

1 2 3 4   36. am indifferent to the needs of others.

1 2 3 4   37. am unable to express praise, enthusiasm, or affection.

1 2 3 4   38. am considered arrogant, inconsiderate by others.

1 2 3 4   39. fight or argue a lot.

1 2 3 4   40. am competitive, contrary, and quarrelsome.

Section C: Subtotal _____

Adult Damage Inventory Score: A + B + C Total _____

Appendix

INTERPRETING YOUR SCORE

Go back and look at each of your total scores for parts I and II of the Damage Inventory. For each part the lowest total score is 120 and the highest total score is 480. Now total your two scores.

Part I score + Part II score: Total Damage Inventory Score _____

Use the following table to evaluate your damage in your childhood, adolescence, and adulthood. You can see that the higher the score is, the more thorough the damage.

> 240–399 none to very little damage
> 400–549 moderate damage
> 550–960 extensive damage

In reviewing your scores, keep the following in mind:

First, the score is an informal yardstick—unlike a thermometer or a blood-pressure cuff—that estimates the extent of your damage rather than measuring it precisely. The purpose of the score and the scale itself is to name your damage so that you can begin to conquer it. I hope that reviewing your scores will not alarm you but will give you the distance from your pain that comes from being "heard" and from knowing exactly what you're up against.

Second, keep in mind that on the first administration, this test scores high. Survivors are typically predisposed, by the urgency of pain, to overestimate damage and underestimate the capacity for self-repair.

I suggest that after completing the inventory, you put your score aside for a while and take the scale again after you have finished the book. The knowledge that you accumulate about resiliency as you read will put your damage in the context of your strengths. Seeing the two together may influence you to give yourself different ratings on the individual items in the scale the second time around. You may be surprised and relieved to find that your damage score goes down.

Third, although your scores define signs of damage in you, the Damage Inventory does not show the damaging process in action. To see the harmful influence of your family in action, we need to backtrack to life at home when you were a child.

Brace yourself, and return to Chapter Two (page 22), "To Name the Damage Is to Conquer It."

NOTES AND COMMENTS

In the following notes, the first citation of each book or article includes title, author, publication information, and referenced pages. Subsequent citations are abbreviated.

1. THE CHALLENGE OF THE TROUBLED FAMILY

1. Part II of this book describes seven resiliencies or clusters of strengths observed in successful survivors. For each resiliency, related research from the fields of psychology and clinical and experimental psychiatry is cited.
2. The seven resiliencies were culled from clinical interviews with twenty-five resilient adult survivors. The resiliencies reflect the common themes that emerged as these survivors reviewed the strategies they had used, from childhood through adulthood, to protect themselves and to take strength from their struggles.
3. Dwight Wolter, "Taste of Fire," *A Life Worth Waiting For* (Minneapolis, Minn.: CompCare Publishers, 1989), pp. 212–213.
4. William Shakespeare, *As You Like It*, Act II, Scene I. *The Complete Works of William Shakespeare* (Baltimore: Penguin Books, 1969), p. 252.
5. George Eliot, *Adam Bede* (London: The Zodiac Press, 1984), p. 403.
6. Christina Stead, *The Man Who Loved Children* (New York: Henry Holt and Co., first Owl Book edition, 1980), p. 59.
7. Christina Stead, *The Man Who Loved Children*, p. 527.
8. Lois Murphy, *The Widening World of Childhood* (New York: Basic Books, 1962), p. 2.
9. Joan Kaufman and Edward Zigler, "Do Abused Children Become Abusive Parents?" *American Journal of Orthopsychiatry*, 57 (1987), pp. 186–192. After examining the research evidence, the authors reject the assumption that child abuse is likely to be repeated from one family generation to the next. In addition, they discuss the hazards associated with accepting this intergenerational premise. They state, "Adults who have been maltreated have been told so many times that they will abuse their children that for some it has become a self-fulfilling

prophecy. Many who have broken the cycle are left feeling like walking time bombs." Finally, Kaufman and Zigler observe that the pervasive influence of such a claim has interfered with progress in understanding the causes of abuse and has resulted in misguided interventions and social policies, p. 191.

10. Linda Bennett, Steven Wolin, David Reiss, and Martha Teitelbaum, "Couples at Risk for Transmission of Alcoholism: Protective Influences," *Family Process,* 26 (1987), pp. 111–129.

11. E. James Anthony first pointed to a "challenge-response formulation" to explain how children handle unusual stress. Also predating the Challenge Model, Anthony's colleague Bertram Cohler observed that some people take misfortune as an impetus for increasing effort to set and reach goals. E. James Anthony, "The Syndrome of the Psychologically Invulnerable Child," in E. James Anthony and Cyrille Koupernik, eds., *The Child in His Family: Children at Psychiatric Risk* (New York: John Wiley & Sons, 1974), p. 537; Bertram Cohler, "Adversity, Resilience, and the Study of Lives," in E. James Anthony and Bertram Cohler, eds., *The Invulnerable Child* (New York: Guilford Press, 1987), p. 284.

12. The discovery of a self through the process of mirroring is a theme running through much of the psychoanalytic literature. See, for instance, Margaret Mahler, Fred Pine, and Anni Bergman, *The Psychological Birth of the Human Infant* (New York: Basic Books, 1975). For an overview intended for the lay person, see Judith Viorst, *Necessary Losses* (New York: Simon and Schuster, 1986), pp. 43–65.

13. Alice Miller, *The Drama of the Gifted Child* (New York: Basic Books, 1981), p. 42. Miller introduces the concept of "substitute mirrors" in a case study of a depressed woman. As the woman aged, she lost her appeal to men who had previously provided the admiration her mother had denied. Miller states, "All her substitute mirrors were broken, and she again stood helpless and confused, as the small girl once did before her mother's face in which she did not find herself but her mother's confusion."

14. Relevant research is cited in Chapters Four through Nine in which the developmental unfolding of each resiliency is described.

15. A full description of the Kauai study is made in Emmy Werner and Ruth Smith, *Vulnerable but Invincible* (New York: Adams, Bannister, Cox, 1982). For a more recent follow-up, see Emmy Werner and Ruth Smith, *Overcoming the Odds* (Ithaca, N.Y.: Cornell University Press, 1992).

16. Emmy Werner. "Children of the Garden Island," *Scientific American* (April 1989), p. 111.

17. By recovery movement, I mean the self-help books, therapy groups, workshops, conventions, and media shows that boomed in the eighties and were directed at anyone who believed that he or she suffered from a psychological sickness or addiction as a result of growing up in a dysfunctional family. Examples include the PBS series *Bradshaw on Family;* Melody Beattie, *Codependent No More* (San Francisco: Harper & Row, 1987); John Friel and Linda Friel, *Adult*

Children (Pompano Beach, Fla.: Health Communications, Inc., 1988); Anne Schaef, *When Society Becomes an Addict* (San Francisco: Harper and Row, 1987); Charles Whitfield, *Healing the Child Within* (Deerfield Beach, Fla.: Health Communications, Inc., 1987). For a critical analysis of the recovery movement, see Wendy Kaminer, *I'm Dysfunctional, You're Dysfunctional* (New York: Addison-Wesley, 1992); Stanton Peele, *Diseasing of America* (Lexington, Mass.: Lexington Books, 1989); Charles Sykes, *A Nation of Victims* (New York: St. Martin's Press, 1992).

18. Carl Jung, *Man and His Symbols* (New York: Anchor Books, 1964), pp. 213, 255.

19. Salvador Minuchin, *Family Therapy Techniques* (Cambridge, Mass.: Harvard University Press, 1981), pp. 73–77. The technique of reframing was first used by family systems therapists and theorists such as Minuchin and Fishman to place an individual's symptoms in the context of family dynamics. For instance, a therapist might cast or reframe a child's aggression as an attempt to distract attention from his or her parents' marital conflict and thereby to perform a service for the entire family. The therapist's goal here is to put an end to scapegoating the child and to give everyone in the family the responsibility for effecting positive change.

2. TO NAME THE DAMAGE IS TO CONQUER IT

1. The concept of "match" between a child's needs and a parent's response in healthy families and the equivalent "mismatch" in troubled families is a variation on the process of "mutual regulation" described by Erik Erikson, "Growth and Crises of the Healthy Personality," in *Psychological Issues*, 1 (1959), pp. 58–59, 70, 81. According to Erikson, a well-functioning parent–child relationship is based on each party's capacity to coordinate his or her "means of getting" with the other's "means of giving." When this coordination or mutual regulation breaks down and control is enforced by duress rather than reciprocity, the relationship between parent and child is no longer healthy.

2. "Little Snow White," in *The Complete Grimm's Fairy Tales* (New York: Pantheon, 1972), pp. 249–258.

3. At the present time, no widely accepted standardized test is available to assess the extent of psychological damage in children, adolescents, and adults from troubled families. Partial measures that are respected and broadly used include Thomas Achenbach, *Child Behavior Checklist* (Burlington, Vt.: University Associates in Psychiatry, 1982); *Symptom Distress Checklist (SCL-90)* (Nutley, N.J.: Hoffman-La Roche Inc., 1973); Theodore Millon, *Millon Clinical Multiaxial Inventory* (Minneapolis, Minn.: National Computer Systems, 1982). Each of these three tests served as a model for the Damage Inventory. I consider the inventory a preliminary, informal measure that I developed for the use of readers. Piloted with both therapy patients and a nontherapy group, it is meant

to highlight areas of weakness rather than to serve as a definitive measure of mental health.

4. Leo Tolstoy, *Anna Karenina* (Garden City, N.J.: Garden City Publishing, 1944), p. 4.

5. A definition of family health based on members' capacity to perform the essential tasks of daily living derives from W. Robert Beavers, "Healthy, Midrange, and Severely Dysfunctional Families," in Froma Walsh, ed., *Normal Family Processes* (New York: Guilford Press, 1982), pp. 45–66; Jerry Lewis and W. Robert Beavers, *No Single Thread: Psychological Health in Family Systems* (New York: Brunner/Mazel, 1976); Jerry Lewis, *How's Your Family* (New York: Brunner/Mazel, 1979); Dolores Curran, *Traits of a Healthy Family* (New York: Ballantine Books, 1984).

6. The definition of sexual abuse offered here is based on Steven Farmer, *Adult Children of Abusive Parents* (Los Angeles: Lowell House, 1989), p. 10.

7. I recommend the following readings to those interested in a fuller discussion of sexual abuse: E. Sue Blume, *Secret Survivors* (New York: John Wiley and Sons, 1990); David Finkelhor, *A Sourcebook on Child Sexual Abuse* (Beverly Hills: Sage Publications, 1986); Wendy Maltz and Beverly Holman, *Incest and Sexuality* (Lexington, Mass.: Lexington Books, 1987).

8. Erich Fromm, *The Art of Loving* (New York: Basic Books, 1963), pp. 41–42.

9. Alice Miller, *The Drama of the Gifted Child,* pp. 7–8, 11.

10. Linda A. Bennett, Steven J. Wolin, and Katherine McAvity, "Family Identity Ritual and Myth: A Cultural Perspective on Life Cycle Transitions," in Celia Falicov, ed., *Family Transitions* (New York: Guilford Press, 1988), pp. 211–234.

11. Steven J. Wolin and Linda Bennett, "Family Rituals," *Family Process,* 23 (1984), pp. 401–420; Steven J. Wolin, Linda Bennett, Denise Noonan, and Martha Teitelbaum. "Disrupted Family Rituals: A Factor in the Intergenerational Transmission of Alcoholism," *Journal of Studies on Alcohol,* 41 (1980), pp. 199–214.

12. Nathan Epstein, Duane Bishop, and Lawrence Baldwin, "McMaster Model of Family Functioning: A View of the Normal Family," in Froma Walsh, ed., *Normal Family Processes* (New York: Guilford Press, 1982), p. 118.

3. REFRAMING: HOW TO RESIST THE VICTIM'S TRAP

1. Emmy Werner and Ruth Smith, *Vulnerable but Invincible;* Emmy Werner and Ruth Smith, *Overcoming the Odds;* Emmy Werner, "Children of the Garden Island," pp. 106–111.

2. Paul McHugh and Phillip Slavney, *The Perspectives of Psychiatry* (Baltimore: The Johns Hopkins University Press, 1986), pp. 123–140. McHugh and Slavney identify life story reasoning or the narrative school as one of several perspectives in psychiatry. The narrative school takes the position that one's life story can be told in many ways. Some tellings are beneficial while others are more destruc-

tive. The goal of the therapist is to find the telling that helps a patient to live well in the present and look forward to the future with hope. The concept of reframing, as it is represented in the Challenge Model, conforms to the perspective of the narrative school as described by McHugh and Slavney.

4. INSIGHT: FOREWARNED IS FOREARMED

1. E. James Anthony, "Children at High Risk for Psychosis Growing Up Successfully," in E. James Anthony and Bertram Cohler, eds., *The Invulnerable Child* (New York: Guilford Press, 1987), p. 284.
2. Theodore Lidz, Stephen Fleck, and Alice Cornelison, *Schizophrenia and the Family* (New York: International University Press, 1978), p. 180.
3. Manfred Bleuler, *The Schizophrenic Disorders* (New Haven, Conn.: Yale University Press, 1978), p. 409.
4. The self's capacity to reflect upon itself is a subject of philosophy as well as psychiatry and psychology. A representative philosophical treatment can be found in George Mead, *Mind, Self & Society* (Chicago: University of Chicago Press, 1934). The psychological perspective is described in Arnold Goldberg, ed., *Advances in Self Psychology* (New York: International Universities Press, 1980).
5. Jerome Kagan, *The Nature of the Child* (New York: Basic Books, 1984), pp. 19–25, 275–280.
6. Jerome Kagan, *The Nature of the Child*, p. 276.
7. The following are citations for developmentalists who suggest that children will interpret mistreatment as evidence of their own badness rather than see their parents as flawed. John Bowlby, "On Knowing What You Are Not Supposed to Know and Feeling What You Are Not Supposed to Feel," *Canadian Journal of Psychiatry*, 24 (1979), pp. 403–408 and *Attachment and Loss*, Vol. 3 (New York: Basic Books, 1979); Lawrence Kohlberg, *The Philosophy of Moral Development*, Vol. 1 (San Francisco: Harper & Row, 1981); Alice Miller, *The Drama of the Gifted Child*.
8. I was introduced to the word "insightlessness" by Judith Viorst, *Necessary Losses*, p. 244. It was originally used by Antonio Ferreira to mean an active resistance to seeing through the myths and distortions of reality operating in one's family. See Antonio Ferreira, "Family Myths and Homeostasis," *Archives of General Psychiatry*, 9 (1963), pp. 457–463.
9. Personal conversation with Ruth Davis, director CASPAR (Cambridge and Somerville Program for Alcoholism Rehabilitation) Alcohol Education Program, Somerville, Mass.
10. Robert L. Selman, *The Growth of Interpersonal Understanding: Developmental and Clinical Analyses* (New York: Academic Press, 1980), pp. 147–151, 120–130.
11. Richard Berlin and Ruth Davis, "Children from Alcoholic Families: Vulnerability

and Resilience," in Timothy Dugan and Robert Coles, eds., *The Child in Our Times: Studies in the Development of Resiliency* (New York: Brunner/Mazel, 1989), p. 94.

12. E. James Anthony, "Children at High Risk for Psychosis Growing Up Success-fully," p. 176.

13. William Beardslee and Donna Podorefsky, "Resilient Adolescents Whose Parents Have Affective and Other Psychiatric Disorders: Importance of Self-Under-standing and Relationships," *American Journal of Psychiatry*, 145 (1988), pp. 63–69.

14. Norman Garmezy, "Vulnerability Research and the Issues of Primary Prevention," *American Journal of Orthopsychiatry*, 41 (1971), p. 114.

5. INDEPENDENCE: A DELICATE NEGOTIATION

1. Linda Bennett, Steven J. Wolin, David Reiss, and Martha Teitelbaum, "Couples at Risk for Transmission of Alcoholism," pp. 119–129.

2. Judith Wallerstein, "Children of Divorce: The Psychological Tasks of the Child," *American Journal of Orthopsychiatry*, 53 (April 1983), pp. 230–243; Judith Wallerstein, "Children of Divorce: Stress and Developmental Tasks," in Norman Garmezy and Michael Rutter, eds., *Stress, Coping, and Development in Children* (New York: McGraw-Hill, 1983), pp. 265–302; Judith S. Wallerstein and Sandra Blakeslee, *Second Chances: Men, Women and Children a Decade After Divorce, Who Wins, Who Loses, and Why* (New York: Ticknor and Fields, 1989).

3. Judith Wallerstein, "Children of Divorce: The Psychological Tasks of the Child," p. 235.

4. E. James Anthony, "Risk, Vulnerability and Resilience: An Overview," in E. James Anthony and Bertram Cohler, eds., *The Invulnerable Child* (New York: Guilford Press, 1987), p. 12.

5. E. James Anthony, "Children at High Risk for Psychosis Growing up Success-fully," p. 176.

6. Lois Murphy described the "optimistic bias" of resilient children. She observed that many latch "on to any excuse for hope and faith in recovery," actively mobilizing all thoughts or resources that could possibly contribute to their well-being. Lois Murphy, "Further Reflections on Resilience," in E. James Anthony and Bertram Cohler, eds., *The Invulnerable Child* (New York: Guilford Press, 1987), pp. 103–104.

7. The case of Peter is reported in Richard Berlin and Ruth Davis, "Children from Alcoholic Families: Vulnerability and Resilience," p. 97.

8. Richard Berlin and Ruth Davis, "Children from Alcoholic Families: Vulnerability and Resilience," p. 97.

6. RELATIONSHIPS: THE SEARCH FOR LOVE

1. Several researchers have noted that children's resistance to hardship or resilience is greater when they have access to one healthy caring parent or to a supportive adult outside the immediate family. See for instance Carol Kauffman, Henry Grunebaum, Bertram Cohler, and Enid Gamer, "Superkids: Competent Children of Psychotic Mothers," *American Journal of Psychiatry,* 136 (1979), pp. 1398–1402; Michael Rutter, "Stress, Coping, and Development: Some Issues and Some Questions," in Norman Garmezy and Michael Rutter, eds., *Stress, Coping, and Development in Children* (New York: McGraw-Hill, 1983), pp. 1–41; Emmy Werner and Ruth Smith, *Vulnerable but Invincible,* pp. 69–82. For a comprehensive lay article on attachment theory including the effects of a positive early bonding experience on later resilience, see Robert Karen, "Becoming Attached," *Atlantic Monthly* (February 1990), pp. 49–74.
2. Anthony's example of a resilient child is reported in Maya Pines, "Superkids," *Psychology Today* (January 1979), pp. 54, 57.
3. Carol Kaufman's example is also reported in Maya Pines, "Superkids." p. 57.
4. Marian Radke-Yarrow and Tracy Sherman, "Hard Growing: Children Who Survive," in Jon Rolf, Ann Masten, Dante Cicchetti, Keith Nuechterlein, and Sheldon Weintraub, eds., *Risk and Protective Factors in the Development of Psychopathology* (Cambridge: Cambridge University Press, 1990), pp. 97–119.
5. Marian Radke-Yarrow and Tracy Sherman, "Hard Growing: Children Who Survive," pp. 106–107.
6. Jere Van Dyk, "Growing Up in East Harlem," *National Geographic* (May 1990), pp. 52–57.
7. Linda Bennett, Steven J. Wolin, David Reiss, and Martha Teitelbaum, "Couples at Risk for Transmission of Alcoholism," pp. 119–129.
8. Regina Higgins, *Psychological Resilience and the Capacity for Intimacy: How the Wounded Might "Love Well,"* Dissertation Abstracts International, 46, 11b (1985), degree Harvard University; available from University Microfilm International, Ann Arbor, Mich.
9. Regina Higgins, *Psychological Resilience and the Capacity for Intimacy: How the Wounded Might "Love Well,"* p. 54.
10. Regina Higgins, *Psychological Resilience and the Capacity for Intimacy: How the Wounded Might "Love Well,"* p. 176.
11. Linda Bennett, Steven J. Wolin, David Reiss, and Martha Teitelbaum, "Couples at Risk for Transmission of Alcoholism," pp. 119–129.

7. THE PLEASURE IN PROBLEMS

1. Julius Segal and Herbert Yahres, *A Child's Journey* (New York: McGraw-Hill, 1979), pp. 282–301.

2. Bishop donated his lecture to benefit a local school. My account is true. I have also verified his remarks in a personal interview.

3. The attitudes and actions of resilient survivors that I group together in the term initiative have the same earmarks as "internal locus of control" which was first identified and described by Herbert Lefcourt, *Locus of Control: Current Trends in Theory and Research* (Hillsdale, N.J.: Lawrence Erlbaum Associates, 1982). For a full account of biography, animal and human experiments, and field studies showing the connection between internal locus of control and stress reduction, see Chapters 1, pp. 1–18; 2, pp. 19–41; 3, pp. 100–110.

4. Herbert Lefcourt, *Locus of Control: Current Trends in Theory and Research,* p. 102.

5. Herbert Lefcourt, *Locus of Control: Current Trends in Theory and Research,* p. 101–102.

6. Thomas Thompson, *Lost* (New York: Atheneum, 1975), p. 244.

7. Robert White, "Competence Motivation Reconsidered: The Concept of Competence," *Psychological Review,* 66 (1959), pp. 297–333.

8. Selma Fraiberg, *The Magic Years* (New York: Charles Scribner's Sons, 1959), pp. 23–27.

9. Carol Diener and Carol Dweck, "An Analysis of Learned Helplessness: Continuous Changes in Performance, Strategy, and Achievement Cognitions Following Failure," *Journal of Personality and Social Psychology,* 36 (1978), pp. 451–462.

10. Jean Piaget in Edwin G. Boring, Herbert S. Langfeld, Heinz Werner, and Robert M. Yerkes, eds. *A History of Psychology in Autobiography,* Vol. 4 (Worcester, Mass.: Clark University Press, 1952), p. 238.

11. J. Kirk Felsman, "Risk and Resiliency in Childhood: The Lives of Street Children," in Timothy Dugan and Robert Coles, eds., *The Child in Our Times: Studies in the Development of Resiliency* (New York: Brunner/Mazel, 1989), pp. 56–80.

12. J. Kirk Felsman, "Risk and Resiliency in Childhood: The Lives of Street Children," p. 56.

13. J. Kirk Felsman, "Risk and Resiliency in Childhood: The Lives of Street Children," p. 56.

14. J. Kirk Felsman and George E. Vaillant, "Resilient Children as Adults: A 40-Year Study," in E. James Anthony and Bertram Cohler, eds., *The Invulnerable Child* (New York: Guilford Press, 1987), pp. 289–314.

15. J. Kirk Felsman and George E. Vaillant, "Resilient Children as Adults: A 40-Year Study," p. 306.

16. J. Kirk Felsman and George E. Vaillant, "Resilient Children as Adults: A 40-Year Study," p. 305.

17. Lois Romano and Tom Kenworthy, "The Past and Paradox of Steve Solarz," *The Washington Post,* The Arts/Television/Leisure (May 29, 1991), pp. B1, 8, 9.

18. Lois Romano and Tom Kenworthy, "The Past and Paradox of Steve Solarz," p. B8.

8. CREATIVITY: NOTHING INTO SOMETHING, HUMOR: SOMETHING INTO NOTHING

1. Sigmund Freud, "Humour," in James Strachey, ed., *The Standard Edition of the Complete Works of Sigmund Freud,* Vol. 21 (London: Hogarth Press, 1961), pp. 159–166.
2. Sigmund Freud, "Humour," p. 162, 166.
3. Hanna Segal, "A Psychoanalytic Approach to Aesthetics," in Melanie Klein, Paula Heimann, and R.E. Money-Kyrle, eds., *New Directions in Psychoanalysis* (London: Tavistock Publications Ltd., 1955), p. 390.
4. Melvin Altshuler, "Haven Where Young Wounds Heal," *Washington Post,* Society (September 17, 1950), p. S1.
5. Thank you to Gabriele Rico for leading me to the Japanese proverb, "The reverse side also has a reverse side," the Anaïs Nin quotation cited on Part II of this book, and Sharon Olds's poem "I Go Back to May, 1947" which is cited later in Chapter 9. Gabriele Rico, *Pain and Possibility* (Los Angeles: Jeremy Tarcher, 1991), pp. 183, 265, 284.
6. Sigmund Freud, "Creative Writers and Day-Dreaming," in James Strachey, ed., *The Standard Edition of the Complete Works of Sigmund Freud,* Vol. 9, p. 144.
7. Sigmund Freud, "Creative Writers and Day-Dreaming," p. 143.
8. E. James Anthony, "Children at High Risk for Psychosis Growing Up Successfully," pp. 147–184.
9. E. James Anthony, "Children at High Risk for Psychosis Growing Up Successfully," p. 182.
10. E. James Anthony, "Children at High Risk for Psychosis Growing Up Successfully," p. 182.
11. Albert Solnit, "A Psychoanalytic View of Play," *The Psychoanalytic Study of the Child,* 42 (1987), p. 215.
12. Barbara Hudson, "The Arabesque," in Shannon Ravenel, ed., *New Stories from the South* (Chapel Hill, N.C.: Algonquin Books, 1991), pp. 22–23.
13. Barbara Hudson, "The Arabesque," pp. 33–34.
14. Sheila Harty, *"Iter Vitarium"* (unpublished).
15. Gabriele Rico, *Pain and Possibility,* pp. 213–215. Rico used the term "cosmic perspective" to describe the enlarged frame of reference necessary to see one's troubles with a sense of humor. My use extends the phrase to any enlarged view of oneself, humorous or not.
16. Sharon Olds, "I Go Back to May, 1937," *The Gold Cell* (New York: Alfred A. Knopf, 1989), p. 23.
17. John Rickman, "On the Nature of Ugliness and the Creative Impulse," *International Journal of Psychoanalysis,* 21 (1940), p. 308.
18. Albert Rapp, *The Origins of Wit and Humor* (New York: E.P. Dutton, 1951), p. 170.
19. Norman Cousins, *Anatomy of an Illness* (New York: W. W. Norton & Co., 1979).

20. William Fry, Jr., and Melanie Allen, "Humour as a Creative Experience: The Development of a Hollywood Humorist," in Anthony Chapman and Hugh Foot, eds., *Humour and Laughter: Theory, Research and Applications* (New York: John Wiley & Sons, 1976), pp. 245–258.

21. William Fry, Jr., and Melanie Allen, "Humour as a Creative Experience: The Development of a Hollywood Humorist," p. 252.

22. William Fry, Jr., and Melanie Allen, "Humour as a Creative Experience: The Development of a Hollywood Humorist," p. 253.

23. Albert Rapp, *The Origins of Wit and Humor,* p. 172.

24. Hermann Hesse, *Steppenwolf* (New York: The Modern Library, 1963), pp. 60, 108–109.

9. MORALITY: HOLINESS IN AN UNHOLY WORLD

1. James Anderson and Ezra Jones, *The Ministry of the Laity* (San Francisco: Harper & Row, 1986), p. 5.

2. Coles reports his experience observing the desegregation crisis in New Orleans in Robert Coles, *The Moral Life of Children* (Boston: Houghton Mifflin, 1986).

3. Robert Coles, *The Spiritual Life of Children* (Boston: Houghton Mifflin, 1990), pp. 303–304.

4. Robert Coles, *The Spiritual Life of Children,* p. 304.

5. Robert Coles, *The Moral Life of Children,* p. 140.

6. Robert Coles, "Moral Energy in the Lives of Impoverished Children," in Timothy Dugan and Robert Coles, eds., *The Child in Our Times: Studies in the Development of Resiliency* (New York: Brunner/Mazel, 1989), pp. 44–55.

7. Robert Coles, *The Moral Life of Children,* p. 36.

8. Sharon Herzberger, Deborah Potts, and Michael Dillon, "Abusive and Nonabusive Parental Treatment from the Child's Perspective," *Journal of Consulting and Clinical Psychology,* 49 (1981), pp. 81–90.

9. The statements made by the abused children who participated in Herzberger's study can be found in Sharon Herzberger, Deborah Potts, and Michael Dillon, "Abusive and Nonabusive Parental Treatment from the Child's Perspective," pp. 86–87.

10. Regina Higgins, *Psychological Resilience and the Capacity for Intimacy: How the Wounded Might "Love Well,"* p. 255.

11. Sharon Herzberger, Deborah Potts, and Michael Dillon, "Abusive and Nonabusive Parental Treatment from the Child's Perspective," p. 86.

12. Jerome Kagan, *The Nature of the Child,* pp. 124–126.

13. Robert Selman, *The Growth of Interpersonal Understanding,* pp. 149–150.

14. John Cheever, "The Sorrows of Gin," in *The Stories of John Cheever* (New York: Ballantine Books, 1980), pp. 234–248. Thank you to Richard Berlin and Ruth

Davis for directing my attention to this story. Richard Berlin and Ruth Davis, "Children from Alcoholic Families: Vulnerability and Resilience."

15. John Cheever, "The Sorrows of Gin," p. 246.
16. Robert Coles, *The Moral Life of Children*, pp. 109–110.
17. James Anderson and Ezra Jones, *The Ministry of the Laity*, pp. 5–8.
18. James Anderson and Ezra Jones, *The Ministry of the Laity*, pp. 30–33.

EPILOGUE. THE INTERNAL IMAGE OF A SURVIVOR: ONE WHO PREVAILS

1. *City Slickers* (New Line Home Video, 1991).

APPENDIX. THE DAMAGE INVENTORY

1. For background information on The Damage Inventory, see note 3 to Chapter 2.

INDEX

Index

Allen, Melanie, 178–79
Allen, Woody, 165
Anatomy of an Illness (Cousins), 178
Anderson, James, *The Ministry of the Laity,*
  199–200
André, 127
anger, 38, 44, 50, 51, 53, 83–84, 89, 97,
  105–7, 129, 130, 169, 181
Anna, 92, 94–95, 96, 101, 102, 105, 127
Anna Karenina (Tolstoy), 25–26
anniversaries, 102
Anthony, E. J., 67–69, 77, 100, 116–17, 170
"The Appealing Child Meets the Potentially
  Interested Adult," 113, 114
"The Arabesque" (Hudson), 171–72, 173
archetypes, 20
Art of Loving, The (Fromm), 30
arts, 10–12, 166–67, 172–78
attaching, 111, 124–28, 135
Audrey, 159
authenticity, 177

baby-sitting, 121, 191
balance, 20
Barbara, 3–4, 6, 18, 51, 55, 83–85, 97–98,
  101, 105–6, 116, 120, 126, 127, 129,
  131, 132, 201–2
Beardslee, William R., 79, 81
behavioral science, 10
Bennett, Linda, 90
Berlin, David, 74, 77, 103
Bible, 30–31, 178
birthdays, 26, 27, 44, 89, 102, 132, 133,
  196
Bishop, Barry, 137–39
blame, 74, 79
Bleuler, Manfred, 69
Boston, 150–51
Boston Children's Hospital, 186
boundaries, 31
Brazil, 193–95
Bridges, Ruby, 186–88, 193

Cali, Colombia, 153–55
California, 151–55
calm, maintaining, 100
career choices, 89, 104
Catholicism, 133
Challenge Model, 15–21, 50, 57–59, 69–71,
  113, 137–40, 207
  research on, 18–19

challenge of the troubled family, 3–21
charity, 198
Cheever, John, "The Sorrows of Gin,"
  191–92
child-development theory, 74
childhood, 7
  in Challenge Model, 15–21, 57–59,
    69–71, 113, 137–40, 207
  and challenge of the troubled family,
    3–21
  communication in, 27, 34–39
  creativity and humor in, 167–71
  Damage Inventory of, 209–11
  in Damage Model, 12–15, 16, 18, 20, 51,
    55–57, 69, 71, 113
  emotional needs provided in, 27, 30–34
  and independence, 96–98
  and initiative, 140–46
  and insight, 72–76
  mirroring in, 16–18, 21, 23–25
  and morality, 188–92
  and positive identity, 27, 40–44
  and relationships, 116–20
  safe environment for, 27, 28–30
"Children Who Will Not Break" (Segal and
  Yahres), 136
City Slickers (film), 205–6
civil rights movement, 185
clinical failures, 14
Coles, Jane, 185–88, 193
Coles, Robert, 185–88, 193, 197
  The Moral Life of Children, 186–88, 193
  The Spiritual Life of Children, 185
college, 3, 4, 12, 41, 54, 68, 82, 93, 102,
  120, 122, 124, 129, 157
Colombia, 153–55
communication, 27, 34–39
community, 40, 55, 132
compassion, 193–202
composing, 163, 175–81, 183
confidence, 89, 112, 127, 143
connecting, 111, 116–20, 134–35, 178
control, 178
  internal locus of, 139–40
Core City High Risk Group, 155–56
courage, 49
Cousins, Norman, *Anatomy of an Illness,* 178
Creative Writers and Daydreaming (Freud),
  168
creativity, 6, 8–9, 52, 62, 97, 163–83
  definition of, 163

230

PERMISSIONS ACKNOWLEDGMENTS

Grateful acknowledgment is made to the following for permission to reprint previously published material:

ATLANTIC MONTHLY PRESS: Excerpt from *The Moral Life of Children* by Robert Coles. Copyright © 1986 by Robert Coles. Reprinted by permission of Atlantic Monthly Press.

BASIC BOOKS: Excerpt from *The Widening World of Childhood* by Lois Barclay Murphy. Reprinted by permission of Basic Books, a division of HarperCollins Publishers.

CAMBRIDGE UNIVERSITY PRESS: Excerpt from "Hard Growing: Children Who Survive" by Marian Radke-Yarrow and Tracy Sherman from *Risk and Protective Factors in the Development of Psychopathology* by Jon Rolf, Ann S. Masten, Dante Cicchetti, Keith H. Nuechterlein, and Sheldon Weintraub. Reprinted by permission of Cambridge University Press.

TIMOTHY DUGAN, M.D.: Excerpts from "Children from Alcoholic Families" by Richard Berlin and Ruth Davis and from "Risk and Resiliency in Childhood: The Lives of Street Children" by J. Kirk Felsman. These selections are excerpted from *The Child in Our Times* edited by Timothy F. Dugan, M.D., and Robert Coles, M.D. Reprinted by permission of Timothy Dugan, M.D.

GUILFORD PRESS: Excerpt from "Resilient Children as Adults: A 40-Year Study" by J. Kirk Felsman and George E. Vaillant from *The Invulnerable Child* by E. James Anthony, M.D., and Bertram J. Cohler, Ph.D., 1987. Copyright © 1987 by Guilford Press. Reprinted by permission of Guilford Press.

ABOUT THE AUTHORS

Steven J. Wolin, M.D., is clinical professor of psychiatry at the George Washington University Medical School, a long-time researcher in the department's Center for Family Research, and director of family therapy training. He also maintains a private practice in psychiatry.

Sybil Wolin, Ph.D., holds a doctorate in child development. Since 1980, she has been in private practice seeing children and families experiencing school failure. She has also been the educational consultant to the Parent Educational Advocacy Training Center in Alexandria, Virginia, and has taught English in high school, adult education, and in urban rehabilitation programs.

Steven and Sybil Wolin have been married for twenty-eight years. They have two children and live in Washington, D.C. Together they founded Project Resilience; a program of consultation, training, and treatment in the Challenge Model.